Major Destinations in Yahoo!

Yahoo! Finance

quote.yahoo.com
An incredible range of investment news, plus personalized portfolios.

Yahoo! Sports

sports.yahoo.com
A data-rich compendium of current sports information.

Yahoo! Chat

chat.yahoo.com
A continual global party! Create your own room and search for friends.

My Yahoo!

my.yahoo.com
Customize the Yahoo! experience.

Yahoo! Travel

travel.yahoo.com
From the comfort of home, explore destinations or buy tickets for your next trip.

Yahoo! News

dailynews.yahoo.com
Exhaustive (and exhausting) coverage of current events.

Yahoo! Games

games.yahoo.com
Play cards and board games with other Yahoo! members.

Yahoo! Clubs

clubs.yahoo.com
Mini-societies of folks who share an interest.

Exercise Your Right to Buy

Fill your shopping cart from Yahoo! stores.

Bid on stuff at Yahoo! Auctions.

Browse the "used" marketplace at Yahoo! Classifieds.

Comparison-shop the Internet at Yahoo! Shopping.

How to Meet People

Join the party at Yahoo! Chat.

Develop groups of friends with Yahoo! Messenger.

Join in the discussion on Yahoo! message boards.

Join a Yahoo! Club or start your own.

Meet other gamers at Yahoo! Games.

Yahoo!® For Dummies®

Cheat Sheet

Make the Most of Messenger

Chat with friends voice-to-voice for free.

Receive e-mail alerts.

Follow your local sports teams.

Read your customized news.

Track your stock portfolio.

See which friends are online at any time.

Look up profiles of other Yahoo! members.

Set up group chats.

Search Yahoo! with keywords.

Games to Play in Yahoo!

Backgammon

Blackjack

Bridge

Checkers

Chess

Gin

Go

Hearts

MahJong

Poker

Solitaire

Things to Put on My Yahoo!

Your horoscope

Local sports scores

Your TV or cable listings

Selected stocks

Movie times at local theaters

Best airline fares to selected cities

E-mail and friend alerts

News and more news

Health tips

The IDG Books Worldwide logo is a registered trademark under exclusive license to IDG Books Worldwide, Inc., from International Data Group, Inc. The ...For Dummies logo is a trademark, and For Dummies and ...For Dummies are registered trademarks of IDG Books Worldwide, Inc. All other trademarks are the property of their respective owners.

...For Dummies®: Bestselling Book Series for Beginners

™

BESTSELLING BOOK SERIES

References for the Rest of Us! ®

Are you intimidated and confused by computers? Do you find that traditional manuals are overloaded with technical details you'll never use? Do your friends and family always call you to fix simple problems on their PCs? Then the *...For Dummies*® computer book series from IDG Books Worldwide is for you.

...For Dummies books are written for those frustrated computer users who know they aren't really dumb but find that PC hardware, software, and indeed the unique vocabulary of computing make them feel helpless. *...For Dummies* books use a lighthearted approach, a down-to-earth style, and even cartoons and humorous icons to dispel computer novices' fears and build their confidence. Lighthearted but not lightweight, these books are a perfect survival guide for anyone forced to use a computer.

> *"I like my copy so much I told friends; now they bought copies."*
>
> — Irene C., Orwell, Ohio

> *"Quick, concise, nontechnical, and humorous."*
>
> — Jay A., Elburn, Illinois

> *"Thanks, I needed this book. Now I can sleep at night."*
>
> — Robin F., British Columbia, Canada

Already, millions of satisfied readers agree. They have made *...For Dummies* books the #1 introductory level computer book series and have written asking for more. So, if you're looking for the most fun and easy way to learn about computers, look to *...For Dummies* books to give you a helping hand.

®

IDG BOOKS WORLDWIDE

1/99

YAHOO!®
FOR
DUMMIES®

YAHOO!® FOR DUMMIES®

by Brad Hill

IDG Books Worldwide, Inc.
An International Data Group Company

Foster City, CA ◆ Chicago, IL ◆ Indianapolis, IN ◆ New York, NY

Yahoo!® For Dummies®

Published by
IDG Books Worldwide, Inc.
An International Data Group Company
919 E. Hillsdale Blvd.
Suite 400
Foster City, CA 94404
www.idgbooks.com (IDG Books Worldwide Web site)
www.dummies.com (Dummies Press Web site)

Library of Congress Catalog Card No.: 99-64593

ISBN: 0-7645-0582-3

Printed in the United States of America

10 9 8 7 6 5 4 3 2

2O/SV/QY/ZZ/IN

Distributed in the United States by IDG Books Worldwide, Inc.

Distributed by CDG Books Canada Inc. for Canada; by Transworld Publishers Limited in the United Kingdom; by IDG Norge Books for Norway; by IDG Sweden Books for Sweden; by IDG Books Australia Publishing Corporation Pty. Ltd. for Australia and New Zealand; by TransQuest Publishers Pte Ltd. for Singapore, Malaysia, Thailand, Indonesia, and Hong Kong; by Gotop Information Inc. for Taiwan; by ICG Muse, Inc. for Japan; by Norma Comunicaciones S.A. for Colombia; by Intersoft for South Africa; by Eyrolles for France; by International Thomson Publishing for Germany, Austria and Switzerland; by Distribuidora Cuspide for Argentina; by LR International for Brazil; by Galileo Libros for Chile; by Ediciones ZETA S.C.R. Ltda. for Peru; by WS Computer Publishing Corporation, Inc., for the Philippines; by Contemporanea de Ediciones for Venezuela; by Express Computer Distributors for the Caribbean and West Indies; by Micronesia Media Distributor, Inc. for Micronesia; by Grupo Editorial Norma S.A. for Guatemala; by Chips Computadoras S.A. de C.V. for Mexico; by Editorial Norma de Panama S.A. for Panama; by American Bookshops for Finland. Authorized Sales Agent: Anthony Rudkin Associates for the Middle East and North Africa.

For general information on IDG Books Worldwide's books in the U.S., please call our Consumer Customer Service department at 800-762-2974. For reseller information, including discounts and premium sales, please call our Reseller Customer Service department at 800-434-3422.

For information on where to purchase IDG Books Worldwide's books outside the U.S., please contact our International Sales department at 317-596-5530 or fax 317-596-5692.

For consumer information on foreign language translations, please contact our Customer Service department at 1-800-434-3422, fax 317-596-5692, or e-mail rights@idgbooks.com.

For information on licensing foreign or domestic rights, please phone +1-650-655-3109.

For sales inquiries and special prices for bulk quantities, please contact our Sales department at 650-655-3200 or write to the address above.

For information on using IDG Books Worldwide's books in the classroom or for ordering examination copies, please contact our Educational Sales department at 800-434-2086 or fax 317-596-5499.

For press review copies, author interviews, or other publicity information, please contact our Public Relations department at 650-655-3000 or fax 650-655-3299.

For authorization to photocopy items for corporate, personal, or educational use, please contact Copyright Clearance Center, 222 Rosewood Drive, Danvers, MA 01923, or fax 978-750-4470.

is a registered trademark or trademark under exclusive license to IDG Books Worldwide, Inc. from International Data Group, Inc. in the United States and/or other countries.

About the Author

Brad Hill is a well-known evangelist of the online experience who has written eleven books about the Internet and personal technology. His titles include a *Publishers Weekly* bestseller and a Book of the Month Club catalog selection.

Get Brad talking about the Internet and you can barely shut him up — as a result, he has appeared widely on television and radio, including CNN, "Good Day L.A.," Turner Entertainment Network, and more than 50 radio programs. His loquaciousness makes him an easy mark for journalists, and Brad is quoted often in magazine and newspaper articles about the Net and cyberculture.

As a columnist, Brad is let off his leash to rant in such publications as *ComputorEdge Magazine, PC World's* TipWorld, and *Raging Bull*. He puts on his virtual tweed jacket to teach online courses at ZDU.

Brad is listed in *Who's Who* and is a member of the Author's Guild. He enjoys hearing from people and can be found (virtually) at his electronic home: www.bradhill.com.

ABOUT IDG BOOKS WORLDWIDE

Welcome to the world of IDG Books Worldwide.

IDG Books Worldwide, Inc., is a subsidiary of International Data Group, the world's largest publisher of computer-related information and the leading global provider of information services on information technology. IDG was founded more than 30 years ago by Patrick J. McGovern and now employs more than 9,000 people worldwide. IDG publishes more than 290 computer publications in over 75 countries. More than 90 million people read one or more IDG publications each month.

Launched in 1990, IDG Books Worldwide is today the #1 publisher of best-selling computer books in the United States. We are proud to have received eight awards from the Computer Press Association in recognition of editorial excellence and three from Computer Currents' First Annual Readers' Choice Awards. Our best-selling ...*For Dummies*® series has more than 50 million copies in print with translations in 31 languages. IDG Books Worldwide, through a joint venture with IDG's Hi-Tech Beijing, became the first U.S. publisher to publish a computer book in the People's Republic of China. In record time, IDG Books Worldwide has become the first choice for millions of readers around the world who want to learn how to better manage their businesses.

Our mission is simple: Every one of our books is designed to bring extra value and skill-building instructions to the reader. Our books are written by experts who understand and care about our readers. The knowledge base of our editorial staff comes from years of experience in publishing, education, and journalism — experience we use to produce books to carry us into the new millennium. In short, we care about books, so we attract the best people. We devote special attention to details such as audience, interior design, use of icons, and illustrations. And because we use an efficient process of authoring, editing, and desktop publishing our books electronically, we can spend more time ensuring superior content and less time on the technicalities of making books.

You can count on our commitment to deliver high-quality books at competitive prices on topics you want to read about. At IDG Books Worldwide, we continue in the IDG tradition of delivering quality for more than 30 years. You'll find no better book on a subject than one from IDG Books Worldwide.

John Kilcullen
Chairman and CEO
IDG Books Worldwide, Inc.

Steven Berkowitz
President and Publisher
IDG Books Worldwide, Inc.

VIII
WINNER

Eighth Annual
Computer Press
Awards ≥1992

IX
WINNER

Ninth Annual
Computer Press
Awards ≥1993

X
WINNER

Tenth Annual
Computer Press
Awards ≥1994

XI
WINNER

Eleventh Annual
Computer Press
Awards ≥1995

IDG is the world's leading IT media, research and exposition company. Founded in 1964, IDG had 1997 revenues of $2.05 billion and has more than 9,000 employees worldwide. IDG offers the widest range of media options that reach IT buyers in 75 countries representing 95% of worldwide IT spending. IDG's diverse product and services portfolio spans six key areas including print publishing, online publishing, expositions and conferences, market research, education and training, and global marketing services. More than 90 million people read one or more of IDG's 290 magazines and newspapers, including IDG's leading global brands — Computerworld, PC World, Network World, Macworld and the Channel World family of publications. IDG Books Worldwide is one of the fastest-growing computer book publishers in the world, with more than 700 titles in 36 languages. The "...For Dummies®" series alone has more than 50 million copies in print. IDG offers online users the largest network of technology-specific Web sites around the world through IDG.net (http://www.idg.net), which comprises more than 225 targeted Web sites in 55 countries worldwide. International Data Corporation (IDC) is the world's largest provider of information technology data, analysis and consulting, with research centers in over 41 countries and more than 400 research analysts worldwide. IDG World Expo is a leading producer of more than 168 globally branded conferences and expositions in 35 countries including E3 (Electronic Entertainment Expo), Macworld Expo, ComNet, Windows World Expo, ICE (Internet Commerce Expo), Agenda, DEMO, and Spotlight. IDG's training subsidiary, ExecuTrain, is the world's largest computer training company, with more than 230 locations worldwide and 785 training courses. IDG Marketing Services helps industry-leading IT companies build international brand recognition by developing global integrated marketing programs via IDG's print, online and exposition products worldwide. Further information about the company can be found at www.idg.com.   1/24/99

Dedication

This book is dedicated to Susan Pink, its editor and my collaborator on many projects. Susan's humor and expertise lighten the stresses of a book's many deadlines, and she is a joy to work with.

Author's Acknowledgments

Mary Bednarek and Steve Hayes engaged in a flattering conspiracy to involve me in this project. Many thanks to them both for their confidence.

Mary Corder got me writing these bright yellow books in the first place, and I won't ever forget it.

Allen Wyatt's contributions to this book are essential.

Many thanks to my agent, Nicholas Smith.

Publisher's Acknowledgments

We're proud of this book; please register your comments through our IDG Books Worldwide Online Registration Form located at http://my2cents.dummies.com.

Some of the people who helped bring this book to market include the following:

Acquisitions, Editorial, and Media Development

Project Editor: Susan Pink

Acquisitions Editor: Steve Hayes

Technical Editor: Allen Wyatt, Discovery Computing Inc.

Editorial Assistant: Beth Parlon

Production

Project Coordinator: E. Shawn Aylsworth

Layout and Graphics: Thomas R. Emrick, Angela F. Hunckler, Dave McKelvey, Barry Offringa, Brent Savage, Michael A. Sullivan, Jacque Schneider, Brian Torwelle

Proofreader: Arielle Carole Mennelle

Indexer: Sharon Hilgenberg

Special Help
Suzanne Thomas

General and Administrative

IDG Books Worldwide, Inc.: John Kilcullen, CEO; Steven Berkowitz, President and Publisher

IDG Books Technology Publishing Group: Richard Swadley, Senior Vice President and Publisher; Walter Bruce III, Vice President and Associate Publisher; Steven Sayre, Associate Publisher; Joseph Wikert, Associate Publisher; Mary Bednarek, Branded Product Development Director; Mary Corder, Editorial Director

IDG Books Consumer Publishing Group: Roland Elgey, Senior Vice President and Publisher; Kathleen A. Welton, Vice President and Publisher; Kevin Thornton, Acquisitions Manager; Kristin A. Cocks, Editorial Director

IDG Books Internet Publishing Group: Brenda McLaughlin, Senior Vice President and Publisher; Diane Graves Steele, Vice President and Associate Publisher; Sofia Marchant, Online Marketing Manager

IDG Books Production for Dummies Press: Michael R. Britton, Vice President of Production; Debbie Stailey, Associate Director of Production; Cindy L. Phipps, Manager of Project Coordination, Production Proofreading, and Indexing; Shelley Lea, Supervisor of Graphics and Design; Debbie J. Gates, Production Systems Specialist; Robert Springer, Supervisor of Proofreading; Laura Carpenter, Production Control Manager; Tony Augsburger, Supervisor of Reprints and Bluelines

◆

The publisher would like to give special thanks to Patrick J. McGovern, without whom this book would not have been possible.

◆

Contents at a Glance

Cartoons at a Glance

By Rich Tennant

Fax: 978-546-7747 • E-mail: the5wave@tiac.net

Table of Contents

Introduction

● ●

1 know what you're thinking. A whole book about a Web site? If that question crossed your mind, a major surprise is headed your way.

Yahoo! began as a mere Web site, though an important one. Yahoo! was one of the first attempts to index the World Wide Web when the Web was little more than a small, quirky, mostly noncommercial network of personal pages. Because you could search Yahoo!'s index, the site was everyone's favorite launching point for a night of Web surfing.

That was then. Yahoo! grew, adding features to its core index and search service. In time, Yahoo! began to resemble a distinct network of sites: sports, finances, communities, entertainment, chat. Like planets orbiting a sun, these discrete destinations made up a self-contained system of impressive dimensions.

The growth and evolution continued. When certain Internet measuring firms began keeping track, they found that the vast and burgeoning Yahoo! was one of the most popular destinations on the entire Web. Now, with many millions of registered users and an astonishing number of Web pages displayed each day, Yahoo! is clearly a full-fledged online service. Great content and a vibrant community add up to one of the dominant and most-used domains in cyberspace.

Yahoo! still has its index and its search engine. Those features retain their high status among experienced and new Internet users. But Yahoo! has evolved light-years beyond its roots. This book takes you on a tour of unexpected depth and breadth. Do you think you know Yahoo!? Prepare to be amazed.

About This Book

This book is your companion to the Yahoo! experience. It exposes you to information and introduces you to communities. It makes your life easier by explaining Yahoo!'s sources of free e-mail, free stock portfolios, free interactive gaming, free sports coverage, free clubs, free auctions — in fact, the money you spent for this book might be the cheapest introduction you ever bought to one heck of a lot of free services and content.

You might be familiar already with some Yahoo! services. If you've been around the Web for a while, you almost certainly have used Yahoo! in some capacity. So don't read this book like a novel. I'll tell you right now, the butler committed the crime and the guy gets the girl. So feel free to skip around or even read the book backwards. (Sense make will that sentence only the is this, backwards it read do you if.)

This book is best used as a reference and a companion to your on-screen explorations. The book isn't going anywhere. (Unless you let your dog have it, in which case it will soon be buried under the geraniums.)

Conventions Used in This Book

Being the conventional type, I thought I'd put some conventional conventions in this book. I've use different typefaces to help you pick up certain on-screen elements, as they are presented on the page, in a glance.

URLs (Uniform Resource Locators), which are Web addresses, are indicated in this kind of type:

```
chat.yahoo.com
```

When I introduce a term for the first time, I *italicize* it to get your attention, and notify you that there's no reason for you to know what it means.

Often I point out links to look for, and they appear <u>underlined</u> in the text.

How This Book Is Organized

This book uses a radical and innovative organization system. Text is printed on pages, and pages are bound into a portable folio! And that's not the half of it. The book's content is divided into distinct parts called . . . well, they're just called *parts*, a term that might not win any prizes for originality. What's amazing is that each part has chapters! I feel confident that this startling idea will spread to other books, revolutionizing the entire publishing industry. Either that, or the sun will rise tomorrow. Place your bets.

This section tells you what's in each part. Here goes.

Part I: Starting the Yahoo! Experience

Part I explains how to join Yahoo!. Joining costs nothing and is not necessary if you use the service casually. But if you hang around Yahoo! enough, you inevitably find a good reason to get a Yahoo! ID, and Chapter 1 describes what that gets you and how to do it. Chapter 2 details how to set up a personalized My Yahoo! page — one of Yahoo!'s most valuable features, in my opinion. The final chapter in this part is devoted to Yahoo! E-mail, a free and sophisticated Web-based e-mail system.

Part II: Letting Yahoo! Be Your Guide

Yahoo!'s traditional services of indexing and searching the Web are intact and thriving. The first two chapters in Part II instruct you in using the Yahoo! directory and search engine. More than that, they offer little-known tips from my Bag of Tips (which is kept in my Tip Vault, located in my Secret Fortress of Tips) on how to maximize your use of these features. Chapter 5 gives you some expertise in using search keywords.

Part III: Information and More Information

When it comes to raw information, nobody beats Yahoo!. Cooked information is available, too. The four chapters in Part III take you on expeditions to the Yahoo! news, sports, finances, and entertainment news sites. Each information portion of Yahoo! deserves a book of its own — especially Yahoo! Finance, which is a foundation site for wired investors. Although it's impossible to cover every nook and cranny of these profound information sources, I isolate and point you toward the important features.

Part IV: Meeting the Yahoo! Community

Yahoo! goes way beyond information. In and around the millions of information pages served up every day, a community lurks restlessly, emerging into the forefront in the chat, message-board, and club domains of the Yahoo! service. The chapters in Part IV get specific about how to meet people and how to operate the slick features of Yahoo!'s community features. Yahoo! Chat is an extraordinary, Java-powered chatting empire. Yahoo! Messenger is an incredible free gadget that allows you to talk — really talk, with your voice — to any other user, anywhere in the world, free of charge. Yahoo! Clubs are wonderful prefab Web sites that anyone can easily build and share. All these wonders and more are divulged in these chapters.

Part V: At Your Service, Yahoo! Style

Information, community, and services: the three parts of any complete online service. Part V steps you through travel planning, car buying, job hunting, reservation making, ticket purchasing, game playing, and real estate hunting. In addition, a separate chapter explains the excellent Yahoo! Companion, a little-known feature for the Internet Explorer browser that I think is the cat's meow (without those annoying claws digging affectionately into your skin).

Part VI: Buying and Selling

Ah, shopping. Isn't that the point of life, when you get right down to it? Even if you're less superficial than I, you might find some use and a lot of fun in this part. The three chapters in Part VI describe not only shopping in the Yahoo! online mall, but also how to set up your own virtual auction and run a classified ad. Did you know you can comparison-shop the entire Internet with a click of the mouse in Yahoo!? Chapter 20 tells you how.

Part VII: The Part of Tens

Part VII is where I share my laundry and shopping lists. No, wait — that's another book. The two chapters in this part are lists of a sort. One recommends ten Yahoo! directory pages worth bookmarking. The other chapter points out ten Yahoo! Clubs worth visiting and perhaps joining.

Foolish Assumptions

Some of my assumptions about you, the reader, might be mistaken. For example, I assume I'll get a holiday greeting card from you. That might be merely a vain hope. Chocolate in the mail? Wishful thinking for sure.

In the area of reasonable assumptions, I have a few. This book doesn't require very much Internet or Web experience. But I do assume you have online access. I don't describe how to get on the Internet, but if you are on, I take it from there and guide you to the splendor of Yahoo!. It doesn't matter to me *how* you get to the Net — through an ISP, or America Online, or a connection from work, or WebTV. Yahoo! is open to every online citizen.

I also assume you know how to operate a Web browser in the most basic way. This book doesn't explain how to click a link, for example, though it does tell you *which* link to click. You should know how to use the Back button — click it once, you'll find out.

Icons Used in This Book

This book wouldn't be a ...*For Dummies* book without goofy pictures in the margins. Those little designs are called *icons*, and each one signals something different. Here's the rundown:

The Tip icon flags a nugget of wisdom that you will remember for a lifetime (or at least until your next snack). These tips are worth their weight in gold. Needless to say, they don't weigh anything.

This icon, if recollection serves, reminds you of something you shouldn't forget. Like turning off the oven before the muffins burn. Or more likely, some on-screen item that's easily forgotten.

I don't devolve into my innate geekhood very often, at least not publicly. When I do, it isn't a pretty sight. Accordingly, the editors of this book have placed this warning icon next to such paragraphs to warn you away. Heed the warning.

Occasionally, if you do something wrong on the Web, your computer liquefies into a steaming puddle. Just kidding. It's hard to do any damage on the Net. Still, my sense of drama prompted me to include a few dire warnings in the text.

Where to Go from Here

If you're an occasional Yahoo! user, but not a registered member, I recommend starting with Chapter 1. Get yourself a Yahoo! ID — you'll be using it plenty as you browse through this book. If you already have the ID, but haven't customized Yahoo! to your preferences, you might want to start with Chapter 2.

Besides the first two chapters, your best bet is to examine the Table of Contents, choose a chapter that looks interesting, and start exploring. Remember, this book doesn't have to be read page by page. Dart in and out according to your interest at any moment.

At some point in your surfing, visit me at my site and drop me a line. I'm always home at

```
www.bradhill.com
```

And now . . . let the fun begin. Yahoo! awaits. It's better than you imagined.

Part I
Starting the Yahoo! Experience

The 5th Wave   By Rich Tennant

"It's a letter from the company that installed our in-ground sprinkler system. They're offering Internet access now."

In this part...

You might think Yahoo! is just another Web site, but in this part I describe how to register in the Yahoo! community, get an ID, create a My Yahoo! personalized page, and begin using Yahoo!'s free e-mail system. The complete, integrated, awesome Yahoo! experience begins here.

Chapter 1

Making a Name for Yourself

*B*ecause Yahoo! is a Web-based service equally available to all Internet users, it does not require membership but it does encourage it. In fact, Yahoo! withholds certain functions from nonmembers. Getting a Yahoo! membership is simple and free. The process amounts to filling in a few bits of information and clicking an on-screen button. Yahoo! members are defined by their Yahoo! IDs, which are like on-screen membership badges that I refer to repeatedly throughout this book.

I encourage you to create a Yahoo! ID as well. Doing so is the first step in making the most of the service. With a Yahoo! ID, you can mold the service around your information needs and tastes. Each Yahoo! ID, if taken advantage of to the max, can create an entire customized service, especially through the use of Yahoo! Messenger, Yahoo! Companion, My Yahoo!, and Yahoo! E-mail.

This chapter explains how to make your ID (it takes only a minute or so); how to create a Public Profile; and how to search for other member Profiles.

Finding Yourself

Frequent Yahoo! users almost always end up establishing a Yahoo! identity (ID). Each Yahoo! ID is paired with a password, and you must know both to sign in and view your personalized settings. Many services are available only to people with Yahoo! IDs — in particular, the interactive services that allow you to create something within Yahoo!.

You need a Yahoo! ID to buy something in a Yahoo! store; make travel reservations; place a Yahoo! Classifieds or Yahoo! Personals ad; chat; play games;

open a Yahoo! e-mail account; use Yahoo! Messenger; personalize the service with My Yahoo!; create a stock portfolio; post a message; use the calendar; make a Yahoo! Profile; and take advantage of other functions and services.

It's important to emphasize that joining Yahoo! with an ID and a password is entirely free. Your membership gives you access to many interactive portions of Yahoo! and doesn't cost a dime, ever. You have no limit on how much you can use your ID. Everyone in your family can have his or her own Yahoo! ID, with its own set of personalized features, and never incur charges.

If you explore Yahoo! enough, you're bound to encounter invitations to join. The following steps work no matter where you start from:

1. **Enter the following URL in your browser:**

   ```
   login.yahoo.com
   ```

   The Welcome to Yahoo! page appears.

   Surprisingly, the Yahoo! home page doesn't have a Create a New Account button. When wandering around the service, however, you are repeatedly prompted to sign in or create a Yahoo! ID. So you can start your free account from many places, but one of those places isn't necessarily on your screen when you want it to be. Use the preceding URL.

2. **Click the <u>Sign me up!</u> link.**

   The sign-up page appears (see Figure 1-1),

3. **Under Create Your Yahoo! ID and Password, fill in the fields.**

   You choose your own user name (Yahoo! ID) and password. If you choose an ID name already in use, Yahoo! prompts you to choose another after you submit the form. You must complete all the fields in this section.

4. **In the Personal Account Information section, complete all required fields.**

   Only the first two fields (first and last name) are optional. Curiously, Yahoo! cares more about your birthdate, gender, occupation, and zip code than about your name. Yahoo! uses this information to provide relevant and personalized information.

5. **In the Tell Us About Your Interests section, check any boxes that apply.**

   This section is optional and important only if you don't personalize the service manually. Chapter 2 describes how to create a My Yahoo! page, which I recommend for getting the most out of the service. If you do get involved with My Yahoo!, these check boxes are irrelevant.

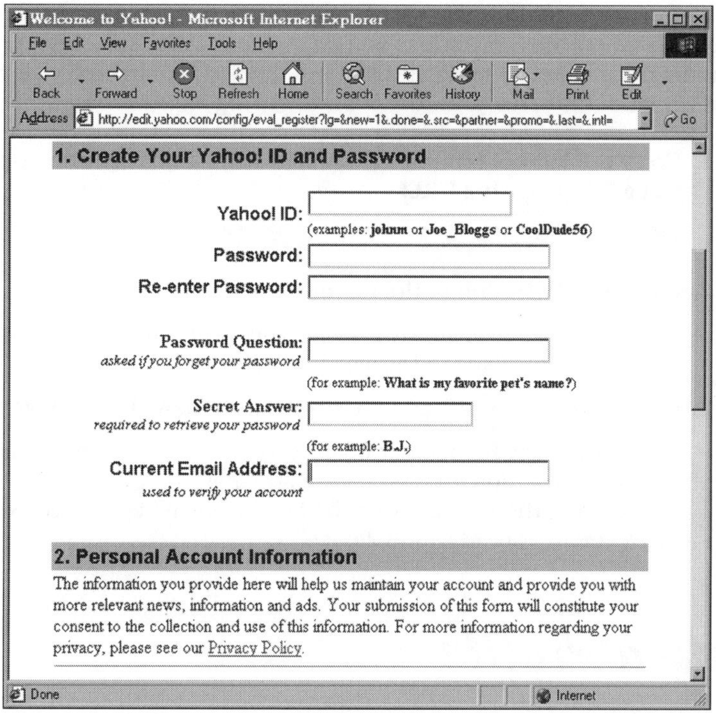

Figure 1-1:
The sign-up
page for
creating a
Yahoo! ID
and pass-
word.

6. Click the Submit this form button.

That's it! You now have a Yahoo! ID and password. A page appears with those two crucial bits of information — it's a good idea to write them down somewhere or commit them to your flawless photographic memory.

When you sign in to Yahoo! with your ID and password, you stay signed in for the duration of your session. You have to sign out manually (using a Sign Out link, which appears on almost every page of the service) or shut down your browser to end your session. However, there's no harm in remaining signed in, even if you're elsewhere on the Web and not using Yahoo!. You're not incurring any charges by being signed in. Normally, signing into Yahoo! is the first thing I do when I go online, and I never have a reason to sign out.

The Sign Out links are useful if your computer lives in a household with more than one Yahoo! user, each with an individual Yahoo! ID. (Because the service is free and Yahoo! is not your Internet service provider, there's no limit to how many IDs can be initiated from a single computer.) Every Yahoo! ID in your household can have its own identity, e-mail account, Personals mailbox, My Yahoo! pages, and so on.

After you have a Yahoo! ID, you can sign in any number of ways in Yahoo!. Booting Yahoo! Messenger logs you on automatically (see Chapter 13), and the Yahoo! Companion (Chapter 19) has a dedicated Sign In button. If you don't use either of those features, the best way to log on is to follow these steps:

1. **Go to the Yahoo! home page by following a browser bookmark or using the following URL:**

   ```
   www.yahoo.com
   ```

2. **Click the My button at the top of the page.**

   The My Yahoo! for [Guest] page appears. On the Yahoo! home page, the My Yahoo! link leads to the same place.

3. **Enter your Yahoo! ID and password, and then click the Sign in button.**

   If you check the Remember my ID & Password box, Yahoo! places your sign-in information on your computer's hard drive, where Yahoo! can find it. From then on, clicking the My button in Step 2 signs you in and takes you to your My Yahoo! page.

Creating a Profile

Figure 1-2 illustrates the page that greets you immediately after you create your Yahoo! ID and password. Notice the two links. One invites you to begin creating your My Yahoo! pages, which I explain in Chapter 2. The other suggests you make a Yahoo! Profile.

The Yahoo! Profile tells other Yahoo! members a bit about you. How much you reveal is up to you. (You don't have to create a profile at all.) Many profiles are basic, including the member's name, perhaps a general location, and nothing else. But if you really get motivated, you can put in your gender, location, age, marital status, real name (not your ID name), occupation, e-mail address (different from your Yahoo! e-mail), a statement of your interests, personal news, a favorite quote, a home page URL, and other Web links you enjoy visiting. Oh — and a picture, if you have one scanned.

You must have a Yahoo! ID to create a Profile. After you've established your ID, follow these steps:

1. **Click the Create Your Public Profile link.**

   The Public Profiles for (yourID) page appears. You can try the View link, and you'll see a Profile page with the information you included when creating your Yahoo! ID (see the preceding section). Notice the Create New Public Profile button — each Yahoo! ID may have several Profiles. Many people create separate profiles for chatting, posting messages, creating an auction, and so forth. I have a few myself, but I don't like the trouble of keeping them straight, so I end up using just one.

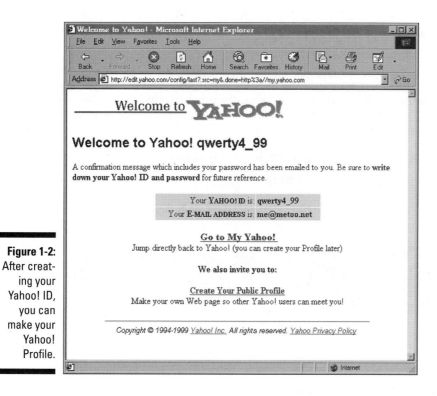

Figure 1-2:
After creating your Yahoo! ID, you can make your Yahoo! Profile.

Use the check box to hide your comings and goings from Yahoo! members who have your ID on their Friends lists. Chapters 11 and 13 (Yahoo! Chat and Yahoo! Messenger, respectively) explain about Friends. For now, you need to know that checking the box makes you more anonymous and invisible. You can re-edit your profile any time, checking and unchecking that box as you please.

2. **Click the Edit link.**

The Edit Public Profile for: (yourID) page appears.

3. **Fill in any or all information fields.**

All the fields on this page are optional. There is no requirement to give more information about yourself than you want. Remember, you may re-edit your profile information at any time. Some people enjoy playing games with the information, such as entering "Mars" or "right here" for the Location field, or "old enough to know better" for Age. Yahoo! doesn't care about any of this; these Profiles are for fun. Yahoo! does have the right to delete anything you create, so don't type anything libelous, illegal, hateful, slanderous, or fundamentally obnoxious in other ways.

4. **Use the Click Here When Done button.**

Cruising the Profiles

You can become acquainted with other Yahoo! members in several ways, chatting perhaps being the most obvious (see Chapter 11). Searching for Public Profiles that meet certain criteria can give you some ideas of who to look for in those chat rooms. It's also a way to get ideas for your own profile. Here's what to do:

1. **Enter the following URL in your browser:**

   ```
   profiles.yahoo.com
   ```

   The Member Directory Search page appears (see Figure 1-3).

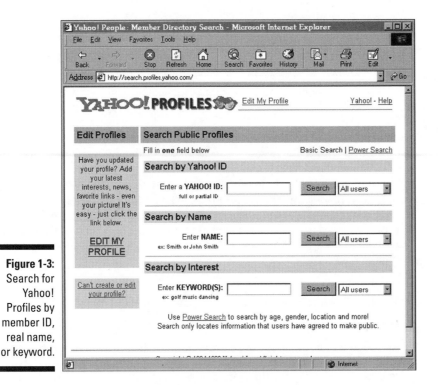

Figure 1-3: Search for Yahoo! Profiles by member ID, real name, or keyword.

2. **Use the keyword fields and drop-down menus to search for Public Profiles.**

   If you know a person's Yahoo! ID, use the top search form. The middle form is an excellent way to search for a person by his or her real name, which may or may not be entered in that person's Profile information. Use the bottom search form to locate people who may match your interest. Yahoo! compares your keyword(s) to every work in every Profile.

Use the drop-down menus to distinguish between a search of all Yahoo! members (every member has a default Public Profile, even if that person hasn't added anything to it), and a search of members who indicate in their Profile that they use Yahoo! Messenger. The Messenger is a good way to chat with people you find through a Profile search.

3. Click the Search button.

The Public Profile Search Results page appears (see Figure 1-4).

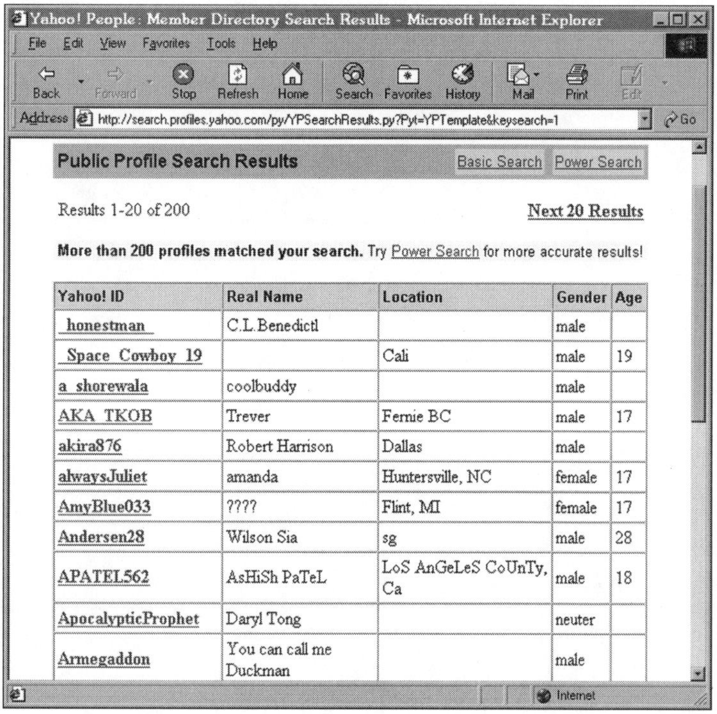

Figure 1-4:
Search
results for
a Profile
search.

Yahoo! ID	Real Name	Location	Gender	Age
honestman	C.L.Benedictl		male	
Space Cowboy 19		Cali	male	19
a shorewala	coolbuddy		male	
AKA TKOB	Trever	Fernie BC	male	17
akira876	Robert Harrison	Dallas	male	
alwaysJuliet	amanda	Huntersville, NC	female	17
AmyBlue033	????	Flint, MI	female	17
Andersen28	Wilson Sia	sg	male	28
APATEL562	AsHiSh PaTeL	LoS AnGeLeS CoUnTy, Ca	male	18
ApocalypticProphet	Daryl Tong		neuter	
Armegaddon	You can call me Duckman		male	

Public Profile Search Results — Basic Search Power Search

Results 1-20 of 200   Next 20 Results

More than 200 profiles matched your search. Try Power Search for more accurate results!

4. Click any Yahoo! ID to see that Profile.

If you get too many search results, you might want to try a power version of the Profiles search engine. Use your browser's Back button to return to the Member Directory Search page, and click the Power Search link. The page that appears gives you several more searching options, including the ability to search for only profiles with pictures, profiles indicating one gender, or profiles within a certain age range.

Chapter 2

It's Yours! Customizing the Experience

In This Chapter

▶ Understanding the customization process

▶ Changing the look and content of a My Yahoo! page

▶ Making your own Yahoo! portal

I like an accommodating online service, don't you? One that takes an interest in my needs and preferences, and doesn't make it hard to find them. Yahoo! is so accommodating that it devotes a substantial part of its service to something called My Yahoo! — but for the purposes of this chapter we'll pretend it's yours. (But it's mine! All mine!) In fact, My Yahoo! belongs to anybody who cares to personalize it, which is pretty easy to do.

Yahoo! places a great deal of its content into the personalization basket. That means you have a grand array of choices to make when customizing your Yahoo! experience. Fortunately, you need never etch a choice in stone (in fact you can't, and I discourage using chisels near computers); you can change your personal settings as often as you please. I tweak mine almost daily.

This chapter instructs you in choosing and configuring your personal Yahoo! choices. In addition, I recommend certain choices as good starting points. That doesn't mean I discourage you from making any of the available selections — I just like to see people getting started on the right foot. Feel free to ignore my advice and explore on your own.

If I were to create detailed explanations of every feature available in My Yahoo!, this book would deal with nothing else and a scandal would ensue. (Ha! Wishful thinking from someone who has never been pictured in a tabloid.) So instead, I offer a quick rundown of all the features, pointing you to other parts of this book if I explain them in detail elsewhere.

Some users ignore My Yahoo!, and indeed, you don't have to use it. The design of Yahoo! makes it pretty easy to click your way anywhere you want without much delay. But I feel certain that any Yahoo! user who creates a My Yahoo! page (or two) will quickly become dependant on it (or them). It's a great way to consolidate the Yahoo! experience, which can be overwhelming in its vastness, and put frequently visited parts of the service within easy reach. Give it a try.

Explaining the Not-So-Obvious

Right about here, you might be thinking, "What the heck is personalization, anyway? And what's in it for me?"

Good questions. Every online service presents its members with content — lots and lots of content in big services such as Yahoo!. *Content* is simply stuff that appears on your screen — information, forums, entertainment, and various services. There can be so much of this content, in so many categories, that grappling with it all is daunting. You might find a great feature one day, and then forget how you got to it the next day. You need some way of customizing the experience to suit your taste, needs, and discoveries.

On the Web, the most common customization feature is the Bookmarks or Favorites list in your Web browser. America Online users have used Favorites for years to keep track of online destinations worthy of repeat visits. Internet Explorer also has a Favorites feature, and the Navigator browser offers a customizable list called Bookmarks. In all these cases, the lists enable you to assemble pointers to favorite virtual places, but they don't change the basic interface of the online service or Internet browser you're using.

Yahoo! goes a step further, thanks to its convenient Web-based foundation. Because every Web browser on the planet understands HTML, the software language that Yahoo! (and every other Web site) is built on, Yahoo! can let you change the actual interface — in other words, the way Yahoo! looks on your screen. You do have limits to how you can change its appearance, and some large features of Yahoo! are off-limits to customization, but the important point is that you are empowered to create your own custom Web pages of Yahoo! features. That's far more control than you have in America Online or any other non-Web service.

Untangling a few terms

In television ads, you hear phrases like "Internet online service." In this chapter, I refer to online services and Web-based online services. It's a good idea to clarify these everyday terms because they can cause so much confusion about what online services are and how they differ from each other.

An *online service*, speaking in the most general way, is any collection of information and interactive features that you view and use by logging your computer into a network. Whether you use a phone-line modem, a cable modem, or a network connection from an office is immaterial. The important thing is that you connect a personal computer to another computer, and view something on your screen that was designed to be accessed by you and others. Generally, online services present pages of information, interactive features such as message boards and chat rooms, and services such as e-mail and shopping. An online service can be large or small; public or private; free or subscription based; on a private network or on the Internet.

The phrase *Internet online service* is a marketing buzzword that traditional online services began using when the Internet became popular. It indicates that the online service has the capacity to connect you to the Internet. Thousands of online services, large and small, were around before the Web brought the Internet into the mainstream. Each one was a little network of features unto itself, providing members with phone numbers for their modems to dial in to so that members could see stuff and talk to other members.

The Internet is like an ocean surrounding each of these online service islands. When the Web made that ocean a popular place to swim, some of the larger online services started offering their members virtual surfboards (by which I mean Web browsers and connections to the Internet). As people began valuing Web content more highly than private online service content, companies such as America Online and CompuServe started calling themselves Internet online services to show how cool they were.

The important thing to remember is that an Internet online service such as America Online is not really located on the Internet — it's still an independent network. It offers its members a gateway to and from the Internet, like a revolving door. On the other hand, a service such as Yahoo! is truly an Internet online service because it started on the Web and uses the Web's natural language (HTML) in all its features. It is, basically, a gigantic Web site — and by *gigantic* I mean that it consists of millions of Web pages. A *Web-based online service*, then, is any collection of features that exists on the Web, not on a private computer network.

Using a Web-based online service has several advantages, the biggest is that you don't need special software (besides your Web browser) to see its content. America Online members must download or acquire new software to view overhauls to the AOL service, whereas Yahoo! could redesign the entire service and you wouldn't need anything more than your good ol' Web browser to be up to date.

Customizing This and That

Yahoo! is vast. It's enormous. The service is massive, prodigious, and colossal. I hope I'm conveying the impression that Yahoo! is big. It has features within features, and still more features within those. You might compare it to a planetary system, with several large bodies orbiting the home page, each of which contains its own atmosphere, topographical features, and society. If you do make such a comparison, don't be surprised if people edge away from you at parties.

The sheer magnitude of Yahoo! is what makes the My Yahoo! feature so useful in getting a grip on it all. At the same time, you can't possibly squeeze the whole shebang onto a few customized pages. Yahoo! doesn't even let you try. My Yahoo! touches on many main feature satellites and some little feature asteroids, and lets you consolidate them onto screen pages formatted to your taste. But in almost every case, you're customizing just the tip of an iceberg, with plenty of depth waiting to be explored. I cover the depth in later chapters.

Following are the main types of content you can gather together using My Yahoo! and the instructions in this chapter:

- ✔ **Web searching.** Searching the Internet is Yahoo!'s traditional function — the service started as a simple directory and search engine. (See Chapters 4 and 5 for explanations of these terms and a guide to using the features.) Although Yahoo! has grown beyond its original scope to enormous proportions, many people still think of it primarily as a Web directory. Yahoo! itself doesn't seem to deny its lineage, positioning the directory front and center on the home page at www.yahoo.com. In My Yahoo!, you can put that directory, or a variation of it (with fewer, more, or different browsing categories), on your personal page. You may also place the Yahoo! keyword entry form on your page for searching by word, phrase, or name. Furthermore, My Yahoo! expands on the bread-and-butter searching of the main service by enabling you to create and save custom-made searches.

- ✔ **Finances.** Yahoo! Finance is a major realm unto itself — one of the most popular and trafficked money sites on the Web. (Chapter 9 gets deep into the heady atmosphere of high finance.) My Yahoo! takes features from the financial portion of the service and feeds them to your personal page if you want. Personalized stock quotes and portfolios are the main features available to My Yahoo!. If you set up a Business page, a few more choices become apparent, such as Earning Surprises, Upgrades/ Downgrades, Currency Converter, and financial headlines from a few different sources.

- ✔ **News.** News headlines can take up a major portion of your personalized page. My Yahoo! offers all kinds of news categories, and you can even set up clipping folders (called News Clipper) based on keywords, names, or places. (News Clipper is highly recommended if you are following a hot news story, or a sports team, or want to read everything about a favorite movie star.) News has become a free commodity, for the most part, on the Internet. It's not called the Information Highway for nothing — and we users benefit from the glut of free information from a wide variety of sources. My Yahoo! helps pull it all together and focus the information stream to meet your interests.

✔ **TV and movies**. If you're willing to part with a bit of personal information — namely, the zip code of your residence — you can get some real-time, local entertainment information. A complete television schedule of broadcast and cable listings might not be more convenient than looking in your paper or *TV Guide,* unless your computer is almost always logged onto the Web, like mine is. (I have a long-standing New Year's resolution to get a life.) But the TV listings are presented in a color-coded grid that's easier to interpret than the pages-long, ad-interrupted listings in *TV Guide.* As for movie showtimes, perusing all the movies showing in all your local theaters, consolidated onto a single on-screen page, is splendidly useful. Furthermore, you can click on any movie title for more information about the film. It beats, by a mile, calling the theater by phone.

✔ **Sports.** Yahoo! delivers sports news with the same attention to detail that you find in USA Today and other information-rich publications. Yahoo! Sports is a major Web sports site but far more streamlined than ESPN.com or many other athletic watering holes on the Net. With few pictures and lots of text, Yahoo! concentrates on scores, standings, schedules, wrap-ups, and some columnists. (See Chapter 8 to explore Yahoo! Sports in depth.) On My Yahoo!, you may configure sports headlines to match your passions and a sports scoreboard that revises games in progress whenever you update the page. The News Clipper, which I mention a few paragraphs up, is also put to good use following the press on a certain team or player.

✔ **Community.** Like any online service, Yahoo! is part information resource, part mall, and part community. For my money, the community aspect of any online service is just as important as the other features, if not more so. First and foremost, an online service is a gathering of members. Cyberspace would be a dreadfully impersonal realm if its citizens couldn't talk to each other. Yahoo! takes several approaches to community interaction; all of which are described through reams of literary prose in Part IV. My Yahoo! lets you position a hook into the vast community features of the service by placing links to favorite message boards and chat rooms on your personalized page. In addition, Yahoo! Messenger is linkable from your page, and you can set things up to deliver e-mail alerts when something arrives in your Yahoo! mailbox.

✔ **Tips and tidbits.** There's no reason your personal page shouldn't be fun. You can sprinkle lottery results, recipes, and other nuggets through your My Yahoo! design. If you're willing to divulge your birthday, you can have your page deliver a fresh, uncannily accurate (maybe) horoscope each day.

✔ **Weather.** I read recently that America is the only country whose citizens take weather beyond mere small talk and establish it as an important news topic in daily life. Yahoo!, being an American company, must resonate with this priority, because it puts the weather on My Yahoo! as a default item. Of course, you can configure it and even remove it if you want. Personally, I like to keep track of my local forecast, the weather in Florida (fueling my fantasies of far-off retirement), and Paris (because I'm a hopeless dreamer).

✔ **Travel.** Speaking of travel fantasies (see the preceding paragraph), Yahoo! runs an online travel agency whose reservation pages (for flights, hotels, and rental cars) can be linked to your My Yahoo! page. The Destinations feature keeps your travel reveries in the forefront by displaying current low airline prices to cities of your choice.

✔ **Organization.** Keeping your feet on the ground and your mind neatly compartmentalized is part of the value in personalizing Yahoo!. You can keep your e-mail address book and interactive calendar on your page. The calendar (whose workings I detail in Chapter 19) is especially useful and flexible.

✔ **Bridge to the offline world.** Online services display a unique effectiveness when they help us cope with the offline world. In so doing, they often mimic traditional aids such as phone books. In fact, that's pretty much what My Yahoo! offers in this department: white pages and yellow pages. The addition of keyword searching makes the computer version of these mainstay lifesavers even more efficient.

✔ **Daily features.** Like a newspaper, My Yahoo! can enliven your page with an array of items whose content changes daily. The Lead Photo adds a small, thumbnail picture of the day's top news story (you can expand it if you want); Today's Fitness Feature is a question-and-answer self-help bite; Computer Tip is exactly that; and Daily Briefing is an audio news update.

Much of Yahoo! is left untouched by My Yahoo! — in other words, tons of features and content that you can't place on your personalized page. For example, the Computer Tip is a fine feature, but only a drop in the bucket of information available in the Yahoo! Computers area. Likewise, the stock quotes are good to have in a glance, but they represent the riches of Yahoo! Finance in only the most meager way. Yahooligans! and Internet Life, two major portions of the service, are not available as links on a My Yahoo! page.

Even those portions of Yahoo! that can be placed on your personal page are reduced, in most cases, to simple links that lead to the full features. The value of My Yahoo! is in providing shortcuts to areas of the service that you use over and over, and in highlighting a few tidbits (such as horoscopes and the Daily Fitness Feature) that you might otherwise find once and never again.

Have It Your Way

Although you can customize the look and content of My Yahoo! pages, they all have the same fundamental design. Figure 2-1 shows a My Yahoo! page as it appears before customization. Notice that it has two columns of features. All the features you select for your page are either left-side features or right-side features.

Left-side features   Right-side features

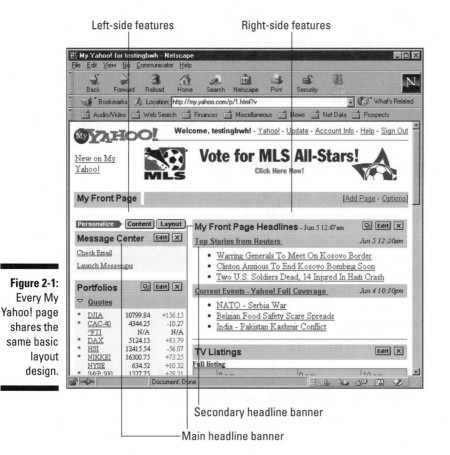

Figure 2-1:
Every My Yahoo! page shares the same basic layout design.

Secondary headline banner

Main headline banner

My Yahoo! features are like modules you plug in and out of your page, and arrange in whatever order you please. (Except that you can't move a right-side module to the left side, or vice versa.) Each column (left side and right side) can be extended as far as you like down the page. A page can be as long as you like, though at some point it makes more sense to create another page because each My Yahoo! design may consist of more than one page.

You may have more than one Yahoo! ID, but you can make only one My Yahoo! page per account. A Yahoo! account is defined by password. Every account may have multiple Yahoo! IDs (see Chapter 1). But all the IDs under one password share a single My Yahoo! personalization.

Every content module has a main headline banner, and some have secondary headline banners. Look at Figure 2-1, and you can see that the Message Center, a left-side module, is a main headline. My Front Page Headlines, a right-side feature, has several secondary headline banners for different types of news. When designing your page, you decide which modules (main banners) you want, and, whenever applicable, which secondary features within those modules you want to appear.

My Yahoo! always starts out with preselected content modules in place. You may keep them, edit them, or discard them. Then, you may move around what remains to the order you prefer. The following sections walk you through the details of setting up your page's substance and appearance.

Making basic settings

The basic settings of any My Yahoo! page include the page's title; a short greeting that appears at the very top of the page; your color scheme; and the refresh rate.

The best place to begin making your basic settings is on the Options page (Figure 2-2). Let's go through the steps:

1. **On your My Yahoo! page, click the <u>Options</u> link.**

   The Options page appears.

2. **In the Greeting field, type a greeting.**

   Keep it short, or it won't fit on your page. Two or three words, at most. Mine says "Back again, eh?" just to remind myself that I spend too much time online. The greeting appears at the very top of My Yahoo!.

3. **Select your color scheme by clicking the radio button next to your choice.**

   Figure 2-2 doesn't show the colors, and makes each selection look pretty much like every other. Check it out on screen, and you'll get the picture. Each preset color scheme sets a hue for the left-hand column, the background of the whole page, the main headings, and the subheadings. You can test one by choosing it and clicking the Finished button.

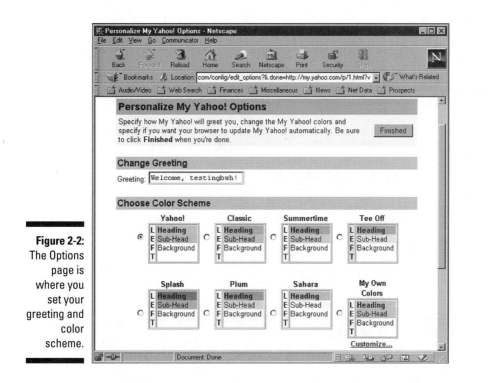

4. Scroll down the page and set the refresh rate for the page using the drop-down menu.

My Yahoo! can be set to automatically reload itself into your browser at a preset interval. It's a good way to make sure your news headlines, stock quotes, and e-mail alerts are current. Because the reload takes only a few seconds in most cases (a little longer for content-packed pages), there's no reason to set the time interval for anything longer than fifteen minutes, the shortest setting.

5. Click the Finished button.

When it comes to setting your page's color scheme, you have more choices than the presets would indicate. To design a custom-made color scheme, click the <u>Customize</u> link on the Options page. Figure 2-3 shows the Custom Colors page. (It's a much more colorful experience on the screen.) On this page, you may choose from a wider selection of hues for the left side of your page, the main heading, the subheading, and the page background. Notice the distinction between 256 Color Mode and High Color Mode. You should use the High Color Mode selections only if your computer is set for color resolution greater than 256 colors. How can you tell? If the color samples on the High Color Mode part of the Custom Colors page look good to you, go ahead and select them. After all, nobody is going to look at your My Yahoo! page except you.

Under each of the four page elements for which a custom color may be selected, you can find a My Own Color radio button with a text entry field. If you're familiar with HTML color codes, you may select a hue that isn't sampled on the page. Every color on a Web page is represented in HTML code by a six-character identifier. You can't effectively guess these identifiers because they're a mix of numbers and letters. This option is for experienced HTML coders.

The next step in making basic settings occurs in the Personalize Page Content page (see Figure 2-4). Here's how to make a name for your page:

1. **On your My Yahoo! page, click the Personalize Content button.**

   The Personalize Page Content page appears.

2. **In the Page Name field, type a name for your page.**

   Your page name can be 20 characters long (including spaces between words). In general, shorter looks better.

3. **Click the Finished button.**

Figure 2-3:
You may personalize your page colors.

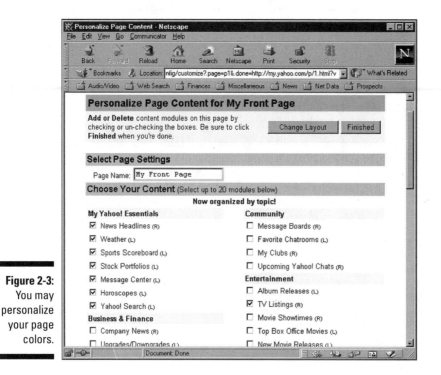

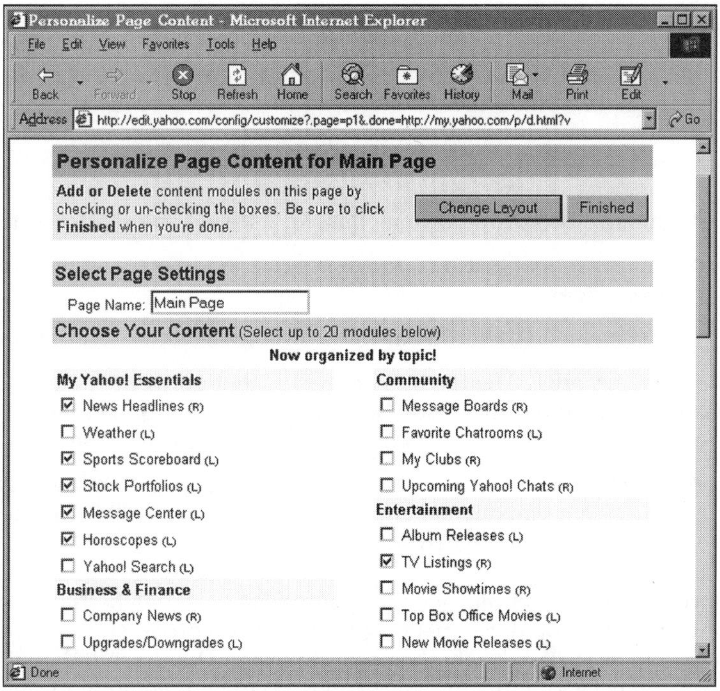

Figure 2-4:
Set your
Page Name
on this
page, and
browse
among the
content
modules.

Before clicking the Finished button in Step 3, you may look over the content selections on the Personalize Page Content page. Notice that each selection is marked R or L, indicating whether it is a right-side or left-side feature. Just click the box next to any feature you want to include. Prechecked boxes currently exist as default content on your page — click to uncheck them and remove them from the page. Adding content isn't a basic setting, and in the next section I describe an easier way to do it. Nevertheless, feel free to experiment here. (Like you need my permission.)

Plugging in some content

Adding content is where the fun really begins. (Assuming you're as easily entertained as I am.) Placing content modules on your page shapes it into something useful. It's best to select features first, and arrange them second. Content precedes layout. For the time being, you might want to leave all the default features on the page — I describe how to get rid of them in the next section.

Using the Personalize Page Content page, described in the preceding section, is one way to add content modules. But I prefer using the drop-down menus at the bottom of My Yahoo! (see Figure 2-5). Scroll down to see them, under the Personalize This Page banner.

Here are the basic facts about adding content using the drop-down menus:

- ✔ You have two drop-down menus, for left-side and right-side features.
- ✔ The two sets of features do not overlap, and you can't make any of them switch sides.
- ✔ Each menu has a scroll bar for browsing the entire list of features.
- ✔ You may add 20 features to your page, but only one feature at a time. Click the Add button after selecting a module from either drop-down list. After the page reloads, add another feature to either side.
- ✔ You may stack features on either side of the page, up to the limit of 20 overall, but you might want to arrange the page so it's balanced fairly evenly between the two sides.

As your modules get plugged into your page, you get a better sense of what they are. The drop-down menus give you only a broad clue; you need to see the modules to decide whether you want them. Keep reading to find out how to customize within the modules and what to do if you don't want them.

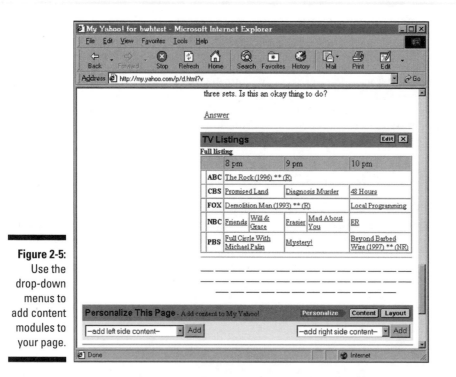

Figure 2-5:
Use the drop-down menus to add content modules to your page.

If you'd rather add several modules at once, without waiting for your page to reload between each addition, use the Personalize Page Content page described in the preceding section. There, you may use the check boxes to make whole-sale changes to your page, and then view the entire alteration at once.

Editing your content

If you look back at Figure 2-1, you can see that the content modules include some combination of editing buttons in the main heading banner. The three buttons are:

- ✔ **Edit button.** The function of the Edit button varies depending on the module. Click it to discover what specific content features are available for that module and to choose among them. I describe the Edit selections of a few major content modules in a later section.

- ✔ **Remove button.** The button with an X in it deletes the module from your page.

- ✔ **Detach button.** The button with little squares in it rips the content module right off your page and establishes it in a new, small browser window. You may resize the window to whatever dimensions are best.

When you detach a content module into its own window, it remains on your main My Yahoo! page. So, when you're ready to get rid of the dedicated window, just close it as you would any window on your screen. No need to add the content again to My Yahoo!. It's still there.

All three editing buttons aren't present on all content modules. Some features can't be detached into separate windows, and some features can't be internally edited. But all features sport the Remove button.

Playing art director

After you have a number of content modules placed on your page, it's time to arrange them in the order you prefer. Of primary importance is moving to the top whatever features you want displayed when you *first* enter My Yahoo!. It's nice to make the important stuff visible without scrolling the page downward. I like to put the Message Center and Portfolios near the top of the left-hand column, and certain news headline groups atop the right-hand column. But you may prefer seeing a horoscope on the left and the Fitness Feature on the right. Sports scores are also a good "up-top" left-hand candidate.

You can't mix and match right-side and left-side features. They are locked to their respective sides.

Follow these steps to arrange your page's layout:

1. **On your My Yahoo! page, click the Personalize Layout button.**

   The Personalize Page Layout page appears, as shown in Figure 2-6.

2. **In the window titled Left Side (narrow), click to select any content module listed.**

3. **Use the up or down arrow button to move the selected module higher or lower on your page, or use the X button to eliminate it.**

   You may move any module as many steps upward or downward as you like. Just keep clicking the arrow button of your choice.

4. **Repeat Steps 2 and 3 for the window titled Right Side (wide).**

5. **Click the Finished button.**

The links under the Other Personalization Options banner take you to pages described in previous sections of this chapter.

Searching Yahoo! from My Yahoo!

Because Yahoo! is well known as a Web index and directory, you'd think there would be some way of browsing and searching Yahoo! from My Yahoo! There is. The keyword entry form for searching the Yahoo! directory (see Chapters 4 and 5) appears by default in the left column of your main My Yahoo! page. If you delete the search form from the left column (I explain how to delete things in this chapter), the form reappears at the top of the page. (Use the <u>move to bottom</u> link to shift the search form to the bottom of the page.)

You may also add categories from the Yahoo! directory to My Yahoo!, but the process is more complicated. Here's what to do:

1. **On your My Yahoo! page, use the right-hand drop-down content menu to select Yahoo! Categories.**

2. **Click the Add button.**

3. **On your My Yahoo! page, scroll down to the Yahoo! Categories banner and click the Edit button.**

4. **On the Choose your favorite categories page, click the Start Here link.**

   The main Yahoo! home page is displayed, showing the top-level directory categories (see Chapter 4).

5. **Browse through the Yahoo! directory, clicking the <u>Personalize</u> link at the top of any category you want to add to My Yahoo!.**

   You don't need to follow the first four steps every time you want to add new categories. Any time you're in the Yahoo! directory, you may select the <u>Personalize</u> link to add a category. You'll see that category added to the Yahoo! Categories content module next time you visit your My Yahoo! page.

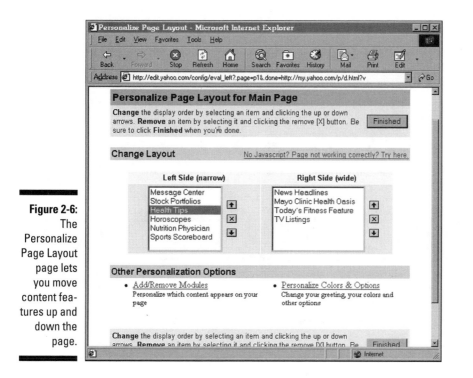

Figure 2-6:
The Personalize Page Layout page lets you move content features up and down the page.

Playing news editor

My Yahoo! is many things, but its default format devotes most of the screen space to news headlines. You can choose from a lot of news covering current events, sports, and finances. Many of the smaller features are newsy, too. This section talks you through some of the editing choices you have for your page.

Selecting the main news portions of your page is probably the biggest editing job you have, simply because so many news sources are available. The following steps familiarize you with adding and removing specific news features:

1. **On your My Yahoo! page, click the Edit button on the Main Page Headlines banner.**

   The My Front Page Headlines banner is at the top of your right-side content when you begin creating a My Yahoo! page. If for some reason it's not there (perhaps because you deleted it), scroll to the bottom of the page, use the right-side drop-down menu to select News Headlines, and then click the Add button. Look at the previous "Plugging in some content" section for complete instructions.

2. On the Edit your Headlines Module page, click any topic link from the list.

I chose the Current Events & Politics link.

3. From the Available Topics window (see Figure 2-7), select any topic.

Use the scroll bar to see items lower on the list. Click any item that doesn't appear in the Your Choices window.

4. Click the Add>> button.

Your selection appears in the Your Choices window.

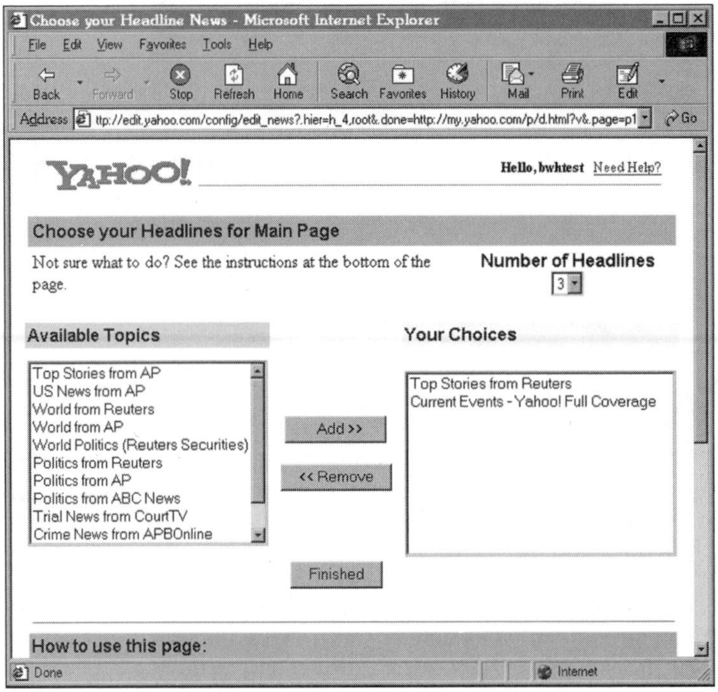

Figure 2-7:
Use this page to select which headline groups appear on your page.

5. Click any item in the Your Choices window that you want to remove.

All the selections in Your Choices currently appear on your page. This is one way to delete them. You may also use the delete button (the X) on the page itself to eliminate any headline topic group.

6. Click the <<Remove button.

The selection disappears from the Your Choices window.

7. **Use the Number of Headlines drop-down menu above the Your Choices window to select how many headlines appear under the topic groups.**

   You can't vary the number of headlines among the groups. So if you choose 3, Yahoo! selects three headlines for each of your topic selections.

8. **When you've finished configuring your news topics, click the Finished button.**

   You may return to this process at any time to adjust your news selections.

Adjusting your scoreboard (if you want a scoreboard on your page) is accomplished by following the preceding steps. You start by clicking the Edit button on the Scoreboard banner, or by creating a Scoreboard module by selecting Sports Scoreboard from the bottom-page drop-down menu on the left side.

When one page isn't enough

Yahoo! starts you off with a single page, but doesn't limit you to just one. You may add up to six other pages, which appear as links in the title banner of your main page. Whenever you surf to My Yahoo!, the main page is displayed first.

To create a second (or third) page, follow these steps:

1. **On your My Yahoo! page, click the Add Page link.**

2. **On the Create a New Page page (see Figure 2-8), click the radio button next to the type of page you want to add.**

   If you don't like the look of any of the new page presets, click the Make My Own link, which takes you to the Personalize Page Content page, described previously in this chapter. There, you may build a new page from scratch.

3. **Click the Create Page button.**

   Your new page is displayed, with preset content modules in place. You may now proceed to personalize the content and layout of the page as described in previous sections.

If you ever want to delete an entire page, you must (paradoxically) click the Add Page link on any of your pages (not necessarily the page you want to delete). On the Create a New Page page, scroll down to the You already have these pages banner, and use the Delete Page link.

Figure 2-8:
Use Create
a New Page
to make up
to five new
pages in
addition to
your main
page.

Chapter 3

Neither Rain, nor Sleet, nor . . .

- -

In This Chapter

▶ Setting up a Yahoo! Mail account

▶ Getting to your mail and writing letters

▶ Creating an address book

▶ Using the Yahoo! Mail search engine

▶ Checking other mailboxes through Yahoo!

- -

*G*uess what the most-used feature of the Internet is. Go on, guess. Okay, I'll tell you — it's e-mail. E-mail is used more than the Web.

E-mail has traditionally existed in its own realm. It's not the Web, it's not Usenet newsgroups, and it's not IRC chat. It has been a separate product of the online experience. When you get an online account (through an online service such as America Online or an Internet service provider), you automatically receive an e-mail box and the capability to exchange letters with anyone else with an account.

Built-in e-mail accounts are convenient and are usually accessed with dedicated e-mail programs such as Outlook Express, Netscape Messenger, or Eudora. In the last few years, though, *Web-based e-mail* has become popular. Web-based e-mail really is part of the Web, and is accessed through regular Web pages, viewed in a Web browser. Although slower and more cumbersome than regular e-mail, the Web-based version has some compelling advantages:

✔ Web-based e-mail is free, though you still need an online access account to get on the Web.

✔ Web mail is accessible from any computer logged onto the Internet, so it's great when traveling.

✔ Such mail accounts can be more permanent than online access accounts. If you switch from America Online to Earthlink to some other Internet provider, you get a new e-mail address each time, but your Yahoo! Mail address remains constant.

This chapter explains how Yahoo! Mail works, and unravels its most important features.

Getting Ready for Yahoo! Mail

Setting up your Yahoo! E-mail account is an easy matter, especially if you've already created a Yahoo! ID. If not, now is a good time to make one — you can't have Yahoo! E-mail without an ID. You get one Yahoo! mailbox per password. Different IDs accessed by one password all share a single e-mail box. You may give out those different IDs as distinct e-mail addresses, each with the @yahoo.com suffix. But all incoming mail lands in the single mailbox assigned to the first ID you created. You can access that mailbox while logged on to any of the IDs.

Follow these steps to set up your Yahoo! mailbox:

1. **At the top of the Yahoo! home page, click the Check Email button.**

   The Welcome to Yahoo! Mail page appears.

2. **Fill in your ID and password, and then click the Sign in button.**

   If you don't have a Yahoo! ID yet, click the Sign me up! link and continue from there, or get some help from Chapter 1 about registering in Yahoo!.

3. **On the setup page, read the Yahoo! Mail Terms of Service Agreement, and then click the I Accept button at the bottom of the page.**

   The mail summary page you see next should bear a strong resemblance to Figure 3-1.

The fine print

Most Web-based e-mail services require that you read (or at least say that you read) a Terms of Service (TOS) agreement, which spells out the basic rules of the service. Yahoo! is no different. Because the e-mail service is free, following the commonsense rules isn't too much to ask. What is it that you're agreeing to?

Basically, you agree to do three things with Yahoo! Mail:

✔ You agree to provide accurate information about yourself in the registration process.

✔ You agree to avoid all illegal, harmful, libelous, abusive, and generally obnoxious uses of the e-mail service.

✔ You agree to not send *spam* (bulk e-mail advertisements) through Yahoo! Mail.

The coup de grace is a clause that says Yahoo! can nuke your account whenever it wants — but don't worry, nobody gets the plug pulled for normal e-mail usage.

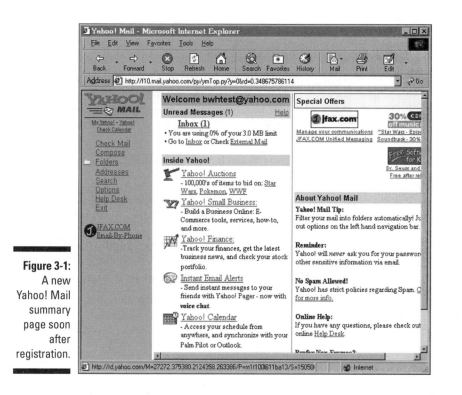

Figure 3-1:
A new
Yahoo! Mail
summary
page soon
after
registration.

Yahoo! Mail has its own log on and log off procedure, distinct from the ID sign in and off process. When you click the Exit link (see the left column in Figure 3-1), you exit Yahoo! Mail, but you do not sign out from your Yahoo! ID account. By the same token, you sometimes need to take an extra log on step to get your mail, depending on the length of time since you last got it. Yahoo! Mail has a *timeout* feature that closes your mailbox after a certain time, requiring you to type your password to get back in. This extra security is for your protection; if you leave your computer unattended for an extended period, others won't be able to peek at your letters.

E-Mail Coming and Going

I'm a much more active correspondent in the realm of e-mail than I ever was with paper letters. This discrepancy could be due to my latent fear of post offices, but more likely it's because e-mail is so easy. No envelope. No stamp. No arm-wrestling with the mailman. But best of all, no delivery delays. E-mail is fast, and I have fun chatting with friends and acquaintances throughout the day. E-mail is informal and conversational.

To check your Yahoo! Mail:

1. **On the Yahoo! home page, click the Check Email button at the top of the page.**

   The mail summary page (Figure 3-1) appears. If it has been a while since you last checked your mail, you might have to enter your password. If you're not logged on to your Yahoo! account ID, you definitely need to enter both it and your password.

2. **On the mail summary page, see whether any unread messages are waiting for you.**

   Figure 3-1 shows a single unread message, indicated in parentheses next to Unread Messages and also by the <u>Inbox (1)</u> link. You can set up multiple incoming-mail folders (I explain how later in this chapter), and each folder shows up in the Unread Messages list with the number of unread messages. But at the beginning, new mail comes into the Inbox.

3. **Click the <u>Inbox</u> link, or click the <u>Check Mail</u> link in the left sidebar.**

   Your Inbox page appears (see Figure 3-2), showing all mail in the Inbox, both read and unread. Read mail is shaded gray, and unread mail isn't shaded. Furthermore, the titles of unread letters are in bold type, which thins out to regular type after you read the letter.

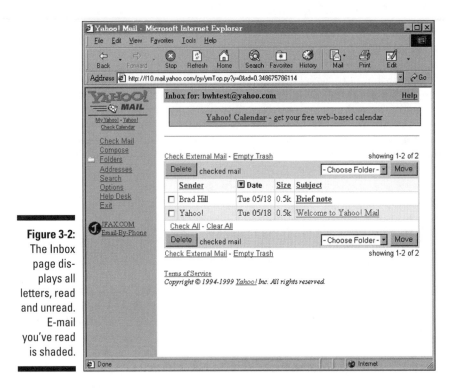

Figure 3-2:
The Inbox page displays all letters, read and unread. E-mail you've read is shaded.

4. Click the subject of any letter to read it.

Figure 3-3 illustrates what a letter (albeit an extremely brief and vapid one) looks like in Yahoo! Mail.

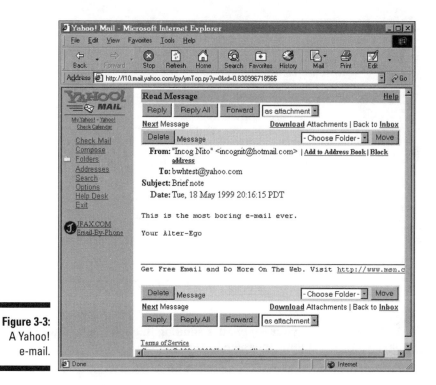

Figure 3-3:
A Yahoo!
e-mail.

To respond to e-mail:

1. On any Read Message page (see Figure 3-3), click the Reply button.

The Compose Mail page appears (see Figure 3-4).

2. Use the large text entry form to type your letter.

Notice that the text of the letter you're replying to is placed in the text entry box. In all e-mail formats, it's typical to *quote back* the letter you're responding to, so the recipient doesn't have to remember what the conversation is about. Typically, you type your response above the quote. Quoting back is not a requirement, though, so feel free to highlight and delete the quoted letter before sending your reply.

3. Click the Send button.

If you're not ready to send the letter yet, but are tired of working on it (or can't think of how to finish your missive), click the Save Draft button. The letter-in-progress is placed in your Draft folder. (Every mailbox has a draft folder — you don't have to create it.)

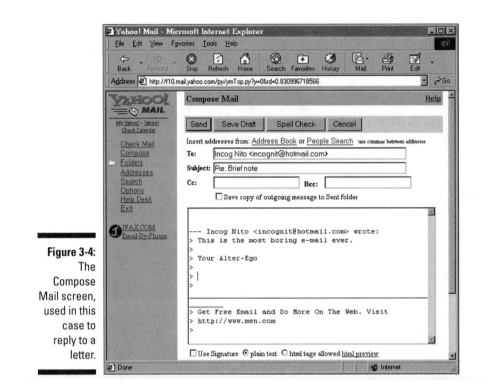

Figure 3-4:
The
Compose
Mail screen,
used in this
case to
reply to a
letter.

4. To keep a copy of your reply after sending it, click the box next to Save copy of outgoing message to Sent folder.

As with the Draft folder, the Sent folder already exists.

You can use the Spell Check feature on outgoing messages. On the Compose Mail page, click the Spell Check button before sending the mail. Figure 3-5 illustrates what happens if you have a misspelling in your outgoing text. (Perhaps unfortunately, Yahoo! Mail checks the spelling of e-mail addresses as well as the message texts, resulting in almost inevitable spelling "errors" because the system doesn't recognize e-mail aliases as real words. Because the system automatically addresses the e-mail for you, the chance of a misspelling is virtually nil, and you can safely ignore spelling "errors" in mail addresses.

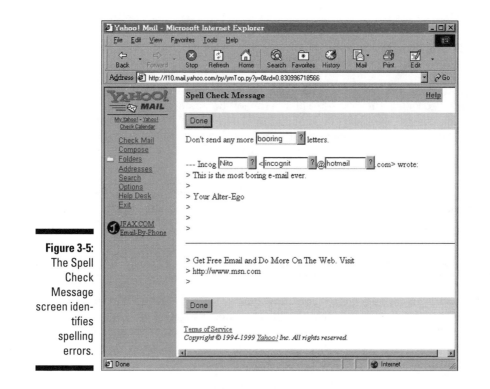

Figure 3-5:
The Spell
Check
Message
screen iden-
tifies
spelling
errors.

To fix a legitimate spelling error, do this:

1. **Click the question-mark button next to any suggested error.**

2. **In the pop-up window, select a correct spelling from the drop-down menu (see Figure 3-6).**

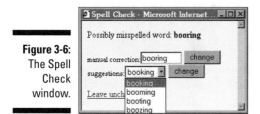

Figure 3-6:
The Spell
Check
window.

If you don't see a correct spelling in the drop-down menu, and you know what the correct spelling is, just type the replacement manually.

3. **Click the change button.**

If you prefer the misspelling for some reason or you realize it's not a misspelling after all, click the <u>Leave unchanged</u> link.

4. On the Spell Check Message page, click the Done button.

Clicking the Done button returns you to the Compose Mail page, where you can edit the letter, add to it, or send it.

To start an e-mail from scratch (as opposed to replying to an e-mail you've received), click the <u>Compose</u> link in the left-hand sidebar. The Compose Mail page appears, as when you're replying to a message, but without an address in the To: field. You must enter the recipient's e-mail address yourself, and type a subject for the letter also. Use the Send, Save Draft, and Spell Check buttons as described previously.

You may enter the recipient address of a letter you're composing directly from your Yahoo! Address Book, which I describe a bit later in this chapter.

Organizing Your Mail

If you're an active e-mailer, you know how letters can pile up and the ol' Inbox can become a cluttered mess. Dedicated e-mail programs let you create multiple folders for organizing mail, and Yahoo! Mail emulates that system in its Web mail.

If you're relatively new to e-mail, or if you already have e-mail and just aren't sure how you're going to use your Yahoo! mailbox, it might not be immediately apparent what folders you need to create. Not a problem — you can make them at any time, as you need them. I'm always creating folders, moving mail around, deleting old folders, and generally wasting more time organizing my mail than if I left it in one big stack. But I'll proceed on the assumption that you're better at this than I am. Here's how to create a new folder in Yahoo! Mail:

1. In Yahoo! Mail, click the <u>Folders</u> link in the left-hand sidebar.

The Folders For page appears.

2. In the Create a personal folder field, type a folder name.

A *personal folder* is any folder added to the collection of default folders Yahoo! provides to every mailbox. The default folders are Inbox, Draft, Sent, and Trash.

3. Click the Create new folder button.

The Folders For page reloads, this time listing your new folder and a new Edit a personal folder section. Whenever you return to this page, you may use the drop-down menu to select one of your personal folders, and rename it or delete it.

Immediately after you create your first personal folder, incoming mail still goes directly to your Inbox. From there, you may move it to any folder, default or personal. Here's how:

1. **On your Inbox page, click the check box next to any message you want to move.**

2. **In the Choose Folder drop-down menu, select the folder you'd like to use to hold the selected letter.**

3. **Click the Move button.**

   The Inbox page reloads, with your selected message no longer present in your Inbox list. To view the contents of any of your folders, click the <u>Folders</u> link in the left-hand sidebar.

Your Virtual Black Book

It's so easy to make friends in Yahoo!, through chatting, the message boards, and Yahoo! Messenger, that you might quickly develop a large and varied correspondence. It's impractical to keep your e-mail addresses on paper. The best system is to have an online address book. Yahoo! E-mail provides such a thing. Here's how to get it started:

1. **In Yahoo! Mail, click the <u>Addresses</u> link in the left-hand sidebar.**

   The Address Book For window appears (see Figure 3-7).

2. **Click the Add Contact button.**

   The New Address Book Entry page appears (see Figure 3-8).

3. **Fill in the fields.**

   All that's really necessary is a name and an e-mail address. You don't need to use the Yahoo! Address Book to keep track of phone numbers and company names if you don't feel so inspired. If you really do get inspired, click the Add More Detail button — the Add/Edit Contact Details page gives you enough information fields to spend the night entering everything you know about someone. Use the Category drop-down list to select which portion of your book to place this address.

4. **Click the Done button.**

Figure 3-9 illustrates an address book with a few entries. This option-packed page has a number of features:

Figure 3-7:
A brand new address book, waiting for new names to be added.

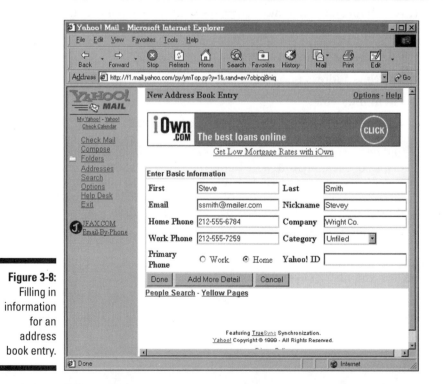

Figure 3-8:
Filling in information for an address book entry.

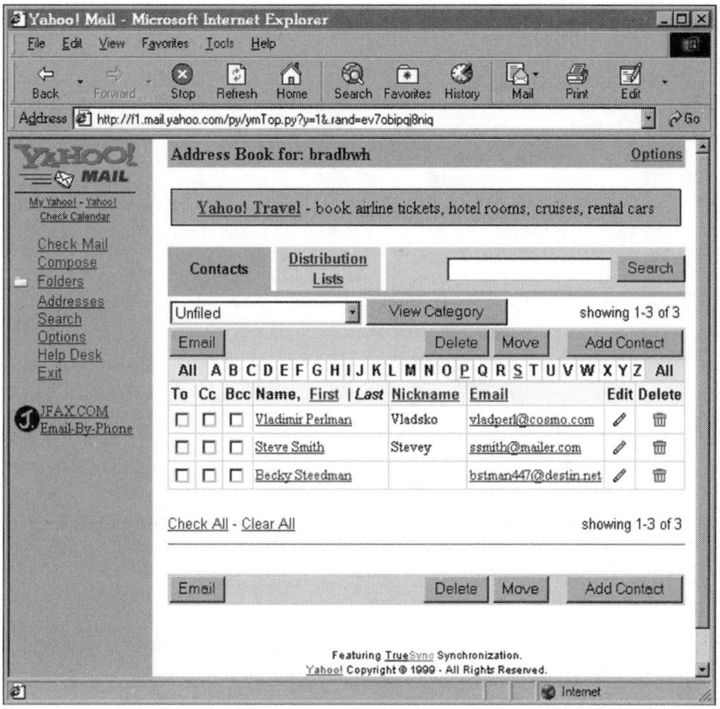

Figure 3-9:
A working
address
book with a
few entries.

✔ Use the Search field to enter a name or part of a name if your address book is large and you've lost someone. The search engine is pretty smart — you can enter a name, a nickname as entered in the address book, a fraction of a name, an e-mail address, or a portion of an e-mail address such as the domain name.

✔ Use the View Category drop-down list if you have addresses in different categories, and click the View Category button to see those entries.

✔ Use the Email button to open the Compose Mail page. If you don't click a check box next to someone's name, you must type an address manually. (The perils of modern life, I tell you.)

✔ Click the check boxes next to names, turning them into recipients of your outgoing mail when you click the Email button. You may check as many as you like. The Cc column is for copies sent to addresses besides the main recipient(s). The Bcc column is for recipients whose names _will not_ appear to all other recipients. (Bcc stands for Blind carbon copy.)

✔ Click any letter to see address book entries for that letter only.

✔ Click the First, Nickname, or Email links to sort the list by that criterion, alphabetically. (If First is clicked, then Last becomes a link.)

✔ Use the Check All link to select every name on the current page as a recipient.

✔ Use <u>Clear All</u> when you realize using the <u>Check All</u> link was a terrible mistake and you want to start over.

✔ Click any name to see all the information you have entered for that person.

✔ Use the Edit icon to change the information entered for any name.

✔ Use the Delete icon to kick someone out of your address book. (You may also use the Delete button to mass-annihilate any number of checked names.)

✔ Use the Move button to shift any entry to a new category.

You might want to organize your names into group lists, if you mail repeatedly to certain groups of names in your address book. Here's how to create your first group:

1. In your address book, click the <u>Distribution Lists</u> link.

2. On the Distribution Lists page, click the Add New List button.

The Edit Distribution List page appears (see Figure 3-10).

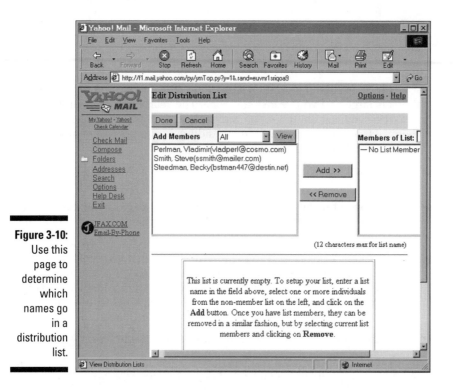

Figure 3-10:
Use this page to determine which names go in a distribution list.

3. **Click any name from the address book list on the left side.**

   You may use the Shift key to include all names between two clicks, or the Ctrl key to select noncontiguous names.

4. **Click the Add> button.**

   Your selected names move, as if by psychic powers, to the Members of List window.

5. **Select names and click the <<Remove button to eliminate names from your list.**

6. **In the Members of List field above the right-hand list, type the name of your new list.**

   You might need to scroll your browser window to the right to see this field.

7. **Click the Done button.**

   Your distribution list is now added to the Distribution Lists page. When you want to send an e-mail to the entire list, simply click the To check box, and all list addresses are automatically inserted as recipients. You may also click the Cc or Bcc check box for an entire list of names.

Search for the Lost Letter

It's come to this: You have so much e-mail stashed in your Yahoo! mailbox folders that you can't find that crucial invitation to the office party. Fortunately, a search engine lurks inside Yahoo! Mail to bail you out of just such a gaffe. Here's what to do:

1. **In Yahoo! Mail, click the <u>Search</u> link in the left-hand sidebar.**

   The Search page appears (see Figure 3-11).

2. **Use the first drop-down menu to select what portion of the message you want to search.**

   The default selection, "the message," means all text plus the address and header information. You can also select just the header or just the text body of the message.

3. **Use the second drop-down menu to select whether the search engine is looking for messages that contain, don't contain, begin with, or end with your keyword(s).**

4. **In the text field, type your phrase or word.**

5. **If you want Yahoo! to search literally, including matching capital letters, click the match case check box.**

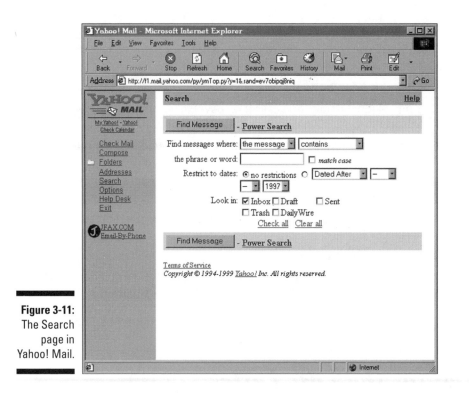

Figure 3-11:
The Search
page in
Yahoo! Mail.

6. **If you'd like to restrict the search to messages dated before, after, or on a certain date, click the second radio button next to Restrict to dates.**

   Use the drop-down menus to specify the date range for the search.

7. **Use the lower check boxes to determine which of your folders Yahoo! will rummage through to find your keyword(s).**

8. **Click the Find Message button.**

   Yahoo! Mail displays a list of all message headers whose messages match your search criteria.

If normal searching doesn't do it for you, try the Power Search link. It displays the Power Search page (Figure 3-12), which uses a series of drop-down menus to fine-tune what Yahoo! is looking for and where it looks.

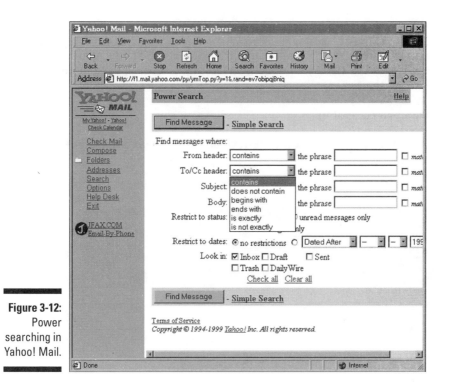

Figure 3-12:
Power
searching in
Yahoo! Mail.

The Way You Want It

Yahoo! Mail has evolved considerably since its introduction, and it's now one
mean, extremely useful tool. Nowhere is the evolution more in evidence than
when perusing the range of options now available. You can apply such features to your account as auto-responses when you're on vacation; receiving
color-coded mail from other Internet mailboxes; filtering incoming mail and
directing it into folders before you read it; and blocking reception of mail
from specific addresses.

The following sections explain two of the most important options.

Getting your mail from all over

If you have Yahoo! Mail, chances are you have another mailbox. You might
use other Web-based mail services, and almost certainly you have an Internet
mailbox associated with your online service or Internet service provider. You
can receive your mail from other mailboxes through the Yahoo! Mail interface
if you like.

Under normal circumstances, you might have little reason for reading non-Yahoo! mail in your Yahoo! mailbox. But I can tell you from experience, the feature comes in handy when you're traveling. Using Yahoo!, you can check your mail from a library computer, an Internet café, or any computer connected to the Net.

Here's how to set it up:

1. **In Yahoo! Mail, click the <u>Options</u> link from the left-hand sidebar.**

   The Options page appears (see Figure 3-13).

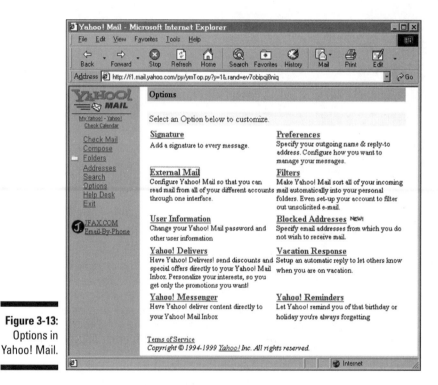

Figure 3-13:
Options in
Yahoo! Mail.

2. **Click the <u>External Mail</u> link.**

   The External Mail page appears.

3. **Click the Configure New Server button.**

   The next External Mail page appears (see Figure 3-14).

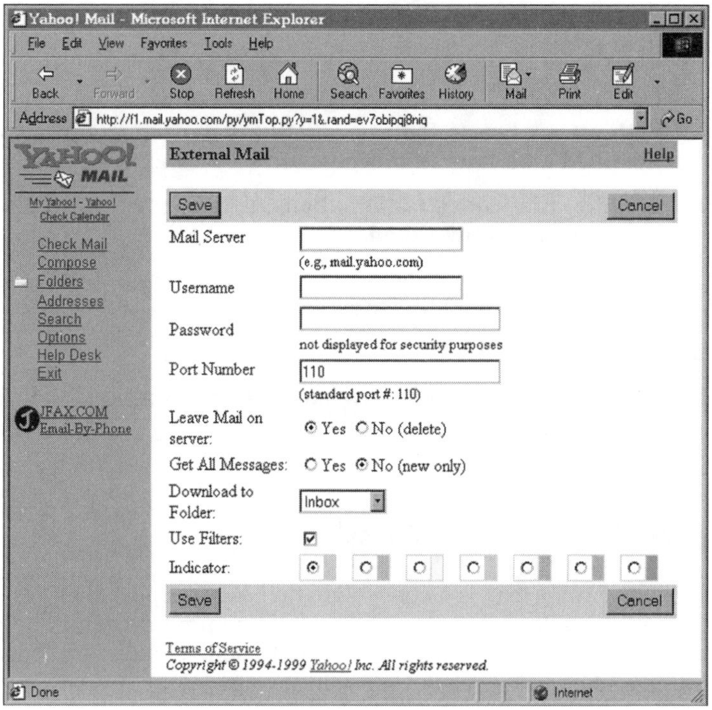

Figure 3-14:
Configuring
your
external
mailbox for
collection
by Yahoo!
Mail.

4. **Fill in the fields that define your external mailbox.**

   The Mail Server is probably the trickiest. You might need to ask your
   Internet service provider for the mail server domain name. Usually, the
   format is *mail.server.com* (or *mail.server.net*). The *server* in this example
   is normally the name of the Internet service provider.

   In most cases, your Username is the first part of your e-mail address,
   before the @ symbol. Only you know the Password. Leave the Port
   Number set at the default, 110.

5. **Using the radio buttons, decide whether you want your mail left on
   the server.**

   I always click Yes because I know I'm going to want the mail in my
   normal e-mail program eventually. But if that isn't important to you, click
   No so your mail doesn't pile up on the server, forcing you to download it
   all again at some point.

6. **Using the radio buttons, decide whether to get all messages or new
   messages only.**

   Yahoo! Mail keeps track of which messages you've collected from your
   server. This selection is relevant only if you selected to leave mail on the
   server (Step 5).

7. **Using the drop-down menu, select which folder to use for your external mail.**

   I find it a good idea to create a new folder exclusively for external mail.

8. **Use the check box to indicate whether you want to apply your filters (described a bit later in this chapter) to your external mail.**

9. **Using the color-coded radio buttons, decide how you would like your external mail distinguished.**

   The color-coding is a good feature, but necessary only if you don't create a dedicated folder for external mail.

10. **Click the Save button.**

11. **To get your external mail, click the <u>Check External Mail</u> link on your Inbox page.**

Controlling the flow

Filtering incoming mail is a convenient timesaver, especially if you receive a predictable flow from certain sources. You can predetermine where that mail will end up, and create dedicated folders to hold it. Filters place mail in selected folders before you ever see it, saving you the trouble of moving it around manually. Follow these steps to set up a filter:

1. **In Yahoo! Mail, click the <u>Options</u> link in the left-hand sidebar.**

   The Options page appears.

2. **Click the <u>Filters</u> link.**

   The Filters page appears.

3. **Click the Create button.**

   The New Filter page appears (see Figure 3-15).

4. **Use the drop-down menus to specify what Yahoo! Mail should look for in your incoming mail.**

   This step might take a bit of experimentation. The most important field is the From header, which includes the sender's e-mail address. That is how most mail is filtered — items from certain sources go here, and letters from other senders go there. So one possibility is to leave "contains" in the drop-down menu, and type the source's e-mail address in "the phrase" field.

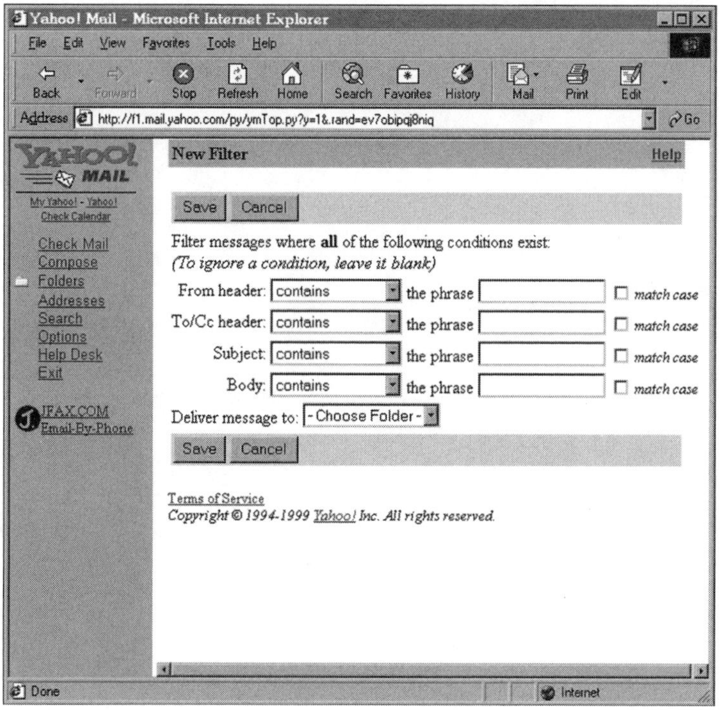

Figure 3-15:
Use this
page to
create a
new
incoming-
mail filter.

5. **Use the Deliver message to drop-down menu to select the target folder for filtered mail.**

6. **Click the Save button.**

Because one of the destination folders is the Trash folder, you can use the filter to automatically discard mail from unwanted sources.

You may make as many filters as you like. Just repeat the preceding steps whenever another good filtering idea occurs to you. Remember to create any dedicated folders before making the filter.

Part II
Letting Yahoo! Be Your Guide

The 5th Wave   By Rich Tennant

"IT'S JUST UNTIL WE GET BACK UP ON THE INTERNET."

In this part...

You may have used the Yahoo! directories and search engine before. The chapters in this part revisit Yahoo!'s traditional indexing and search services, and make anyone a better navigator of the Web.

Chapter 4

Ordering from the World's Biggest Menu

*T*hink of it. The Internet can be considered the planet's largest library. And Yahoo!, which started as a directory of the Web, is arguably the most comprehensive card catalogue to the Internet. *Arguably* is a key word, though, because several other directories would lay claim to the honor of being the most detailed and thorough menu of Web pages. The argument has been raging for years, but it's pointless. The Web is so huge and so kaleidoscopic in its tendency to shift and evolve that no online service in the world can take the ultimate snapshot of all Web pages at any given moment.

Yahoo! built the reputation of its directory on the ideas that big is good and that inclusion beats discrimination. Although some other directories provide editorial guidance by selecting sites to be included while leaving others out, Yahoo! became famous for its lengthy directory pages that seem to link every Web site ever created on a certain topic. That's not exactly true, but I'll get more detailed about Yahoo!'s inclusion methods a bit further on in this chapter.

The upshot is that Yahoo!'s directory remains a core feature of the entire online service, and it still carries an encyclopedic cachet. When you want an overview of Web destinations on a certain topic, general or detailed, good and bad, corporate or personal, famous and obscure — Yahoo!'s directory is the place to turn. Although the directory isn't a difficult feature to use, it is massive to the point of intimidation. Luckily, it succumbs nicely to a few tricks and shortcuts. That's the purpose of this chapter. Here, I tackle Yahoo!'s sprawling, magnificent information menu, which played a huge part in popularizing the Internet and still provides a daily virtual map to millions of online citizens.

Understanding the Yahoo! Directory

I might have titled this section "Understanding the Toaster" because the Yahoo! directory is somewhat easier to comprehend than piloting an airliner. This isn't brain surgery or even a relatively simple appendectomy. (For information on those topics, please see "Scalpel Technique For Dummies.") But this is where the aforementioned tricks and shortcuts come in. I'll guide your mouse through the points and clicks of Yahoo!'s directory, adding my personal tips along the way.

Start with the main directory page, as pictured in the lovely Figure 4-1. Get there by using the primary Yahoo! URL:

```
www.yahoo.com
```

The main Yahoo! directory page doesn't waste any space on decoration or unnecessary prettiness. Perhaps that's a kind way of saying it's ugly but useful. Its plain look brings an advantage to the user, though — without graphics and lots of advertisements, the directory is quick loading, easy to navigate, and down to earth.

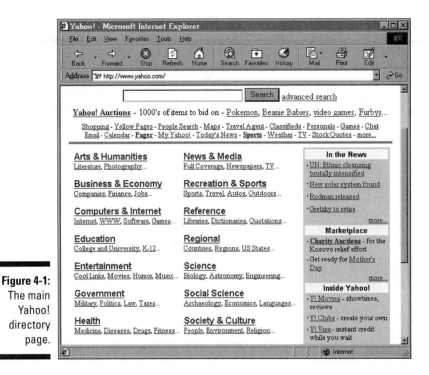

Figure 4-1: The main Yahoo! directory page.

You can see a search entry form and a Search button above the directory topics, but ignore them for the time being. (I explain how to use keywords and the search form in Chapter 5.) Likewise, disregard the auction links and all those other tempting links immediately below the Search button. I get into each one of those features later in the book.

Scroll down to those big, fat directory topics — Arts & Humanities, News & Media, and the twelve others. These are the *top-level,* or *first-level,* directory topics. Each one is a link leading to a *second-level* directory page. Each second-level page contains subtopic links leading to *third-level* pages, and so it goes for several levels. How many levels, exactly? It depends on the topic. Figure 4-2 shows a sixth-level directory page in the Computers and Internet topic.

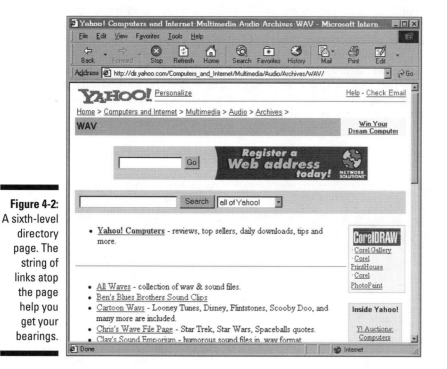

Figure 4-2:
A sixth-level directory page. The string of links atop the page help you get your bearings.

Site links versus directory links

It's a fight! Not really. Site links and directory links work together to bring sparkle and joy to many directory pages. Well, they work together, anyway. My point is to draw a distinction between when you're linking to a Web site (leaving Yahoo! to visit another site) and when you're linking to a lower-level page in the Yahoo! directory.

Some directory pages have only directory links. (They tend to be upper-level pages representing broad topics.) Some directory pages have only site links. (They're lower-level pages representing highly specific topics, containing links to other sites on those topics.) The middle ground is populated with pages that have both directory and site links, and in those cases the directory links are always above the site links and are displayed in **bold type**.

Figure 4-3 shows a hybrid directory page. The figure illustrates the Trivia portion of the Entertainment topic. Trivia subcategories are placed above the site links. Clicking a subcategory leads to another directory page (third level in this case), and clicking a site link takes you to that site, outside Yahoo!.

The numbers next to directory links throughout the Yahoo! directory give you an indication of how many site links are within that topic and its subtopics. As you begin working with the directory, it might seem that those numbers are inaccurate. Next to **Chat** in Figure 4-3, for example, four site links are indicated. Yet clicking that directory link reveals only one site link on the next page. That's because *another* directory link (with a 3 in parentheses) is featured on that page, and clicking it reveals the missing site links on the next page. In other words, the site links indicated in parentheses might be distributed among several layers further down in the directory.

Directory links

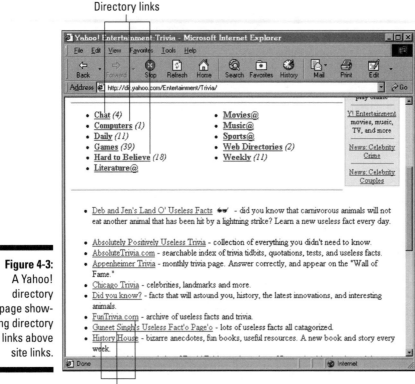

Figure 4-3:
A Yahoo! directory page showing directory links above site links.

Site links

Getting your bearings

The Yahoo! directory is as complex as a labyrinth. It's a marvel of organization, actually, but even highly organized structures can leave your head spinning if they're complicated enough. The Yahoo! directory is definitely complex. Fortunately, it delivers a helpful feature that marks your place in the overall structure at any given moment. And you can use this feature to quickly get out of any tangled trail.

Near the top of every Yahoo! directory page is a succession of links, the leftmost of which is a Home link to the top page of the directory (Yahoo!'s home page). The links get more topic specific as you track them to the right, and the last one represents the page you're on. Moving up to a higher-level directory page is as simple as clicking any of the links.

It's tempting to think that the string of links represents a trail of your journey into the directory, but in fact it doesn't always work that way. As you navigate through the directory, you might notice that the entire string changes from one page to another, when you'd expect only the last link to be added to the previous string. This discrepancy is due to the cross-referencing of the directory, wherein some very specific topics might be listed in more than one main topic's directory pages.

Here's an example of cross-referencing. The directory page in Figure 4-2 contains links to archives of sound files. As you can see from the string of directory links, the list is located in the Multimedia portion of the Computers and Internet main topic area. However, I didn't follow that path to arrive at this page; it's listed also in the Music portion of the main Entertainment topic. So one second I was at the Home > Entertainment > Music > Recording > Sampling directory page, and the next second I had been slung over to Computers and Internet. (Fortunately, I was uninjured.)

Fun with shortcuts

When I was a kid, I cut through a neighbor's yard on the way to school, trampling flowerbeds in my haste to educate myself. Who knew that a life of juvenile crime would prepare me to be a famous author? (I'm still waiting for the fame part.) Anyway, Yahoo! lets you take shortcuts for the sake of education, too.

If you look back at Figure 4-1, you see a few links in small type beneath the main topic categories. Each link takes you directly to a third-level directory page, skipping over the second level with the same blithe spirit I felt when thrashing through tulips as an eager young lad. Yahoo! attempts to place the most popular, in-demand subcategories as these shortcut links. But if you don't see what you're looking for, you might need to click the main category, get to the second-level page, and find your subtopic there. On the other hand, if your goal falls within one of the shortcut links (like a film title falls within the Movies shortcut), you'll save some time by cruising directly to the third level.

I told you that would be fun. I'm great at parties, too.

Little tiny icons

Did I mention that the icons are small? Cute, too. These diminutive icons are sprinkled through the Yahoo! directory like sprouts on a healthy salad. The figure shows the three types of icon likely to catch your attention:

✔ **NEW!** The yellow NEW! icon, displayed next to directory links, can mean only one thing — something is NEW! It's not the sub-category link that's new, though. The NEW! icon indicates that new site links have been added to the category.

✔ **GLASSES.** The glasses icon is a miniature graphic of a pair of glasses (sunglasses, it appears). It indicates that a site link is worth investigating — worth a closer look, you might say. The glasses are sometimes, but not always, next to a reviewed link (see the next item).

✔ **REVIEW.** Sites reviewed in Yahoo!'s Internet Life e-zine feature this icon. To see the review, don't click the site link — that takes you to the site itself, not the review. If you want to read the review before trying the site, click the REVIEW icon.

Browser window: Yahoo! Entertainment:Movies and Film - Microsoft Internet Explorer

Address: http://dir.yahoo.com/Entertainment/Movies_and_Film/

- Cultures and Groups *(455)* NEW!
- Databases *(16)*
- Employment *(220)*
- Events *(9)*
- Fan Fiction@
- Film Festivals *(330)* NEW!
- Film Music *(252)* NEW!
- Film Schools *(78)*
- Filmmaking *(879)* NEW!
- Genres *(1884)* NEW!
- History *(43)*
- Home Video *(57)*
- Humor@
- Independent *(32)*

- Personal Pages *(168)*
- Previews *(20)*
- Release Schedules *(13)*
- Reviews *(495)*
- Screenplays *(150)*
- Showtimes *(8)*
- Studios@
- Theaters *(46)* NEW!
- Theory and Criticism *(18)*
- Titles *(4261)* NEW!
- Trivia *(80)* NEW!
- Web Directories *(41)*
- FAQs *(5)*
- Usenet *(41)*

near you

News: Bollywood

News: Cannes Film Festival

News: Star Wars Episode I

- Film Scouts ᏊᏊ - takes you from Hollywood to the beaches of Cannes. On site you will find Hollywood clips, Indie clips, stars, and other information about films.
- Film.com ᏊᏊ - an independent site devoted to contemporary film review and discussion, film festivals announcements and field reports, and essays on film craft and filmmaking.
- Hollywood Online REVIEW ᏊᏊ - multimedia entertainment, information and previews, hundreds of photos, video, sound and multimedia kits, movie trailers and more.
- Internet Movie Database@ ᏊᏊ
- Yahoo! Movies ᏊᏊ - showtimes, new releases, reviews, and more.

Yahoo! plugs itself

In the far-ago olden days (about two years ago), the Yahoo! directory was strictly self-contained and kept distinct from other features in the broad Yahoo! online service. You knew that when you clicked a link on a directory page, you'd get either another (more specific) directory page or a non-Yahoo! site on your topic of choice.

Now, though, you might spin yourself off into another part of Yahoo! if you're not careful. So be careful! There's no great danger, of course, and you can always use your browser's Back button to get back on track. The links to watch out for are located near the top of every second-level directory page, and some of the deeper directory pages as well. The links invite you to Join a Chat, Start a Club, or Post a Message — all worthy pursuits that I describe in other chapters. Links to Live Net Events and Headline News also appear under many categories.

These self-promotional links are always relevant. For example, the Start a Club link takes you to a topical directory of Yahoo! Clubs, relevant to the directory page you were browsing. But they take you out of the directory, so if you want to continue tracking down a topic, just Back your way into the directory and resume your search.

Steroid-Infused Tips

As the preceding section makes clear, the Yahoo! directory is a marvel of organization and complexity. It contains an astounding number of topics, subtopics, and directory pages. Navigating within the directory isn't hard, after you grasp the multilayered architecture of the thing. (All Web directories are structured in essentially the same way.)

This section highlights some tricks for any would-be power Yahoo!'er. The following points are habits I've incorporated in my constant quest for more, faster, and better content.

Look before you link

It's amazing what you can learn from a URL — the Web address — of any site link in the Yahoo! directory. Examining URLs has become such a habit for me that I almost never click a link blithely, without checking the address for signs of quality first.

In the Yahoo! directory, many sites are linked with no description or explanation whatsoever. Yahoo! invites Webmasters to include such information, but many don't. As a result, when you're browsing for sites under a certain topic, you might be overwhelmed with choices with no sense of where to go first. Only rarely will a URL tell you whether a site will be exactly what you're looking for, but almost all of them offer hints of what is to come if you click that link.

In the Navigator and Internet Explorer browsers, viewing the domain name of a link is simple. Just place the mouse cursor over the link — but don't click! The URL appears in the bottom status bar of the browser window, immediately beneath the page you're currently viewing. In the Opera browser, the URL floats next to the link when you position your mouse cursor on it.

Every URL begins with *http://*, although I have that universal prefix out of all the links in this book (to create space for questionable jokes, silly asides, and unnecessary parenthetical inserts). When typing a URL into your browser, you can likewise leave off the *http://* prefix.

Following are some of the main URL indicators to look for.

Domain name

The *domain name* of a URL is the part after the *www.* and before the first slash. Checking out the domain name gives you a hint as to the professionalism of a site. If the name of the site (or company) is in the domain name, you're probably headed for a more professional online experience than if the site is a personal production hosted by an ISP (Internet service provider). For example, if you were looking for sites about Star Trek, you might run your mouse cursor over the following three URLs:

```
www.startrek.com
members.tripod.com/~Huntster
www.bestoftrek.com/
```

In each case, the domain name follows the *www.* In the first example, the domain name `startrek` is a big indicator of a major site on the subject. Although domain names are freely available to anybody for purchase, the major ones were either snagged first or bought later by the corporate owners of their trademarks — in this case, Paramount Pictures. So if you were looking for highly produced, official information about Star Trek, that would be one link you'd want to click. (Of course, you don't need the Yahoo! directory to find the most obvious URLs; you can simply type them into your browser.)

In the second example — the URL for a site that the Yahoo! directory calls Ben's Star Trek Page — the domain name is that of a well-known and popular Web-page hosting site called Tripod. It's a sure sign that this is a fan page. Now don't misunderstand me — nothing's wrong with fan pages. In fact, to Star Trek (and other show) fans, the homegrown sites are often more satisfying than the slick studio productions. So when you see *tripod* (or *geocities* or *angelfire* or *aol*) in the domain name, you're looking at a hobby-site link. Many other Web hosting companies are out there as well. The ~ symbol (as in the second example) is often another indicator that you have a personal, not a professional, site.

The third example type usually lies between the first two in the hobby-professional continuum. (I use words like *continuum* because I myself am an unrepentant Star Trekker.) Notice that the domain name incorporates the subject, without impinging on the trademark. Such a URL is usually a sign of a serious amateur or semiprofessional Web site, created by someone who went to the trouble (and slight expense) to purchase a dedicated domain name for it. It could also be a small company taking a stab at the new-media business on the Net. Whatever the background particulars, such sites are often good blends of professional design and funky content.

Domain names are like virtual real estate. Anyone can buy one — or, to put it more accurately, lease one. You pay an annual fee to retain possession of a domain. Cyber real estate is just about the least expensive real estate in the world, with an annual rent of only thirty-five dollars per domain — and that fee might go down. After a person or a company acquires a domain name, a Web hosting company is needed to display the Web site, which runs into more money. Still, producing a pro-style site under a good address is a low-overhead business, and many enterprising individuals are getting into the act.

Domain name suffix

The ubiquitous *dot com* (.com) is the most recognizable part of a domain name, but it's not the only domain suffix you see in links. The suffix gives you a broad indicator of the nature of some sites and of the geography in some cases. Currently, six major domain suffixes are used in the United States (and around the world in two cases):

- **.com** is the high-rent suffix. Not that it costs any more than the others do, but it carries the highest status.

- **.net** doesn't mean anything different from *.com* — it's an alternative when a *domain.com* address is taken. Many companies buy the *.com* and *.net* versions of their trademark domain names. This suffix is regarded with a bit less esteem than *.com*. When you see a *.net* URL, it might mean that the site failed to purchase the *.com* address in time. That doesn't necessarily mean it's a second-rate site, though.

- **.edu** is used by verified four-year educational institutions. Sites with *.edu* domains tend to be more academic in nature. There's even an *.edu* Star Trek site:

```
www.hputx.edu/Academics/English/df-trek.htm
```

✔ **.gov** is used by all government sites in the United States (except military sites). It's something to look for if you're searching out official information about government topics such as regulatory issues. Sites such as the White House, the Internal Revenue Service, and the Department of Labor all have the *.gov* suffix.

✔ **.org** may be used by non-profit organizations, but they aren't required to use it. Such sites are sometimes slimmer productions than their *.org* counterparts, though some hefty and entertaining *.org* sites are out there. (National Public Radio has a nice one at `www.npr.org`.)

✔ **.mil** is used by military agencies in the United States.

Every non-United States country has its own two-letter domain suffix, such as *.uk* for the United Kingdom and *.pt* for Portugal. When you see a non-United States domain in a URL, the site might not be in English. More common for American users is the delay sometimes encountered when trying to visit those sites, due to the geographical distance.

Using multiple windows

One important detail that can escape the attention of Internet newcomers, and even folks of greater experience, is that browsers can replicate themselves in multiple windows. Whether you're using Internet Explorer or Navigator, you may at any time generate a new browser window.

In both programs, using the Ctrl+N keyboard command opens up a new window, displaying the same page as the original window. Navigator keeps added windows the same size as the original, but Explorer is more capricious in that regard. Explorer users can always resize the new window to their taste.

When using the Yahoo! directory, I usually open new browser windows in the process of clicking a link. Both popular browsers give you the option of opening a link in a new window by using the right-click menu. Here's how it works:

1. **When you find a site link you'd like to visit, place your mouse cursor over it and click the right mouse button.**

   (Or click the left button if you have reversed the default function of the buttons. At any rate, use the mouse button you don't normally use to click a link.) A menu drops down beneath the mouse cursor.

2. **Move the cursor to the Open in New Window selection, and left-click it. (Use the normal mouse button.)**

   The site you're visiting appears in a new browser window.

3. **Resize the window if necessary.**

   You may switch back and forth between the site and the directory page.

If creating multiple browser windows gives you concern about using up your computer's resources and slowing down its performance, stop worrying. Opening another window doesn't boot up a cloned version of your browser. It's just one program running, with the capability to reach several tentacles into the Net simultaneously. Sort of like one room with many windows. Each extra window does chew up a small portion of your desktop resources, but in most cases you won't notice the difference. If your machine has no more than 32 megs of RAM, however, and you notice slower-than-normal page loads when using more than one browser window, go back to a single window.

Opening multiple browser windows helps you avoid getting lost. Keep in mind that finding good stuff through the Yahoo! directory is a hit-or-miss business. The directory exposes you to a gigantic range of sites on almost any topic, and — even using the URL pointers I explain in the preceding section — bouncing back and forth between Yahoo! and outside sites is commonplace. That bouncing is a lot easier if you keep one browser window dedicated to the directory page you're linking from.

It's easy to get involved in a site, exploring its pages and layers. In so doing, you can lose track of where you were in the Yahoo! directory. Keep clicking for long enough, and even the Back button and History list of your browser won't help you. Anchoring one browser window on the directory page and linking sites into new browser windows is the answer.

Using a fresh browser window isn't a bad idea even while you're staying within the Yahoo! directory. I sometimes link from one subcategory to a lower-level topic in a new window so as not to lose track of the subcategory. Whether you rely on your Back button or keep things organized in different 15-inch monitor's windows depends on how you like to view things, and how big your monitor is. Multiple browser windows on 15-inch monitors (or smaller) can get cluttered and confusing.

Bookmark your Favorites

If you're the adventurous sort, the Yahoo! directory is made for you. During your explorations, you will no doubt investigate many a terrific Web site. One common downfall of surf-loving folks is forgetting to bookmark sites, and then never finding them again.

The Navigator browser has its Bookmark feature, and Internet Explorer uses lists called Favorites. Although the two browsers implement these features somewhat differently, they both serve the same essential function, which is to put reminder links to sites in the browser itself, so you don't have to track them down the hard way a second time. Both Bookmarks and Favorites allow you to accumulate many such links and organize them into named folders.

The rule is bookmark first, sort later. If you go into a site that looks halfway decent, and might possibly be worth a second visit sometime, just add it to your Bookmark or Favorites list immediately. It's a lot easier to remove a bookmark than to find an obscure site a second time.

Adding a Site

Yahoo! is a highly interactive online service. You might be surprised to learn that the directory relies on its visitors for additions to its extensive menu of sites. The Yahoo! editors perform a small portion of the selecting and reviewing of new directory sites, but most additions result from the suggestions of users.

If you have a Web page of your own, submitting it to the Yahoo! directory is free and doesn't take much time. You must follow a certain procedure, however, or you'll get bogged down in error messages. When sending in the name and URL of a site, you must also select a subcategory page where you think the link should be. You must submit a subcategory, not one of the 14 main topic areas that appear on the Yahoo! home page. Note, though, that the Yahoo! Surfers (the Yahoo! team) might change the location before adding your site.

Although you have no assurance that a site will be added to the Yahoo! directory, Yahoo! isn't in the business of turning sites away from the directory. So as long as you have a legitimate URL and follow the procedure, it should get added within a reasonable time. (It sometimes takes a few weeks.)

Finding the category

Choosing a good subcategory page for your site submission enhances your chances of getting the site added, and added quickly. Because of that fact, choosing the subcategory is probably the most important part of the entire process. Don't slight it by taking a hasty or ill-informed guess at where your site belongs. Digging around the directory until you find the best spot is worth the time.

Following are a few pointers for finding the best subcategory:

✔ When choosing a subcategory, the first thing you should look for is the presence of site links on the subcategory directory page. (I explain the difference between site links and directory links earlier in this chapter.) If the page has only directory links leading to more specific subtopics, you're still too high in the directory and need to dig deeper to find your category.

✔ When examining a possible subcategory directory page, look for sites that are similar to the one you're submitting. You might even want to visit a few, but you might be able to see immediately, from the site titles, whether it's the page for you.

✔ When assessing where your site belongs, distinguish between a personal site and a topical site. By this I mean, is your site about anything besides yourself? Is it an online personal scrapbook, or is it about a hobby? Are the pages about your family, vacations, pets, and home? If so, it's a personal site. Are the pages about your hobby, favorite TV show, or research into a medical condition? If it's along some specific subject line, it's a topic page. All personal sites get listed in the **Society and Culture: People: Personal Home Pages** category. Topic sites fit into other directory subcategories.

You might be tempted to try pushing your site as high in the directory as possible. Resist this temptation. Suggesting an inappropriately high placement just makes the Yahoo! editors' job harder, and slows the process of getting the site listed at all. Remember that Yahoo! enjoys a gigantic audience, and any listing in the directory is good exposure for your site.

Once you decide on a subcategory directory page for your site submission, follow these two simple steps:

1. **Click the Suggest a Site link at the bottom of that directory page.**

   The link appears on every level-three and lower directory page.

2. **On the next page, click the Proceed to Step One button.**

Submitting the site

After following the preceding steps, Yahoo! tosses you into a four-part Suggest a Site process. Don't be put off by all the steps — Yahoo! could have just as easily put the whole shebang on one page. The four-page design spreads out the forms you need to fill in, but doesn't make them difficult. Here's what you need to do:

1. **In Step 1, fill in the Title, URL, and Description forms, and then click the Proceed to Step 2 button.**

   Follow the instructions beneath each form. The title does not need to be the page title as it appears in the title bar of a browser visiting that page, but it's probably less confusing to visitors if you keep them the same. In the Description form, take the time to write a concise, positive description of the site. Remarkably, most submissions don't contain descriptions; a short blurb encourages users to link over to your site.

2. **In Step 2, fill in the Category Suggestions fields, and then click the Proceed to Step 3 button.**

   Remember that Yahoo! already knows your first choice for a category in which to list your site. On this page, you have the chance to specify a second (or new) category where your site should *also* be listed. Some sites are cross-referenced in two categories — such as an investment company specializing in local accounts that might be listed in a regional category and a financial category.

   You can't be vague about the alternate category suggestion. Make a suggestion for an alternate listing only if you have the exact category on hand. If you want to do further research in the directory, open a new browser window so you don't lose your place in the submission process.

3. **In Step 3, fill in the Contact and Geographical information, and then click the Proceed to Step 4 button.**

   This page is where Yahoo! learns who you are (in a perfunctory way; you don't have to discuss your troubled childhood), how you can be contacted, and where your site is located.

4. **In Step 4, fill in the applicable fields, and then click the Submit button.**

   The Time-Sensitive Information fields on this page apply only to pages that describe, promote, or host an event. If your page isn't associated with any deadlines or ending times, ignore these forms. The Final Comments form is the place to type anything that will help the Yahoo! team understand or place your site.

You're finished! Have patience as Yahoo! checks out your site.

Chapter 5

Starting Up the Yahoo! Search Engine

*Y*ou've probably heard the slightly intimidating phrase: *search engine.* Sounds like something you don't want to get your hands dirty on. Actually, search engines are extremely sanitary and useful. They help you find things on the Internet without spending all night browsing through directories.

If browsing directories is like window shopping, using a search engine is like striding into a store, plastic in hand, with intent to purchase. Browsing goes for the haystack; searching goes for the needle. (My Bachelor of Metaphor degree is really coming in handy.)

This chapter describes how Yahoo! differs from other search engines, and explains how to use keywords in Yahoo! to find stuff on the Net.

Yahoo! Searching Secrets Revealed

Yahoo! became famous several years ago as an Internet directory with a search engine attached. This chapter describes how searching in Yahoo! works, but it's important to distinguish between two types of search engines you can find on the Web. Many search engines use automated software to continually troll the Net, learning about new sites. Those sites then become part of a massive, searchable index of Internet destinations.

Yahoo! operates differently, without any such automated indexing software (sometimes called *spiders, robots*, or just *bots*). The Yahoo! search engine performs only within the Yahoo! directory. (See Chapter 4 to find out more about the directory.) The difference between Yahoo!'s search engine and others might seem subtle — after all, a directory is nothing more than a big index. Although that's true, a fairly big difference exists in how different indices are compiled. For example, automated Web-trolling software picks up individual pages of multipage sites, whereas Yahoo! — which relies on site owners to submit their URLs to the directory — might contain only the main page of a site.

Other differences distinguish bot-based search engines from Yahoo!'s directory searching feature. When you perform a search in one of the major, non-Yahoo! search engines, the results you get are slanted according to a number of factors that may exist in the pages' underlying code. The search engine in Yahoo!, by contrast, looks only at the page title and description as submitted by the page owner and listed in the directory.

This is all very interesting (or not), but what do these differences mean to us, the users? They add up to one central fact: Each search engine is different and produces distinctive search results for any given query. Yahoo! is unique in that its directory is so gigantic and targeted to main pages of sites. On the other hand, if a site owner hasn't submitted his or her site to Yahoo! for inclusion in the directory (a somewhat time-consuming process described in Chapter 4), it doesn't exist on Yahoo!'s radar. Search engines that run automatically might well turn up that same site, thanks to the work of their tireless software robots.

Going beyond the directory

Recognizing that its users sometimes want to search beyond its directory, Yahoo! provides an automated link to another, Internet-wide search engine. (That engine is called Inktomi, which is a good tidbit of information to forget.)

Every search results page that you see has a Web Pages link near the top. When you click that link, Yahoo! automatically feeds your keyword(s) into the Inktomi search engine and displays the results. Now you're seeing the results of Inktomi's *spider*, which scours the Web all the time finding new sites and multiple

pages within sites. Unlike Yahoo!'s own search engine, the Inktomi engine looks at all the words on every page it finds, so your search runs much deeper into the Web's content.

Generally, a Web Pages search returns more results (sometimes a *lot* more) than the standard directory search. Some of the search results can seem bafflingly irrelevant, if your keywords are matching some bit of text buried deep within the page. Deeper searching is not always better searching, but it's good to have the option.

Sleuthing with Keywords

Keywords are clues. Computers, being the dense creatures they are, need all the clues they can get. Keywords are cryptic hints that lead you to specific topics on the Internet.

Using keywords to search in Yahoo! is the reverse of using the directory, which gives *you* keywords. Consider the categories and subcategories of the Yahoo! directory, as pictured in Figure 5-1. Each topical link provides a keyword that leads you to more detailed subjects. Typing your own keywords in the search form (also pictured in Figure 5-1) lets you cut to the chase by zooming directly to directory pages and site links on highly specific topics.

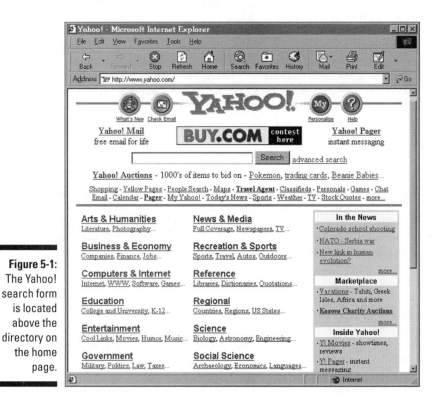

Figure 5-1:
The Yahoo!
search form
is located
above the
directory on
the home
page.

A keyword can be anything related to what you're looking for. You may also enter more than one keyword, called a *keyword string*. A certain craft is involved in determining what keyword(s) will give you the best results. This chapter gets you started on the right foot for the Yahoo! search engine, and provides some helpful tips. In fact, I see a helpful tip coming up next.

To search effectively in Yahoo!, you must attain a literal state of mind. It doesn't do any good to speak colloquially to Yahoo! or to ask it questions. For example, if you're interested in finding a Web page with a stock market summary, you might be tempted to type what's really on your mind, like this search string: *did the stock market close up or down today?* Yahoo!, struggling in its literal-minded way to please you, would search for matches to every one of those keywords, and (I just tried it now) would deliver the official Rice Krispies site because its description matched the greatest number of words. (Including *did* and *today,* which have little to do with what you really want.) Entering the search string *stock market summary,* however, brings up links you can use, unrelated to crunchy breakfast fare.

You need to remember a few basic points if you're just starting to use keywords in Yahoo!. The following might seem obvious, but I'll get to the more sophisticated stuff later in this chapter:

- **No caps.** Capital (uppercase) letters are not important when searching in Yahoo!. It doesn't hurt your search to use them, but there's no point knocking yourself out unnecessarily. The search engine is not *case sensitive.* Even when using proper names as your keywords, feel free to use lowercase letters, as in *kevin costner.*

- **Don't forget the spaces.** Yahoo! may be literal, but it can't understand multiple keywords if you don't have a space between each word. You can enhance your search by inserting things in those spaces. I'll get to them later in this chapter.

- **Watch your spelling.** Spelling counts when searching. You can get away with sloppy spelling in just about every other aspect of the Net — e-mail, chat rooms, message boards — but it'll kill a search. Many times I've scratched my head over a puzzling set of search results, only to finally realize that I made slip of the typing finger.

Just a Simple Search

Getting started with a simple Yahoo! search is so easy it's almost embarrassing. Follow these steps and you'll be lasering into the Web in no time:

1. **Go to the Yahoo! home page (refer to Figure 5-1) at this URL:**

   ```
   www.yahoo.com
   ```

2. **In the keyword entry form, type a keyword or a keyword string.**

3. **Click the Search button next to the keyword entry form.**

In a few seconds, a search results page appears, unsurprisingly called Yahoo! Search Results. Figure 5-2 illustrates the search results for the keyword string *anthony hopkins*. Because I searched for a particular person, as opposed to a general topic, I got a manageable number of results (called *hits*). Had I searched for a more general subject, I would have been deluged with hits (ouch!), which Yahoo! would have organized in groups of twenty hits per page. Whenever you get more than twenty hits, you can move among your Search Results pages using links at the bottom of each page.

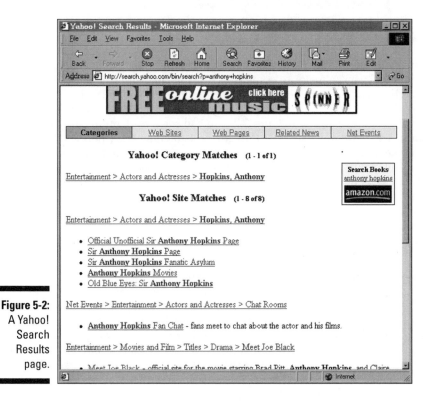

Figure 5-2:
A Yahoo!
Search
Results
page.

Simple searches are a little more complicated than they seem. Yahoo! is really performing two functions. First, it is searching the categories of its directory. Second, it is searching the site links of its directory. The upshot of this two-pronged approach is a results page divided into what are called Category Matches and Site Matches. Figure 5-2 shows how results are organized in a typical simple search.

Category Matches bring up directory categories and subcategories that include all your keywords. Each category link takes you to that directory page, where you may browse for sites and perhaps drill down further into the directory. Site Matches show links to outside sites whose titles or descriptions match at least one of your keywords. (Sites that match *all* your keywords are listed first.) Additionally, the site links are organized by the directory subcategory under which they are listed. As you can see in Figure 5-2, Site Matches may be grouped on directory pages that do not appear in the Category Matches. That's because certain directory page titles might not contain your keywords, but still house links that do contain your keywords.

Getting Your Bearings on the Search Results Page

The Yahoo! Search Results page has a few features worth investigating. In addition, I want to get into some tricks to working with the Category Matches. This section helps you make the most of your search results.

If you look once again at Figure 5-2, you can see a horizontal bar with five links. The left-hand selection, Categories, is highlighted when you first see your search results. These five links are important because they give you new ways of making your keywords work for you. Whenever you use these links, Yahoo! remembers your most recent keywords and matches them to its database in certain ways. Here's how the links work:

- ✔ **Categories.** The default selection when you perform a simple search, the Categories page displays Category Matches to your keywords first, followed by Site Matches.

- ✔ **Web Sites.** If you want to skip the Category Matches, click this selection to display a page containing only the Site Matches to your keywords. This tack is especially useful when using broad, general keywords or just a single keyword. In those cases, it's possible to generate so many Category Matches that your Site Matches don't even appear on the first Search Results page. (Remember that Yahoo! places only 20 results on any page.) Try searching on the single keyword *movies* to see what I mean. Later in this section, I'll show you another way of dealing with extensive Category Matches.

- ✔ **Web Pages.** As I mention in the "Going beyond the directory" sidebar, Yahoo! lets you break out of its directory whenever you want to take advantage of a Web-spider search engine called Inktomi. After performing your simple search, from the Search Results page, click the Web Pages link to apply your keyword to Inktomi. Inktomi inspects every word of all the Web sites in its index, so your results draw a deeper portrait of what's available on the Internet for any topic. The numbers bear out that added depth: In my original simple search for *anthony hopkins*, the Yahoo! directory came up with eight Site Matches, whereas Inktomi delivered over fourteen thousand hits. Remember — bigger is not necessarily better! Those eight Yahoo! directory hits are well targeted because the keywords appear in the site title or description. If you were to investigate all the Inktomi hits (which would probably damage your mental health), you'd find many irrelevancies and dead ends.

✔ **Related News.** Yahoo! maintains an extensive database of up-to-the-minute news stories from a number of wire services and other sources (see Chapter 7). The <u>Related News</u> link sends your keywords into that database and returns hits that match any words in any stories. The searching in this department is thorough, and you're likely to see matches that don't seem, at first, to bear any relationship to your keywords. Then, if you read a seemingly irrelevant news story, you always find your keywords in there somewhere. This feature is good to use when searching on proper name keywords or places.

✔ **Net Events.** This link notifies you of scheduled online events that relate to your keywords. In the *anthony hopkins* search, <u>Net Events</u> hit on a weekly fan chat about the actor. Some searches don't bring up any events; my search for *dump trucks*, for example, though it returned more Site Matches than *anthony hopkins*, failed to uncover any chats about six-wheelers. (Maybe there's not much to say about them.)

When conducting a simple search, you're more likely to get a lot of Category Matches when you use fewer and broader keywords as opposed to more and specific keywords. Knowing that, a strategy should begin to take form in your mind. When you know exactly what you want, and you desire to get outside Yahoo! to the sites that deliver your subject, spell out your need with a string of precisely targeted keywords.

Why would you ever want to broaden the search to get more Category Matches? There's a good reason: From any category page in the Yahoo! directory, you have a choice of entering keywords and searching within *just that category*. This is a great way to weed irrelevancies from your search results and explore a subcategory with precision. Here's a scenario that illustrates how to use this technique:

1. **Perform a simple search from the Yahoo! home page.**

   Follow the procedure I describe in the preceding section. You may enter any keyword and click the Search button, but to follow along with this example, use the keyword *investing*.

2. **On the Search Results page, click one of the Category Matches.**

   You should see a few Category Matches in response to the *investing* search. At the time of this writing, three Yahoo! directory categories match the keyword, but there might be more or fewer when you try it.

3. **On the category page (see Figure 5-3), use the drop-down menu to the right of the Search button to select "just this category."**

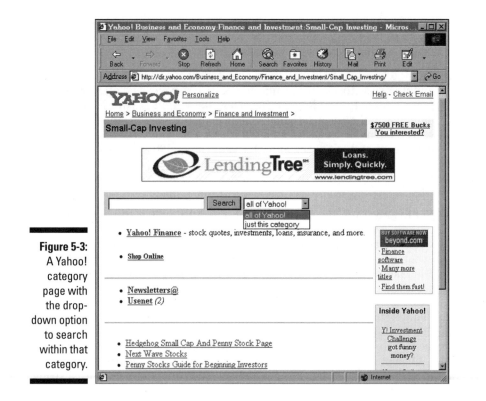

Figure 5-3:
A Yahoo!
category
page with
the drop-
down option
to search
within that
category.

4. Enter new keywords, and click the Search button.

You may enter the same keyword(s) as before — *investing* in this example — but it makes more sense to fine-tune the search at this point.

After following this procedure, you are now searching a small, contained portion of the Yahoo! directory. If you clicked on a low-level Category Match in
Step 2, it could be a very limited portion indeed. You might have trouble finding keywords that generate Site Matches in a particular subcategory. You
have two choices if your frustration mounts:

  ✔ Use the Back button to return to the original Search Results page and
     click a different Category Match (Step 2), or

  ✔ Use the drop-down menu to select "all of Yahoo!" and start your search
     over as if you were on the home page.

You can always start over in the midst of any Yahoo! search. Near the bottom
of every Search Results page is a keyword search form. Yahoo! remembers
your previous keywords, but you can type over them to begin a new search.
By the same token, you may begin a search from any directory page — the
keyword search form is located near the top of each of them.

Show-Off Searching

From any Search Results page or from the Yahoo! home page, you can opt for a more sophisticated set of options for your keywords. On any of those pages, click the advanced search link to see the Search Options page. On this page, you can give Yahoo! more clues than the raw keywords that you use in a simple search. Here, you can

✔ Choose between Category and Site searching

✔ Apply *search operators* to your keywords

✔ Select to avoid the Web entirely in favor of Usenet newsgroups

✔ Alter the time period of your search

Advanced searching works in the same fundamental way as simple searching, in that you type a keyword or three and click the Search button to launch your inquiry. The difference lies in settings that control how Yahoo! treats your keywords, giving you a more precise searching focus. Figure 5-4 shows the Search Options page; you might want to refer to it or get the page on your computer screen as you go through the following sections.

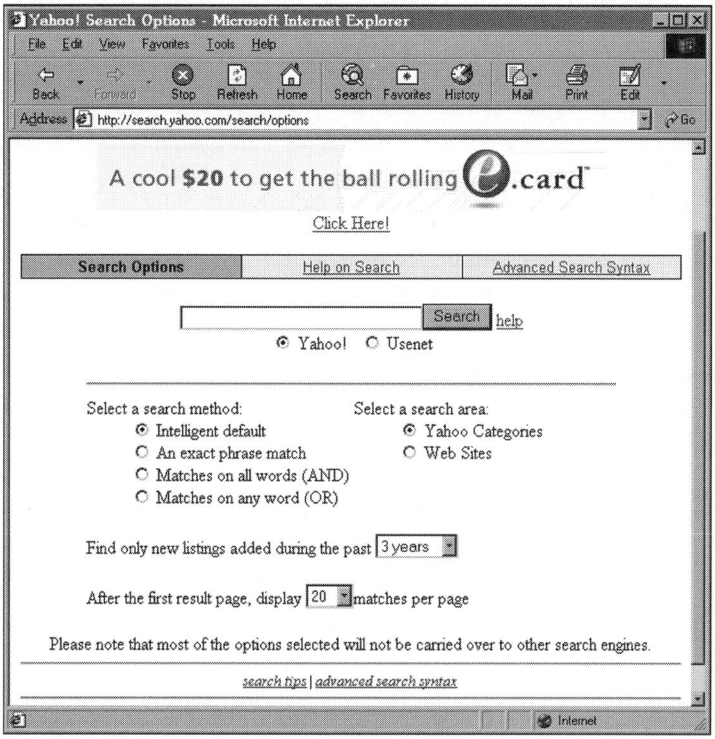

Figure 5-4:
The Yahoo!
Search
Options
page for
advanced
searching.

Setting boundaries

The biggest choice you have in an advanced search is whether to search the Web or Usenet. *Usenet* is the bulletin board system of the Internet — it's older and probably larger than the Web. Usenet consists of many thousands of *newsgroups*, or message-board discussion forums. Such meeting places exist in the Yahoo! service (see Chapter 12), as well as in other Web sites, America Online, and CompuServe. But Usenet preceded them all, and has a rich heritage of Internet pioneerism. The Usenet newsgroups are populated by some of the most long-time denizens of the Net.

The Usenet searching feature prowls through a vast database of newsgroup messages, comparing each word with your keywords. Considering the immensity of the newsgroup database, it's astounding that the search takes only the few seconds that it does.

The Deja News search engine provides Usenet searching on Yahoo!. Deja News has its own site, which provides advanced newsgroup searches as well as other specialized features for angling into Usenet. If you get serious about searching newsgroup messages, try Deja News at the source (www.dejanews.com). For casual Usenet prowling, Yahoo! is fine.

What's the purpose of searching through old discussion messages? First, if you're looking for newsgroups holding talks about particular subjects, it saves time to search for the subject first, not the newsgroup. Then, when you find messages of interest, you can subscribe to the newsgroup through Outlook Express, Netscape Messenger, or whatever newsgroup program you prefer. Second, message-board discussions, informal though they may be, are sometimes extremely informative. In certain subject areas, experts talk with each other through Usenet. Even if you're not trolling for experts, searching the newsgroups is a good way to assess public opinion about an ongoing news story, a current movie, or any other topic. Essentially, searching Usenet lets you look with some precision into the discussions of the Internet community.

On the Yahoo! Search Options page, click the Usenet radio button to search newsgroups, or leave the default Yahoo! setting to search the Web.

Choosing your keyword options

Yahoo! gives you some flexibility in how you package your keyword for the search. When you type more than one keyword, you can instruct Yahoo! to find matches using the following criteria:

✔ **Intelligent default.** This setting is how Yahoo! behaves naturally in a simple search. The search engine attempts to match all your keywords, but also provides matches to fewer than all keywords or even just one. The best hits are the matches to all keywords, and they are grouped at the top of the search results.

✔ **An exact phrase match.** Selecting this radio button forces Yahoo! to take your keyword string literally. The search engine does not match fewer than all the words, and furthermore, it matches only phrases that duplicate your word order. You should use this option when searching for common phrases, proper names, or locations expressed in more than one word.

✔ **Matches on all words (AND).** This option tells Yahoo! that you're interested only in hits that match all your keywords, in any order. The (AND) refers to a standard keyword operator, which I describe in the next section.

✔ **Matches on any word (OR).** Choose this radio button when you want Yahoo! to match any of your keywords, but not necessarily all of them.

Selecting categories or sites

In the "Select a search area" portion of the Search Options page (refer to Figure 5-4), you can choose between Yahoo! Categories and Web Sites. Click the first, and Category Matches — as well as Site Matches — appear on your Search Results page. Choose Web Sites, and only Site Matches appear.

Setting limits

The final two search options let you limit the number of hits you receive in two ways.

First, you can determine how far back in time Yahoo! searches. Because the search engine is crawling through the Yahoo! directory, and Yahoo! keeps track of when listings are added, it's a simple matter (for a smart computer) to filter listings farther back in time. Your choices are defined by the drop-down menu, which lets you go back 3 years, 6 months, 3 months, 1 month, 1 week, 3 days, or 1 day. This option is useful if you're looking for only new sites. Notice the big time gap between 6 months and 3 years — indicating that this feature is implemented to locate relatively new listings.

Second, you may determine how many hits appear on each Search Results page. The default is 20, but you can adjust that to create small pages of 10 hits or larger ones of 50 or 100 hits.

No matter how many hits you place on each Search Results page, Yahoo! always tells you the total number of links that match your keywords. So you always know what lies ahead and whether you need to narrow your search, broaden it, or forget the whole thing and play softball.

Getting Precise with Search Operators

The preceding section on advanced searching provides an introduction of sorts to *search operators*, which are words or symbols added to your keyword string that tell Yahoo! how to interpret your request. On the Search Options page, the AND and OR options refer to two basic search operators that instruct the search engine to find matches for *all* keywords (AND) and *any* keywords (OR). You can bypass the Search Options page by becoming acquainted with the search operators and typing them manually into your search string.

In Yahoo!, symbols and single-letter abbreviations indicate search operators. As always when dealing with simple-minded computers, you must be literal and use the correct spelling and syntax — the symbols must not be varied or positioned in the wrong place. This section summarizes the search operators recognized by Yahoo! and specifies how to type them.

- ✔ **AND.** The AND search operator is symbolized with +, the addition sign, and is placed immediately before any keyword that must be included in the search results. This operator tends to narrow the search, delivering fewer, better targeted results. An example of its use is the search string *baltimore +orioles*, which eliminates sites about the city of Baltimore that didn't include a reference to its baseball team, the Orioles. If you're concerned about getting sites about birds, you could extend the string to *baltimore +orioles +baseball* which would force Yahoo! to return sites that include all three words.

- ✔ **NOT.** The NOT operator is very useful and is not included on the Search Options page. NOT excludes keywords from being matched, and is symbolized by –, the minus sign (the hyphen key of your keyboard). As with the AND operator, the NOT symbol is placed immediately before any word you want to exclude from matching. An example is *orioles –baseball*, which would match to sites about birds but not the baseball team.

- ✔ **Document titles only.** Yahoo! can restrict the search to Web site titles only, disregarding descriptions and URLs. To do so, put **t:** immediately before a keyword or keyword string. (If you're using multiple keywords, you need place only one t: in front of the whole string.) An example is *t:anthony hopkins*, which searches for sites with Anthony Hopkins in the title, but not necessarily in the site description or URL. At the same time, it eliminates matches of Anthony Hopkins in the description, if it doesn't also appear in the title.

✔ **Document URLs only.** As a reverse of the preceding search operator, Yahoo! can limit the search to URLs, excluding Web page titles and descriptions. This is a great option for zooming in on specific Web sites. Simply place **u:** in front of the keyword string (or single keyword). Try it when searching for a company name. A good experiment is to search on the company name without the u: operator and then with it, and compare the results.

✔ **Exact phrases.** The Search Options page allows you to specify exact phrase matches, and you can do the same thing using quotation marks (" and ") around the keyword string. If you're searching for a person's name, for example, and the first and last name could be mistaken for words with other meanings (such as Jack London), the phrase operator comes in handy. Try the *"jack london"* keyword string.

✔ **Wild card.** This search operator lets you get away with not knowing how to spell something, and is also an easy way to broaden a search. The symbol is an asterisk (*), and it must be placed immediately after a word or partial word. An example is *paris**, which matches up with Paris and Parisian.

Search operators can be combined! Stay calm; don't get too excited. I know this is good news. You can mix and match the preceding operators in any way that remains logical. Here are two examples based on keywords I already used:

✔ If you want to find sites about the Baltimore Orioles baseball team but specifically exclude bird information, try

   baltimore +orioles +baseball –birds

✔ If you want pages about Anthony Hopkins, but don't care to read about the "Silence of the Lambs" movie, try

   anthony +hopkins – "silence of the lambs"

Generally, when you combine search operators with the number of keywords, you can drastically enlarge or shrink your search results. Here are two rules:

✔ To get fewer hits, add keywords and use the + search operator.

✔ To get more hits, subtract keywords and use the – operator on the Search Options page.

Chapter 6

Regional and Special Directories

● ●

In This Chapter

▶ Browsing city and world directories

▶ Scheduling your computer for real-time events

▶ Finding Yahooligans! for kids

● ●

*Y*ahoo! began as a Web directory and is still well known for that core service. If this book demonstrates nothing else (such as my appetite for
chocolate in Chapter 20), it reveals that Yahoo! has evolved into far more
than a mere directory. Even its directory services have evolved to global
scope. Bridging the online and offline realms, Yahoo!'s many regional directories provide guidance to metropolitan and national niches of the planet.

This chapter sketches the range of directory services found in Yahoo!. In
addition to the regional directories, Yahooligans! provides safe Web guidance
for kids, and the Net Events listings point visitors to real-time broadcast and
community happenings every day. I don't spend any time in this chapter
explaining basic techniques for navigating Yahoo!'s complex directory structure — those instructions and tips are in Chapter 4.

Local and World Yahoo!s

A glance at the bottom of the Yahoo! home page reveals a bit of Yahoo!'s reach
around the world and into American metropolitan areas. Figure 6-1 shows
what you see by going to the Yahoo! home page and scrolling to the bottom.

The first thing most Americans need to know about the national directories is
that they are presented in the native language of each country. And no software plug-in turns them into English. (The Canadian directory is in English.)
Not only are the directories in the native language, but they represent only
native-language sites. In other words, these aren't travel directories. They are
Web guides for different portions of the planetary Internet community.

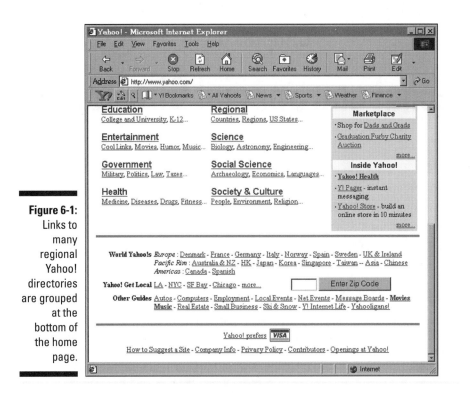

Figure 6-1:
Links to
many
regional
Yahoo!
directories
are grouped
at the
bottom of
the home
page.

The city directories are not meant to be travel guides any more than the national directories, but they serve that function to some degree. You can check out businesses, entertainment, newspapers, sports, weather, and local headlines in each city represented by a directory. Each local directory hooks conveniently into the online Yellow Pages. The degree to which each city is revealed through the directory is partly determined by how many local establishments have Web sites.

Figure 6-2 shows the Los Angeles Metro directory home page. As you can see, the left sidebar is packed with at-a-glance information about weather, current events, and news headlines. The main directory is set up in the usual Yahoo! fashion, with main topic areas leading to finer delineations of subcategories, and then lists of Web sites in the L.A. area. Residents can make particularly good use of the Yellow Pages search form.

The Yellow Pages have a great feature that helps you locate things just outside an area defined in your search. Here's a sample search that shows how it works:

1. **On the Los Angeles Metro home page (or any other city directory), enter a keyword and city in the Yellow Pages search form, and then click the Search button.**

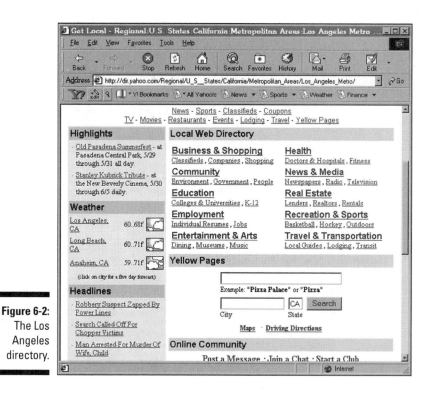

Figure 6-2:
The Los
Angeles
directory.

In this example, I am entering *sushi* and *venice*, looking for some raw fish in the city of Venice, near L.A.

2. **On the Yellow Pages Results page, which lists only one sushi restaurant, click the <u>Beyond Venice</u> link.**

   The next Yellow Pages Results page appears (see Figure 6-3).

3. **Click any restaurant.**

   Note that each search match on the expanded results page indicates how far the restaurant is from Venice. Clicking any restaurant displays a street map and a link that automatically adds the restaurant name and address to your Yahoo! Address Book (see Chapter 3).

From the map page of a Yellow Pages search result, click anywhere on the map to display yet another map page, this one much more interactive. This more elaborate map allows you to zoom in and out to see different bird's-eye views of the locale and includes a link for getting driving directions.

On the Los Angeles directory home page (likewise for all the cities), the menu links above the main directory categories are useful. Each link takes you to a portion of Yahoo! (TV, Movies, Events, Lodging, Sports, and so on) with default settings for Los Angeles (or the city whose directory you linked from).

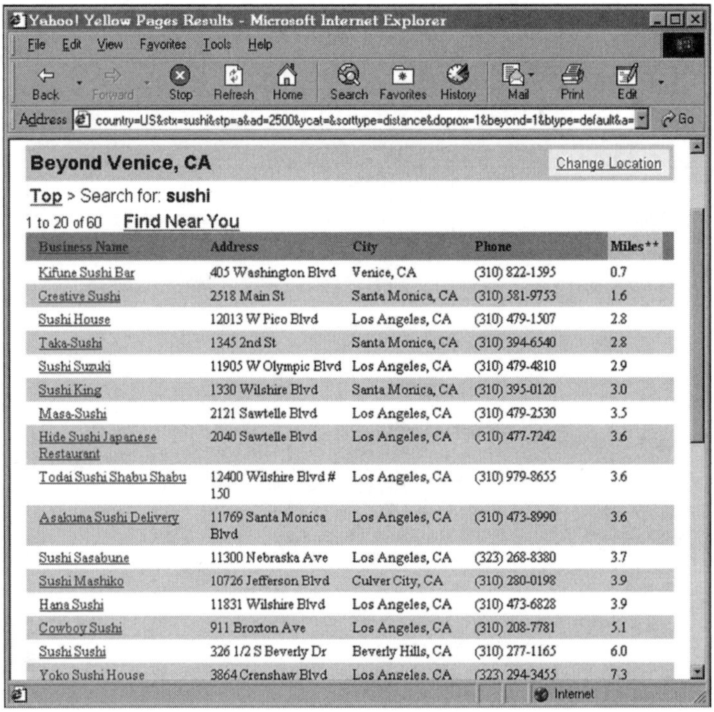

Figure 6-3:
Using the Beyond (City) feature shows more results and their distance to the search city.

Net Events

Net Events is the online realm's preeminent guide to real-time, scheduled events. Net Events can be chat sessions, live interviews with celebrities, and multimedia presentations such as Net-radio broadcasts. In general, the Net Events directory is for power users — or at least semipower users. To cruise into any Net Event without fear that your computer and software setup will shut you out of the fun, you should be equipped thusly:

- ✔ Have a Java-capable Web browser. This means Navigator or Internet Explorer versions 3.0 or later, running on Windows 95, Windows 98, or Windows NT. Java is needed for most chat events.

- ✔ Get the RealPlayer plug-in for your browser from Real Networks. Here's the URL:

  ```
  www.real.com
  ```

- ✔ Some broadcast events require Windows Media Player, part of the Windows 95 and 98 operating systems; it also comes bundled with new versions of Internet Explorer.

The Net Events directory operates like any other directory. Get to it by clicking the <u>Net Events</u> link on the Yahoo! home page or by going directly to the following URL:

```
events.Yahoo.com
```

Each main topic area of the Net Events directory (see Figure 6-4) goes down three or four levels, delivering real-time scheduled events for each subcategory.

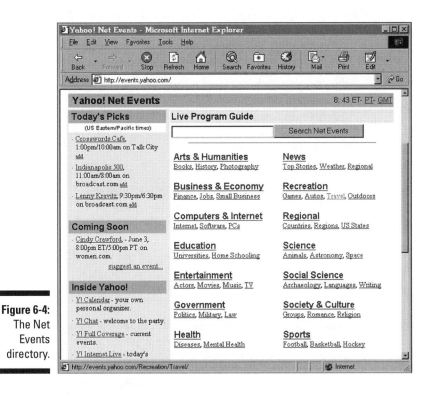

Figure 6-4:
The Net Events directory.

Figure 6-5 shows Finance and Investment events. Notice that you can look several days ahead by clicking a date link. (Events in business categories are usually scheduled on weekdays; entertainment events tend to be grouped on weekends and weekday evenings.)

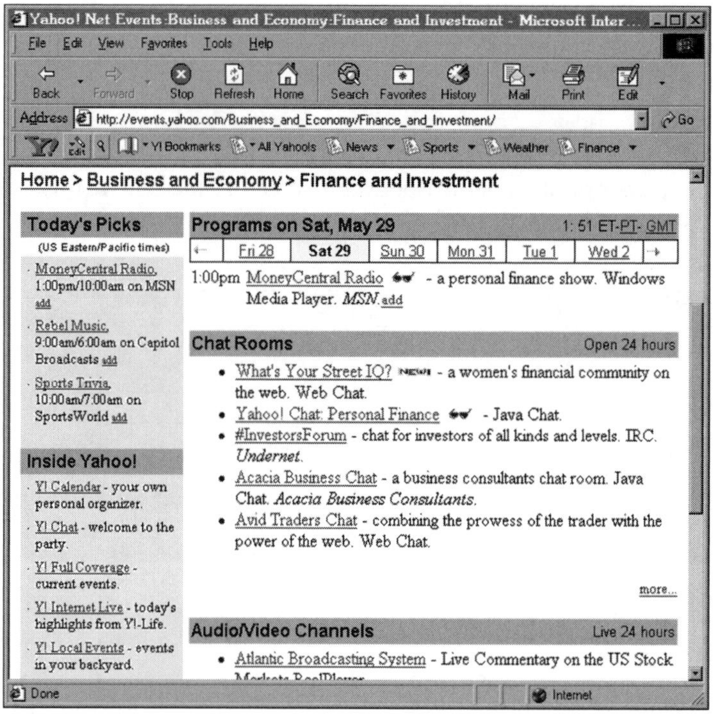

Figure 6-5:
One day's
broadcasts
and chats in
the Finance
and
Investment
category.

Just for Kids

Yahoo! was one of the first online services to recognize the value — and
risks — of the Internet to kids. Yahooligans! (see Figure 6-6), the premier Web
directory for youngsters, has grown and gained in reputation for years and
now stands as a mature online service for the under-18 set. Highly moderated, Yahooligans! accepts sites into the directory only after their content
(and their links to other sites) pass the kid-safe test.

To experience Yahooligans!, grab a kid and head for this URL:

```
www.yahooligans.com
```

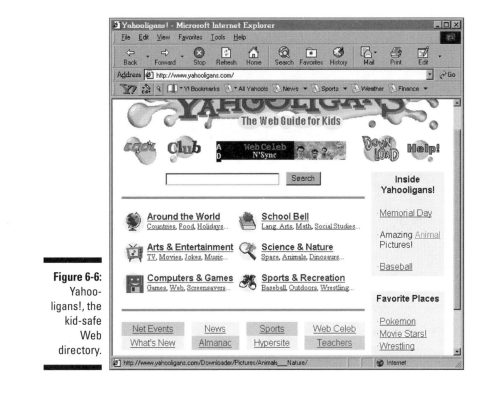

Figure 6-6:
Yahoo-
ligans!, the
kid-safe
Web
directory.

Part III
Information and More Information

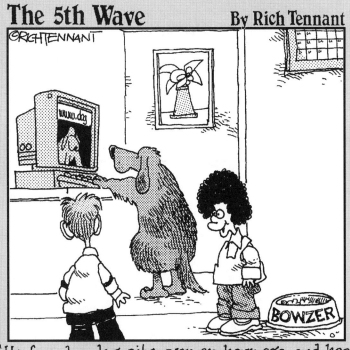

The 5th Wave By Rich Tennant

"He found a dog site over an hour ago and has been in a staring contest ever since."

In this part...

Yahoo! is your source for an unending supply of information. From international news to finances, from sports to movies, Yahoo!'s information sites keep you enlightened up to the minute. The chapters in this part reveal more information than you thought could exist in a single online service.

Chapter 7

All the News That's Fit to Link

*I*nformation wants to be free. That's the motto of the Internet. Whether information actually has desires is a question beyond my metaphysical capacity, but it does seem as if Yahoo! adheres to the sentiment. Free news is provided in almost embarrassing wealth. Big, sloppy buckets of news. Up-to-the-second, comprehensive news. You can get a broad overview or drill deeply into a topic.

Best of all, Yahoo!'s plain, straightforward display style makes the experience fast and generally without hassle. Unlike other news magazines on the Web that force you to load graphics-intense, feature-laden pages, Yahoo! gets most of its news from wire services, and sticks to the stark headline style that characterizes those sources. It's not that Yahoo! News pages are unattractive, but neither are they unnecessarily encumbered with fancy borders, pictures, and advertisements. It's a clean viewing experience. News photos are gathered into separate areas for those who want to take the time to view them.

This chapter walks you through the sometimes labyrinthine hallways of the Yahoo! newsroom.

Finding the Front Page

Getting started is perhaps the trickiest part of enjoying news, Yahoo! style. The home page doesn't make a big deal of the rich news resources that await you, so your mouse might circle the page a bit before knowing how to proceed. Here's the solution:

1. **On the Yahoo! home page, click the <u>Today's News</u> link.**

   Alternatively, you can go directly to the front page with this link:

   ```
   http://dailynews.yahoo.com
   ```

2. **On the Yahoo! News directory page (see Figure 7-1), click any news topic.**

   Clicking a news topic takes you to a Yahoo! News topical front page. The topical pages are the *real* front pages, in my view, the ones that should be bookmarked for the future. I dissect the topical pages in the next section.

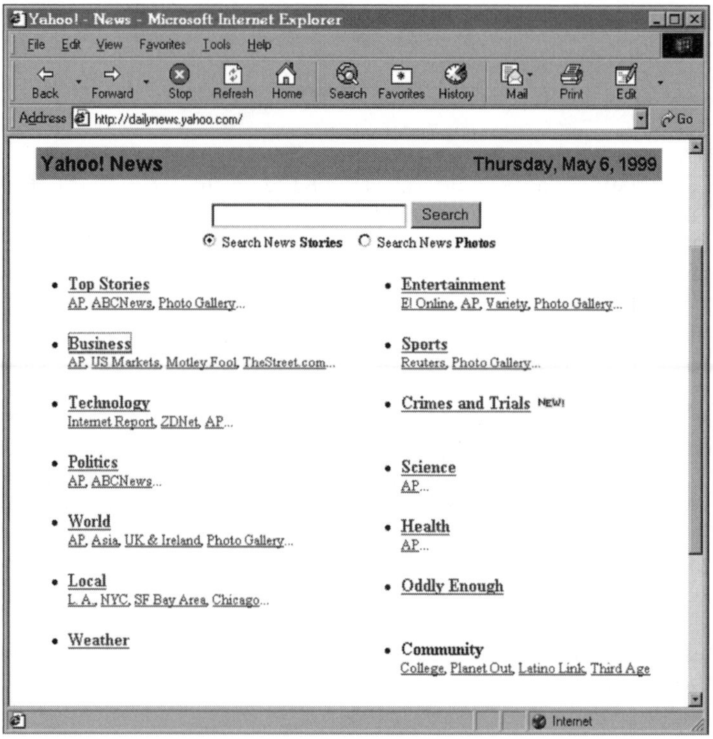

Figure 7-1: The main Yahoo! News directory page.

You can angle into the Yahoo! News section in other ways. The Yahoo! directory features link to news on every second-level directory page (see Figure 7-2). Those directory links take you to the news page relevant to the directory topic you linked from. Such cross-referencing makes it handy to relate your Web surfing to outside-world current events.

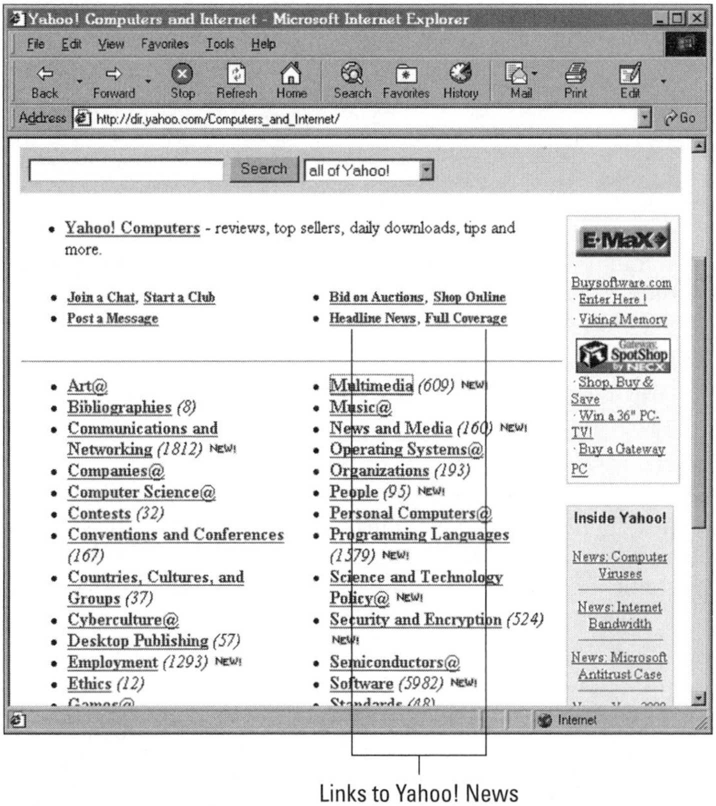

Figure 7-2:
Every
second-
level
directory
page
contains a
link or two
to Yahoo!
News.

Links to Yahoo! News

Yahoo! News also borrows heavily from other sections of Yahoo!. Sports news takes information and pages from Yahoo! Sports; business news borrows from Yahoo! Finance. You shouldn't think of Yahoo! News as an isolated warehouse of current event information. It's best to familiarize yourself with many Yahoo! sections, and treat the whole thing as an organic information entity. How you pursue your interests through Yahoo! and how you bookmark its pages is a matter of taste, and you'll develop your own system over time as your understanding of the whole service grows.

Notice the Search form in Figure 7-1. The form exists on every Yahoo! News page, and searching for news is useful in some situations. It works easily:

1. **In the keyword entry field, type your keyword(s).**

2. **Using the radio buttons beneath your keyword(s), select whether you're searching for stories or photos.**

3. **Click the Search button.**

Here are some hints for productive news searching:

✔ Remember that Yahoo! News searching is literal and detailed. Every word of every story is compared to your keyword(s), including the writer's name. So a search for *O.J. Simpson* might deliver an unrelated story written by Ian Simpson, the writer for Reuters news service.

✔ The Yahoo! News search engine finds every matching story in its archived database, which goes back ten days. If you want to avoid scrolling through page after page of results, and jump further back in time, select keywords that deliver narrower results. (See Chapter 4 for keyword help.)

✔ Very general searches that deliver hundreds of results are not particularly useful — it's better to browse your way through the Yahoo! News pages to find current headlines and stories. General searches for photos, however, work nicely.

✔ Search results in Yahoo! News are displayed on a general Yahoo! Search Results page, which includes links to search results (for your keywords) among Yahoo! directory categories, Web Sites, Web Pages, and Net Events (see Figure 7-3). The upshot is an integrated result to your search that covers categories of Web sites, Web sites themselves, and scheduled Internet events — all related to your search query.

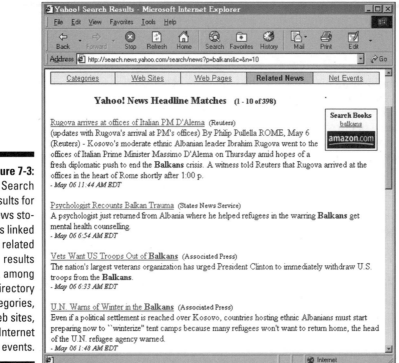

Figure 7-3:
Search results for news stories linked to related results among directory categories, Web sites, and Internet events.

On the Yahoo! News main directory page, near the bottom, is a beguiling Customize Your News link. This link takes you to your My Yahoo! page, if you've created one. From there, you can follow my guidelines in Chapter 2 to personalize the news links on your page. However, Yahoo! News provides a far more comprehensive news experience than My Yahoo! does.

Filling the Tank with High-Octane News

When you proceed past the Yahoo! News main directory page, the search for news gets interesting. You may click any topic you like on the main directory page (aren't you glad you have my gracious permission?). For the sake of illustration, I'm clicking the Politics link. Figure 7-4 shows the Politics news directory page.

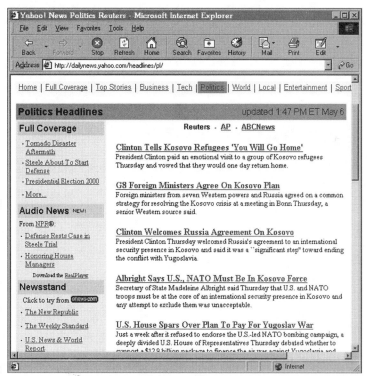

Figure 7-4:
The Politics page. Topical news pages are where news browsing gets interesting.

Each news topic presents a slightly different front page, but some elements appear on most of them:

- ✔ **Headlines.** The meat of every Yahoo! News topical front page, the headlines stretch down the main portion of the page, including the first line from each story. Click any headline to see the full story.

- ✔ **Topic menu.** The main Yahoo! News topics are presented on each topical front page, in a concise banner across the upper part of the page. Use the banner to switch from Politics to Business, Tech, or any other main news topic.

- ✔ **Full Coverage.** Full Coverage is one of Yahoo!'s most shining news features, where information from multiple sources about major news stories is gathered in one place. You can access Full Coverage in two ways. Each news topic front page has a Full Coverage section in the left-hand navigation bar, containing a few Full Coverage items for that topic. The Full Coverage link on the topic menu takes you to a dedicated Full Coverage page (see Figure 7-5). Scroll down the Full Coverage page to see which news items, in all the Yahoo! News topics, get the Full Coverage treatment. (Click the More Full Coverage link in any topic if you don't see the news item you're looking for.)

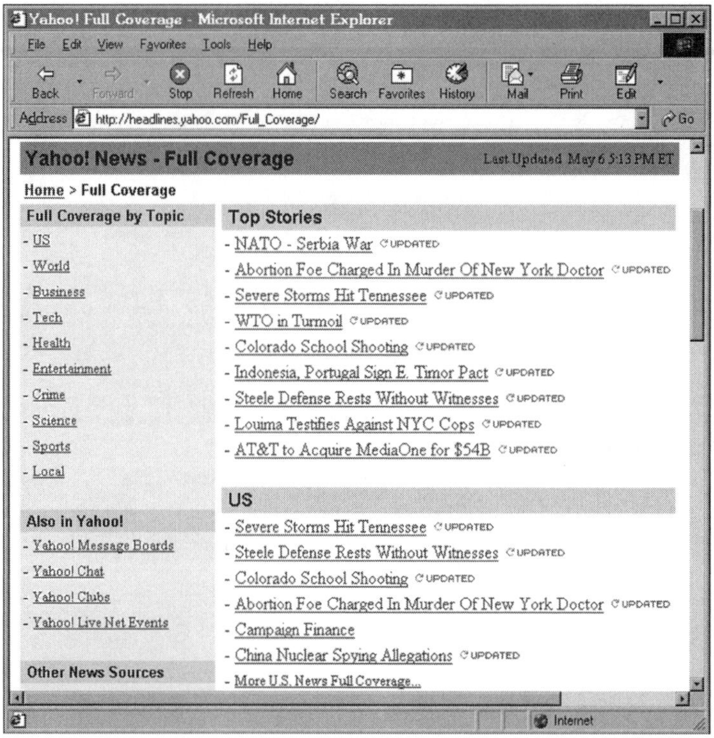

Figure 7-5:
The Full Coverage page links to in-depth coverage of major news.

Each Full Coverage news item is a page of headlines plus links to news sources outside Yahoo! (see Figure 7-6). Yahoo! itself is not a news bureau and doesn't do original news reporting. Its headlines are licensed from wire news sources such as Associated Press and Reuters, and Yahoo! gladly links to sites such as CNN, the BBC, and The New York Times. The value of the Full Coverage pages is that they assemble all these linked sources in one place. If you're tracking an ongoing news item, it makes sense to bookmark its Full Coverage page.

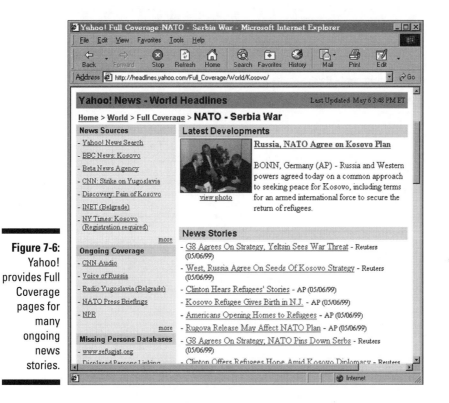

Figure 7-6:
Yahoo!
provides Full
Coverage
pages for
many
ongoing
news
stories.

✔ **Audio News.** Some topic front pages have an Audio News section in the left-hand sidebar, featuring links to netcasts you can listen to with RealAudio or Windows Media Player. In most cases, the links go directly to the audio file, so a minimum of clicking is necessary, and you may not even have to leave the Yahoo! page to hear the netcast.

✔ **Newsstand.** The Newsstand links take you to enews.com, an electronic magazine vendor, where you can read samples of magazines and purchase subscriptions.

✔ **Yahoo! Categories.** This portion of the left-hand sidebar connects you to relevant Yahoo! directory pages.

✔ **Net Events.** The Net Events links are relevant to the topical front page you're looking at, and link you to portions of the Yahoo! Net Events directory. (See Chapter 6 for a discussion of Net Events.) You can find a lot of newsy Internet events, including RealAudio netcasts of press briefings, chat interview sessions with public figures, Internet-only talk shows, and video feeds from TV stations around the world. Figure 7-7 illustrates the Net Events page linked from the Politics news front page.

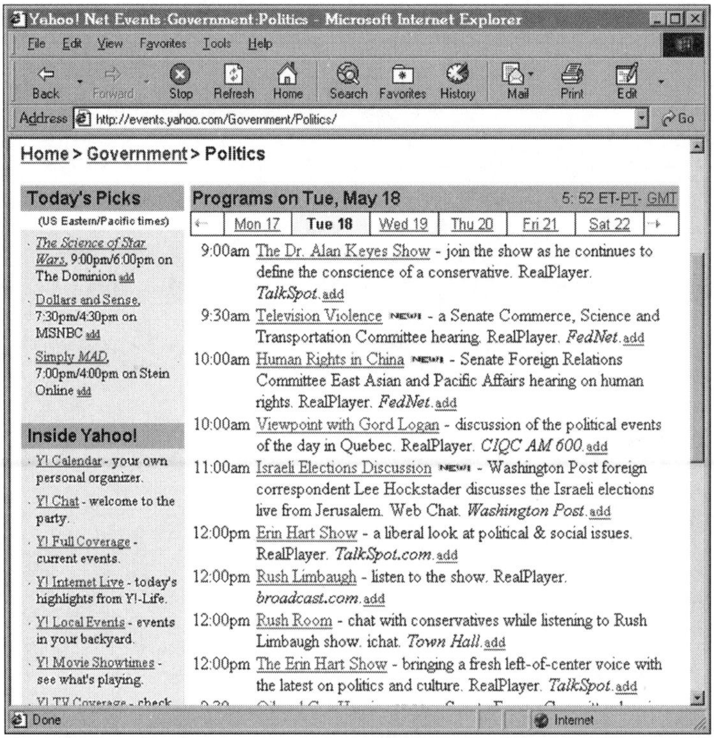

Figure 7-7: Net Events related to the Politics news front page.

✔ **Related Links.** Here, you can find links to major news sites within the topic you're browsing. Sources such as C-SPAN, major newspapers on the Web, and government sites are featured. Each link takes you outside Yahoo!.

Local news isn't given quite the same status as United States and international news in Yahoo!, but the service does take a stab at state-level information for Americans, plus a handful of major cities. Take a look for yourself:

1. From the Yahoo! News front page, click Local.

Or click the Local link from any topical front page.

2. **Under the Local Headlines banner of the next page, use the drop-down menus to select a metro or a state.**

   See Figure 7-8, which shows the headline page for Michigan.

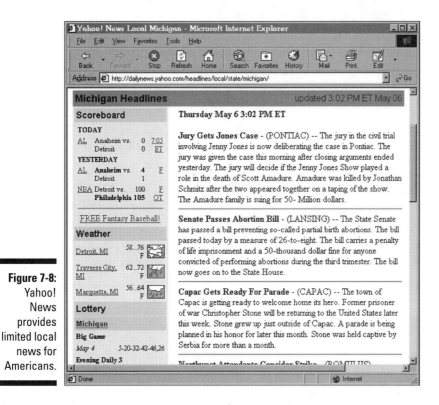

Figure 7-8:
Yahoo!
News
provides
limited local
news for
Americans.

The state-specific Headlines pages actually don't display headlines, but they do provide single-paragraph summaries of local stories. The left-hand sidebar contains bits of sports, weather, and lottery information.

Specialized News

A number of specialized news sources and magazines contribute to Yahoo! News. In most cases, these contributions can be accessed independently from the topical front pages. In each case listed next, the source or magazine links are placed just above the headlines. Clicking a link does not take you away from Yahoo!, which packages the content within its own pages. Here's the lineup:

- ✔ **Entertainment.** From the Entertainment front page, you can link to E! Online, Hollywood Reporter, and Variety.

- ✔ **Sports.** From the Sports front page, you can link to Sports Ticker, The Sporting News, and Yahoo! Sports (which duplicates some of the sports content you find in Yahoo! News).

- ✔ **Business.** From the Business front page, you can link to US Markets, The Motley Fool (investment news and commentary), and TheStreet.com (more investment news and commentary).

- ✔ **Tech.** From the Tech front page, you can link to Internet Report and ZDNet.

In the "hard news" sections, the wire services Associated Press and Reuters are used heavily by Yahoo!, and the headlines for each service are accessible separately. Just click the AP or Reuters link.

If you crave photos, Yahoo! has them, too. But the service doesn't force-feed them down your modem's throat; you must click your way to them. Photo galleries of news items are available in the Top Stories, World, Entertainment, and Sports sections. Just click the Photo Gallery link. Selections of small photos are displayed first; just click any photo or the view photo link to see a blow-up. (A larger photo, that is, not a photo of an explosion.)

Chapter 8

Knowing the Score

● ●

In This Chapter

▶ Getting an overview of Yahoo! Sports

▶ Finding league, team, and game pages

▶ Crunching statistics

▶ Finding photos and fantasies

● ●

*I*t's not hard to find sports on the Web. ESPN, CBS SportsLine, and other media outlets share their news gathering resources with Internet citizens to some extent. But it is unusual to find an information-rich sports location that is completely free and delivers the goods with a minimum of advertisements, modem-choking graphics, registration procedures, and other hassles of Internet life. After all, when it comes to sports, don't you just want the score, and only the score, about half the time? And you don't want to slog through a bunch of glitz to get it.

Now don't get me wrong. Yahoo! Sports provides more than just scores. A broad scope of information from league standings to team updates, photo galleries, and opinion columns is presented. But Yahoo! leads with the data, not with the fat stuff such as pictures, so the pages are displayed quickly. Likewise, Yahoo! Sports doesn't push Java applets through your modem to display streaming game information. Maintaining the steely, lean interface that characterizes Yahoo! in general, Yahoo! Sports delivers the goods quickly and without headaches.

This chapter walks you through the main elements of Yahoo! Sports, and helps you develop paths to certain pages you'll use over and over.

The Back Page

I don't know what it's like where you live, but some of the major New York City newspapers put their sports sections way in the back, with the back page serving as a sports front page. With that in mind, the first thing to do in

Yahoo! Sports is find the front . . . er, back . . . well, the *home* page. Actually, Yahoo! has a few types of front pages, and this section explains their differences, similarities, and uses.

To get to the main Yahoo! Sports front page, click the Sports link on Yahoo!'s home page, or go directly to this URL:

```
sports.yahoo.com
```

Figure 8-1 shows the basic layout of the Yahoo! Sports front page. This page has four basic elements:

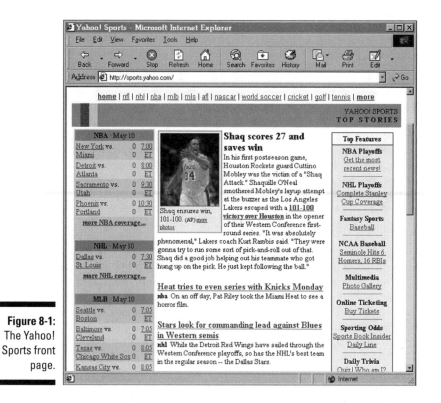

Figure 8-1:
The Yahoo!
Sports front
page.

✔ **Menu bar.** Up top, above the TOP STORIES banner, you see a series of links to sub-sections within Yahoo! Sports. These links are for league pages and sections on NASCAR racing, soccer, cricket, golf, and tennis. Click the more link for a detailed menu of available sports and leagues. Figure 8-2 shows that menu, and provides a site overview in a glance. Some of the second-string sports coverage is impressive, such as the sections for college baseball and women's golf. In other cases, such as cycling and rugby, the respective pages are nothing more than a few headline links, without scores or league standings.

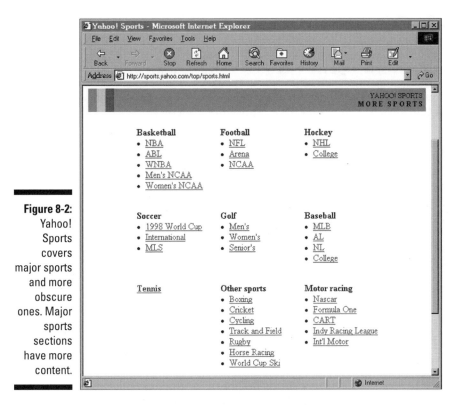

Figure 8-2:
Yahoo!
Sports
covers
major sports
and more
obscure
ones. Major
sports
sections
have more
content.

✔ **Feature stories.** The central portion of the Yahoo! Sports front page is devoted to headlines and story summaries from all sports — whatever is making news at the time you view the page.

✔ **Scores and other links.** Stretching down the left-hand sidebar are scores for finished games and games in progress. Early in the day (for the United States), match-ups for that day's events are listed with their starting times. Links to other sports sites on the Web (The Sporting News, Fox Sports, ESPN.com, and others) are at the bottom of the sidebar.

✔ **Top Features.** The Top Features sidebar is on the right-hand side of the page, and includes links to special sections for playoff coverage, the Photo Gallery, online ticket ordering, betting sheets, and fantasy leagues. I cover these items later in the chapter.

The Yahoo! Sports front page — and every page of Yahoo! Sports that contains quickly changing information such as game scores — updates automatically every few minutes. Your browser simply reloads the page, without any intervention on your part. This is convenient, because you can set up a browser window in a corner of your screen, just large enough to display a game score you're following, and continue using the Internet in another browser window.

It's possible to get lost in Yahoo! Sports, wending your way deeply into end-less pages of statistics and other features. At any time, you can always get a fresh start by clicking the Yahoo! Sports logo, which is at the top of every page. That link takes you back to the main front page.

You can drill into the ever-shifting fund of sports information in Yahoo! Sports at three levels, and a front page represents each one:

- ✔ **League.** At the league level, entire sports are covered. The front pages in the league sections embrace all teams in the league. These pages are similar in design to the front page of Yahoo! Sports, but with a dedicated focus on one sport.

- ✔ **Team.** If you're primarily interested in one team (or a few teams), it's possible to zip directly to team-oriented front pages. These pages cover recent news, standings, game results, and player statistics.

- ✔ **Game.** A good deal of game information is presented for all games in all major sports. Coverage includes previews, highlight articles, starting players, recaps, box scores, and game logs.

In your league

When you want an overview of a sport, complete with links that take you to deeper levels of detail, try the menu links near the top of the Yahoo! Sports home page (see Figure 8-1). Official pro leagues are linked by their acronyms, including National Football League (NFL, from which you may link to the NFC and AFC), National Hockey League (NHL), National Basketball Association (NBA), Major League Baseball (MLB, from which you may link to the National and American Leagues), Major League Soccer (MLS), and American Football League (AFL). The remaining links are for Nascar racing, World soccer, cricket, golf, and tennis — sports not consolidated into ownership leagues per se. (Click the <u>more</u> link to see all the sports covered.)

Figure 8-3 shows the NHL front page. If you compare the illustration to Figure 8-1, you can see that it carries the same design as the main Yahoo! Sports front page (and, at the time these screen shots were taken, some of the same stories and the same picture). The page in Figure 8-3 is devoted to NHL hockey, and all the content beneath the main banner relates to the league and its games.

The league front pages keep game scores posted for a day longer than on the main Yahoo! Sports front page. The main front page wipes the scores off the board early in the morning, replacing them with preview links for the upcom-ing day's games. On the league front pages, though, the left-hand sidebar extends downward to include the previous day's action.

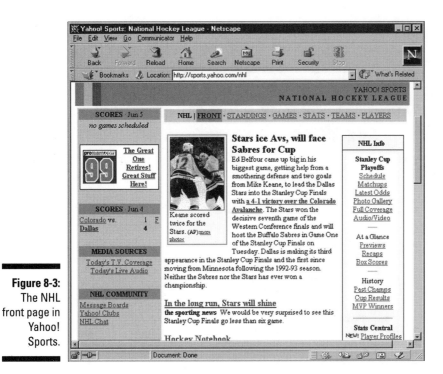

Figure 8-3:
The NHL front page in Yahoo! Sports.

During a sport's off-season, the league front page for that sport doesn't contain game scores, obviously. The left-hand sidebar consists of Resources links to other Web sites. The right-hand sidebar includes some very useful off-season stuff, including links to player draft results, free-agent signings, trades, expansion drafts, as well as next season's calendar. The Photo Gallery remains available during the off-season, and you can link to player statistics as well.

You can peruse links for two weeks of archived news stories. On any league front page, scroll to the very bottom, where some headlines are grouped under EARLIER STORIES. At the bottom of the headline stack is an <u>Archived News</u> link. Click it to see league-related stories grouped by day, stretching back two weeks. (See Figure 8-4.)

Following the home team

All the major sport teams are represented with their own front pages in Yahoo! Sports. What do I mean by a major sport? The big four, of course (NFL football, NBA basketball, major league baseball, and NHL hockey), plus AFL football and NCAA college football. Yahoo! Sports might expand the team-by-team coverage in the future, so keep checking. For now, sports such as college baseball and soccer enjoy general reporting, but lack in-depth team analysis.

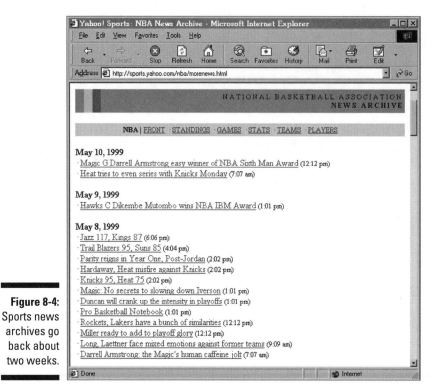

Figure 8-4:
Sports news
archives go
back about
two weeks.

You can reach your team's front page in a few ways:

✔ During your team's playing season, on game days, the team is listed in the left-hand sidebar on the main Yahoo! Sports front page. Click the team name to see the team-specific front page.

✔ During your team's playing season, on game days, the team is also listed in the left-hand sidebar on the league front page.

✔ On any league front page or any page linked from a league front page, click the <u>TEAMS</u> link for a complete list of teams in the league. From this list, you can display any team's front page.

Team front pages provide a current snapshot of team notes, schedules, standings, and game results during the playing season. (Off-season team front pages continue to carry update articles, team notes, and the next season's schedule if available.) Figure 8-5 shows the team page for the Cleveland Indians baseball club.

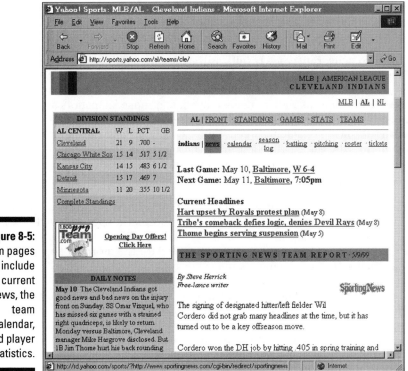

In addition to daily articles and team notes, a menu bar shows links to deeper and more statistical information about the team:

- **Calendar.** The calendar shows the team's playing schedule for the entire season. Unfortunately for fans, player birthdays are not included.

- **Season log.** This page is a game-by-game recap of the team's season. The information included in this wrap-up varies from one sport to another.

- **Roster.** The roster page lists every player on the team with some basic information including — Ta-da! — the players' birthdays.

- **Stats.** A statistics page for the team's players. The numbers provided on this page are not as extensive as the player stats at the league level, which I describe later in this chapter. But this page is an easy solution to basic facts such as the average points per game for an NBA player. The stats pages for major league baseball teams are divided into batters and pitchers.

- **Tickets.** This link displays a page in which you may begin a process of buying tickets to your team's games over the Web. The service is provided jointly by Yahoo! and Ticketmaster.

The play-by-play

The game is where the action is. How does Yahoo! Sports measure up when it comes to delivering game results as they are happening and after the fact? Because Yahoo! does not have multimedia pretensions, don't expect to find any streaming netcasts of games in progress. Yahoo! delivers snapshot reports of games as they're being played, and those snapshots are sometimes not as up-to-the-second as might be desired. Recently, I tested the game page of an NBA playoff game between Phoenix and Portland during the closing minutes of the game, while following the action on TV. Yahoo! was consistently and substantially behind the real-time play, and at one point let six minutes go by without updating the score.

Yahoo! Sports does better with static content such as recaps and box scores of completed games. It gets the statistical information posted quickly, and the editorial commentary arrives whenever Yahoo!'s licensed content providers supply it (certainly sooner than if you waited for the morning paper, which might miss the end of a night game anyway).

For any games in the big four sports happening on a given day, you can click directly to game pages from the main Yahoo! Sports front page. If you refer back to Figure 8-1, you can see that all the listed games in the left-hand sidebar are scheduled for the evening, and hadn't started yet when that screen shot was taken. When a game is in progress, that starting time is replaced by an indication of where the game stands (what quarter, period, or inning it's in). When a game is over (and before the following morning when it's removed from the sidebar), these indications are replaced by an F (for Final score).

Whether a game is yet to start, in progress, or finished, click the indicator to the right of the score to display the game page. For each game, there is (or will be, by the time the contest is over) a preview, box score, and recap, each on its own page. Those elements are all linkable from the main game page. Figure 8-6 shows a game page from an NBA playoff game. Because the game is over, the link automatically displays not the game page but the recap page; the <u>preview</u> and <u>box score</u> links are also available.

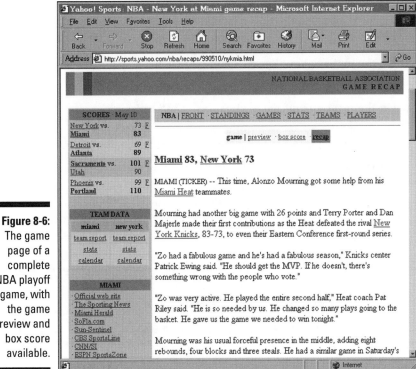

Figure 8-6:
The game
page of a
complete
NBA playoff
game, with
the game
preview and
box score
available.

Crunching the Stats

As a stock chart is to an investor and a recipe is to a chef, so are statistics to a sports fan. Statistics explain, clarify, and reveal by comparison. A particular fascination exists for individual player statistics in team sports. Even in a team effort, each player is competing with himself or herself and with historical standards of excellence. Following a team usually means rooting for individual player accomplishment in addition to team success.

Yahoo! Sports fares pretty well in the stat department. Throughout this section, I use baseball as an example because it is perhaps the most numbers-rich and statistically manic sport.

Yahoo! Sport has two basic types of stats:

- ✔ Team statistics
- ✔ Player statistics

It can be tricky to find exactly the type of numbers you're looking for. Allow me to mark the best paths to the best stats. To start exploring team stats, do the following:

1. **On the main Yahoo! Sports front page, click any league link.**

    In this example, I'm using the <u>mlb</u> baseball link.

2. **On the league front page, click the <u>STATS</u> link.**

    You might think it more intuitive to click the <u>TEAMS</u> link, but that just leads to links for team front pages, as described previously in this chapter.

3. **On the Statistics page, click any category of statistic.**

    Figure 8-7 shows the Statistics page for major league baseball. You can see that the stats are categorized by American and National League, with a column for numbers applying to both leagues. Each category is further divided into batting and pitching categories.

Photos and fantasies

I trust the headline got your attention. Beyond news, team updates, game recaps, and statistics, Yahoo! Sports throws a couple of miscellaneous features into the mix — namely, a collection of sports photojournalism and an interactive fantasy baseball game.

You get to the photos from the main Yahoo! Sports front page or from any league front page. Just click the <u>Photo Gallery</u> to see thumbnail (that is, small) versions of available pictures, with captions. Click any thumbnail to see a larger display of the photo. Naturally, the photo gallery you see when linking from a league front page contains photos of only that sport in action.

Fantasy baseball is a statistician's idea of athletic endeavor. Actually, it's a fun, somewhat cerebral game that requires smarts about the game and the stamina to concentrate on the details of the game over the course of an entire season. It works by selecting real-world players for your imaginary roster, and then calculating the success of your team according to the actual exploits of the players as the season grinds on. Different fantasy leagues implement variations on the basic rules. Yahoo! Sports allows you to create your own league with your own rules, or play the house version.

Get the scoop on virtual baseball by clicking the <u>Baseball</u> link under Fantasy Sports. Obviously, this game can be played only during the baseball season, but you may take advantage of a mid-season entry point. Keep your eyes open for other fantasy sports on the main Yahoo! Sports front page during the rest of the year.

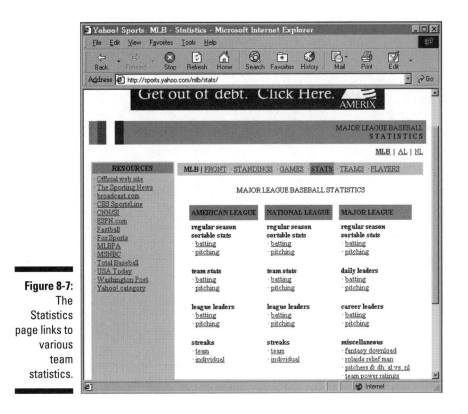

Figure 8-7:
The
Statistics
page links to
various
team
statistics.

A slightly different path leads to the player stats. Here it is:

1. **On the main Yahoo! Sports front page, click any league link.**

   Again, let's go for the <u>mlb</u> link for this example.

2. **On the league front page, click the <u>PLAYERS</u> link.**

3. **On the Players page, click any player's name to see his or her statistical section.**

   The player statistics for major league baseball are more complex than for other sports. Figure 8-8 shows the stats page for Bobby Bonilla.

   If you look at the link menu below the main banner, you can see that the Player Profile is just the first page. A few other stat pages deliver a comprehensive analysis of Bonilla's performance since 1997, the earliest year represented in the Yahoo! Sports statistics as of this writing. The "How Bobby Stacks Up" chart (included for each player) is a nifty at-a-glance indicator of essential performance.

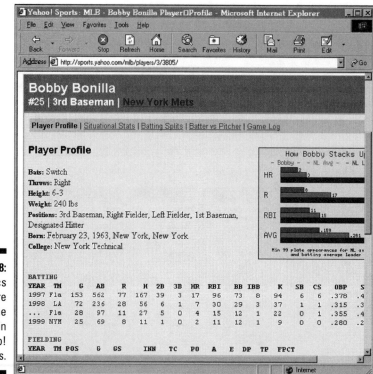

Figure 8-8:
Statistics
get a share
of the
spotlight in
Yahoo!
Sports.

Chapter 9

Taking Stock of Investments

· ·

In This Chapter

▶ Touring the Finance section of Yahoo!

▶ Getting up-to-the-15-minute stock quotes

▶ Tracking your holdings with an online portfolio

· ·

*T*he Yahoo! Finance home page is an anchor site for millions of online investors. What was once primarily a stock quote server has blossomed into a data hub and information resource. Yahoo!'s no-nonsense, fast-moving pages really come in handy for online traders who value quick, reliable information. The range of editorial services has rounded out what was once a fairly dry set of features. The page design remains stark, but that just ensures fast and reliable navigation.

Other Web sites offer real-time stock quotes, whereas Yahoo!'s company quotes are still delayed by at least 15 minutes. For gathering fundamental information about a company, however, no one does the job faster or more thoroughly than Yahoo! Finance.

This chapter runs down the most important features of Yahoo! Finance, including getting stock quotes, creating an online portfolio, and playing a stock-trading game.

A Basic Map of Yahoo! Finance

Following is a quick tour of the main content features of the Yahoo! Finance home page. As you can see in Figure 9-1, the home page has one heck of a lot of links. Many lead to deeply informative sites that would be worth a chapter by themselves. Because I can't do justice to the whole thing, I provide a map of the page's basic topography so you don't miss anything important. Stock quotes and portfolios are described in separate sections later in this chapter.

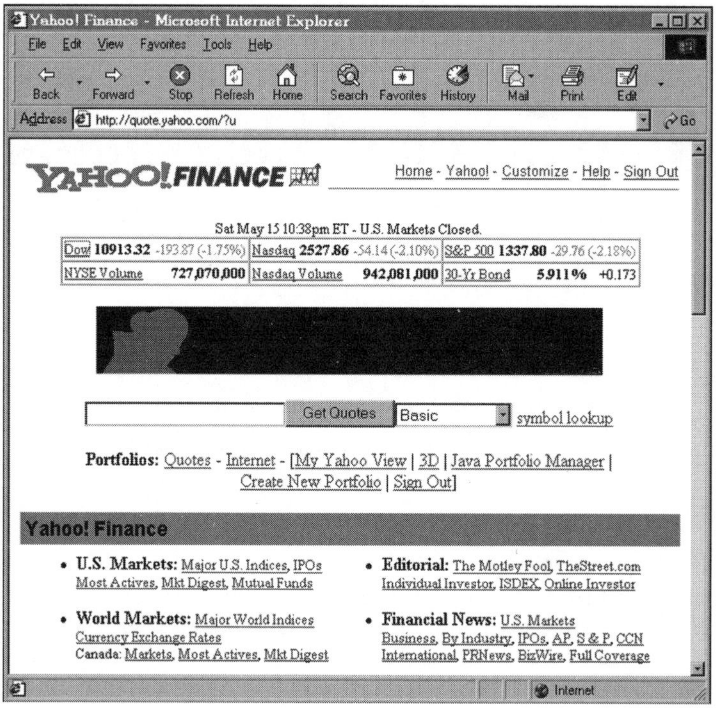

Figure 9-1:
The Yahoo!
Finance
home page.

To get to Yahoo! Finance, click the <u>Stock Quotes</u> link on the Yahoo! home page, or go directly to this URL:

```
quote.yahoo.com
```

Market overview

Most people who follow the financial markets check in periodically throughout the business day to get a snapshot of stock and bond activity. For most people, that snapshot is provided by the major index prices. You've probably heard them quoted on radio and TV stock market reports: "The Dow is up (or down) for the day, and the Nasdaq Composite has rallied (or slumped) throughout the afternoon. The yield on the 30-year Treasury bond is at an all-time high (or low)." Those statistics are presented at the very top of Yahoo! Finance, in real time. If you continually click your browser's Reload or Refresh button, you can see the prices changing.

As you can see in Figure 9-1, the three index benchmarks for measuring stock market performance in the United States are on the page:

✔ **Dow** is the Dow Jones Industrial Average, a measure of large-company performance consisting of 30 big companies from the New York Stock Exchange.

✔ **Nasdaq** is the Nasdaq stock exchange composite average, generally considered a measure of technology companies because of the many such companies traded on the Nasdaq exchange.

✔ **S&P 500** represents the Standard and Poor's index of 500 large and mid-sized companies, widely considered the most accurate barometer of broad stock market performance.

Trading volume numbers for the Dow and Nasdaq are displayed, plus the yield (but not the price) for the 30-year Treasury bond, the benchmark bond product used to evaluate the entire bond marketplace.

Click the index name for a detailed quote of that index's price, including the day's range and the 52-week range (see Figure 9-2). The 30-Yr Bond link divulges the bond yield in basis points — so 5.911 percent, for example, is represented by 59.11.

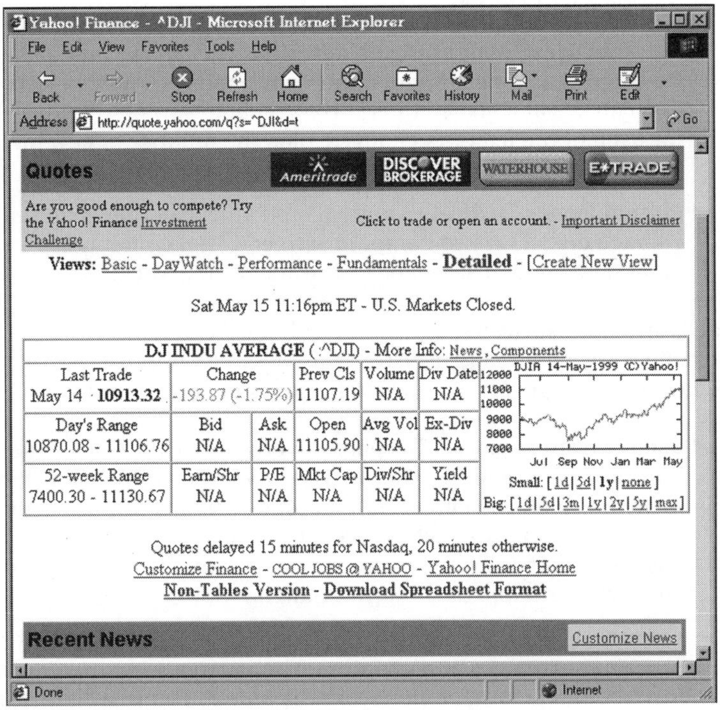

Figure 9-2:
A detailed
quote of the
Dow Jones
Industrial
Average.

Global financial data

Yahoo! Finance is a data-rich resource, and it knows no boundaries. From Asian stock markets to currency exchange rates, Yahoo! has it. Several major sections contain links to data about the United States markets and those abroad.

Under the Yahoo! Finance banner (mid page), the U.S. Markets section offers these features:

- **Major U.S. Indices.** The Dow, Nasdaq, and S&P 500 paint the picture in broad strokes, but dozens of other United States financial market indices assign value to different sectors. Go here to see what's up with the Dow Transportation Average, the Russell 2000 index of small-cap companies, regional stock exchanges, Treasury securities, commodities, and much more. This is index-lover's heaven.

- **IPOs.** The IPO section is a detailed review and forecast of initial public offerings, including performance rankings over different time periods.

- **Most Actives.** Click this link to see the high-volume leaders at any given time for each of the three main United States exchanges; New York, American, and Nasdaq.

- **Market Digest.** Market Digest describes the *market breadth* at any given time and is a subject of great interest to most serious investors. Here, you can see at a glance the ratio of declining stocks to advancing stocks for each of the major exchanges, plus the number of new highs and new lows. The total volume for each exchange is included.

- **Mutual Funds.** Dedicated mutual fund sites can't be beat, but Yahoo! Finance doesn't try to compete with editorial content. Instead, it provides a basic fund screener, performance statistics, and news headlines.

The World Markets section goes beyond United States stock and bond exchanges to cover overseas (from the American perspective) stock exchanges, foreign currency trading, and Canadian stocks:

- **Major World Indices.** This page covers North and South America, Asia, Europe, Africa, and the Middle East. I bet you never knew there were so many financial exchanges. And at times, even the most seemingly obscure ones may affect the stocks of your exchange — this is a good page to keep handy during those nervous midnights when you have to know what's happening on the Shanghai Composite.

- **Currency Exchange Rates.** This handy page features both a static table of major currencies and an interactive currency converter that handles just about any form of money on the planet. Figure 9-3 illustrates the drop-down menu selection that lends the currency converter its flexibility. Using both menus, you can convert any national monetary unit into any other. Even if you don't trade currencies, this gadget is useful if you're interested in traveling to another country.

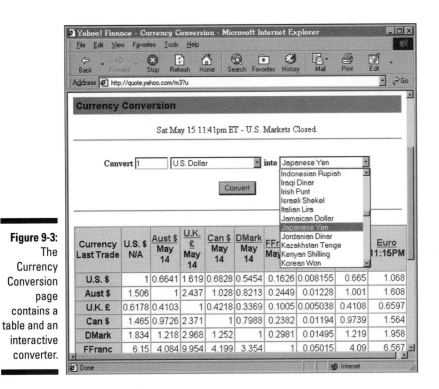

Figure 9-3:
The
Currency
Conversion
page
contains a
table and an
interactive
converter.

✓ **Canadian Markets.** The <u>Market Digest</u> and <u>Most Actives</u> links in this section deliver stock overviews for the many busy regional Canadian stock exchanges.

News and commentary

The main fund of current news headlines is located about halfway down the Yahoo! Finance home page, under the Latest Market News banner. (See Figure 9-4.) This vortex of financial news is one of the most dynamic headline feeds on the Net. Constantly changing, it is best appreciated by clicking your browser's Reload or Refresh button every few minutes. That's not practical, of course, but the point is that Latest Market News is up to the minute no matter when you check in.

In addition to timeliness, Latest Market News doesn't pull any punches in the content department. This is a news service for the serious observer of global financial markets. Stuffed with foreign market responses to United States stocks, thorny reports about corporate boardrooms, and political news with a business slant, this editorial selection doesn't hold anyone's hand.

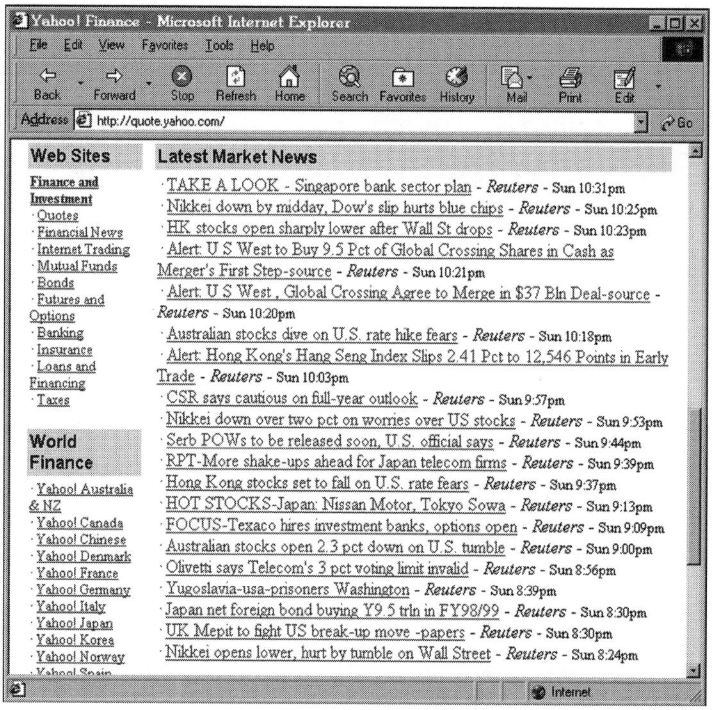

Figure 9-4:
Latest
Market
News is a
shifting
kaleido-
scope of
current
news
stories.

Further up on the page, under the Yahoo! Finance banner, the Financial News section lets you angle into news reports by individual wire service tickers, featuring the Associated Press (AP), Canadian Corporate News (CCN), Standard & Poor's News Service (S & P), PRNews, and BizWire. The Full Coverage link takes you to the Business Headlines page of Yahoo! News.

Yahoo! licenses financial commentary from a few highly regarded sources, and packages it into the familiar Yahoo! page design. Here's what you can find under the Editorial section:

- ✔ **The Motley Fool.** The two brothers who achieved fame and a loyal following among investors began their online career at America Online, and then migrated to the Internet. The Motley Fool blends irreverent humor with a sound investment philosophy. Yahoo! runs the Motley Fool Lunchtime News and Evening News, as well as other columns.

- ✔ **TheStreet.com.** James J. Cramer, who has attained celebrity status through his many opinionated appearances on CNBC (the financial cable channel), runs this site. TheStreet.com contributes Cramer's widely read Wrong! column and other regularly scheduled articles.

- ✔ **Individual Investor Online.** This mix of commentary and news dishes up a stock pick of the day, mutual fund analysis, and ongoing market coverage.

✔ **Online Investor.** Online Investor delivers a daily stock pick and some educational content about investing over the Internet.

Getting Stock Quotes

To get a stock quote from Yahoo! Finance, follow these steps:

1. **On the Yahoo! Finance home page, type one or more stock symbols in the Get Quotes entry form.**

   When entering more than one symbol, separate your entries by a single space. If you know the company name but not its ticker symbol, click the symbol lookup link. On the Ticker Symbol Lookup page, enter the company (or part of it) and click the Lookup button to find the symbol.

2. **Use the drop-down menu to choose the type of quote.**

   Yahoo! Finance offers a varying amount of data along with the simple stock price. Basic quotes are the simplest (see Figure 9-5), while Research quotes display a hefty page of analyst rankings for the stock. The chart selection includes a one-year price chart below the quote. I usually select Detailed quotes (see Figure 9-6). No matter what selection you make, it's easy to switch to another view.

3. **Click the Get Quotes button.**

Every quote page — regardless of whether it's a Simple quote, Detailed quote, or some other view — displays a list of recent company-related headline links.

With most stock quotes you get from Yahoo!, a Profile link is available in the More Info category. This link leads to an extremely useful page (see Figure 9-7) that displays share valuations, per-share data, financial strength, dividend values, and more.

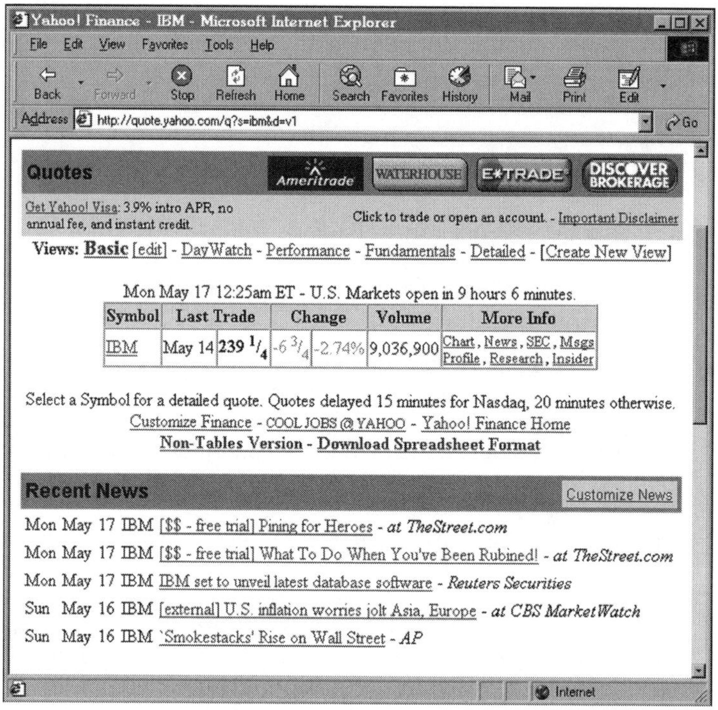

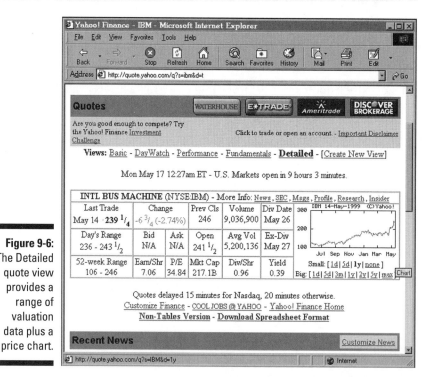

Figure 9-5:
A Basic stock quote view gives basic information plus the news links that appear with all quote views.

Figure 9-6:
The Detailed quote view provides a range of valuation data plus a price chart.

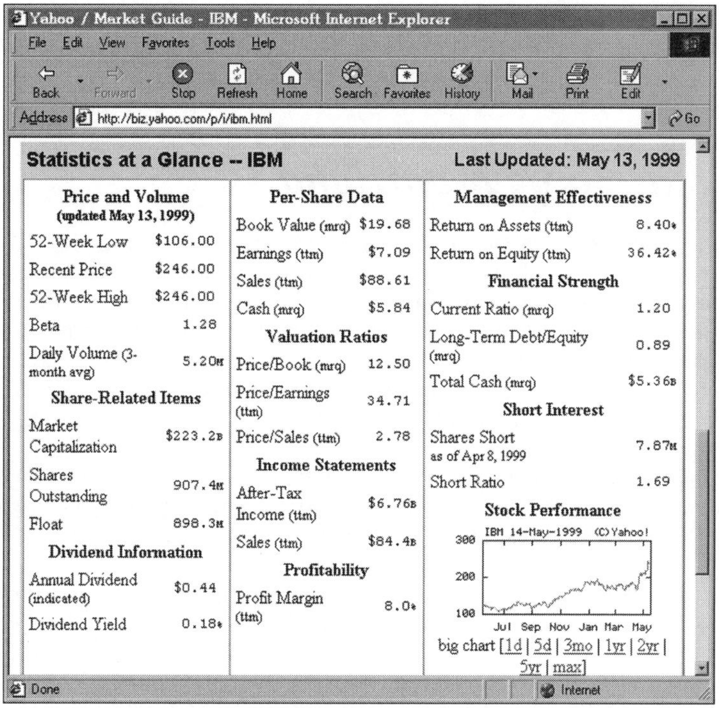

Figure 9-7:
The Profile
page, linked
from a stock
quote,
displays
many stock
valuations.

Statistics at a Glance -- IBM   Last Updated: May 13, 1999

Price and Volume
(updated May 13, 1999)

52-Week Low	$106.00
Recent Price	$246.00
52-Week High	$246.00
Beta	1.28
Daily Volume (3-month avg)	5.20M

Share-Related Items

Market Capitalization	$223.2B
Shares Outstanding	907.4M
Float	898.3M

Dividend Information

Annual Dividend (indicated)	$0.44
Dividend Yield	0.18%

Per-Share Data

Book Value (mrq)	$19.68
Earnings (ttm)	$7.09
Sales (ttm)	$88.61
Cash (mrq)	$5.84

Valuation Ratios

Price/Book (mrq)	12.50
Price/Earnings (ttm)	34.71
Price/Sales (ttm)	2.78

Income Statements

After-Tax Income (ttm)	$6.76B
Sales (ttm)	$84.4B

Profitability

Profit Margin (ttm)	8.0%

Management Effectiveness

Return on Assets (ttm)	8.40%
Return on Equity (ttm)	36.42%

Financial Strength

Current Ratio (mrq)	1.20
Long-Term Debt/Equity (mrq)	0.89
Total Cash (mrq)	$5.36B

Short Interest

Shares Short as of Apr 8, 1999	7.87M
Short Ratio	1.69

Stock Performance

big chart [1d | 5d | 3mo | 1yr | 2yr | 5yr | max]

Creating Portfolios

If you own stocks or mutual funds, creating an online portfolio is an interesting way to track your holdings. If you're accustomed to following your investments more casually, with an occasional glance at the newspaper stock listings and a monthly perusal of your brokerage statement, you might discover the fun of minute-by-minute portfolio fluctuations. Fun? Some might call it obsessive. At any rate, you don't have to watch your portfolio obsessively, but keeping your stocks listed in Yahoo! Finance at least gives you a quick way to check your bottom line, and your individual holdings, whenever you want.

There's another reason to create an online portfolio. If you are considering becoming an online trader — the popular high-risk hobby of the late 1990s — it's a good idea to paper trade first. *Paper trading* means buying and selling stocks in a virtual portfolio, without money. Yahoo! Finance is not a brokerage, and you can't open an account in it. So the service doesn't know or care whether your portfolio reflects actual holdings or pretend holdings. Many beginning online investors practice virtual trading through an online portfolio before putting any real money into play.

This section describes how to create a basic Yahoo! Finance portfolio; introduces you to the free Java Portfolio Manager; and explains the Investment Challenge stock-trading game.

Creating your portfolio

Yahoo! Finance throws a lot of portfolio features in your face, but you don't have to use them all. You may fashion a simple list of stocks or develop a complex tool including upper and lower price alert limits, notes on each holding, commission rates to be subtracted from capital gains, and so on. A portfolio may be set up to track stocks generally (as if you didn't own them), or to track ownership of certain numbers of shares purchased at a certain price (whether you actually own the stock or are just pretending).

You need to display the Edit your portfolio page to begin creating your portfolio. On the Yahoo! Finance home page, click the Create New Portfolio link, and you're ready to start. See Figure 9-8.

You must have a Yahoo! ID to create a portfolio. See Chapter 1 for information about registering as a Yahoo! member.

Figure 9-8:
This is
where you
create a
virtual
portfolio.

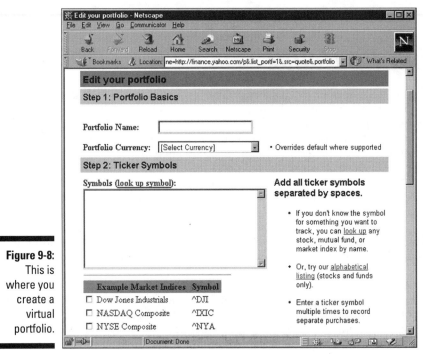

The imaginary method

Most people who use Yahoo! portfolios create imaginary stock-holding scenarios either to test investing strategies or to follow certain companies out of interest. Investors generally track their actual holdings using portfolio tools provided by their online brokerage. Offline investors usually rely on their broker statements and newspaper information. This is changing, though, as more people experiment with managing information online.

Here, I describe how to set up a relatively simple Yahoo! portfolio — not to track actual holdings, but to follow a group of stocks out of experimentation or interest. The next part of this section gets into more complex features.

Follow these steps to create a basic portfolio tracker:

1. **On the Edit your portfolio page, type a name for the portfolio in the Portfolio Name field.**

   Because you might establish a number of portfolios, name this one something that indicates what is in it, or give it a number. (Why am I being so pushy? Name it whatever you want.)

2. **In the Portfolio Currency field, use the drop-down menu to select the currency you want to use.**

   Yahoo! converts the native currency of the exchange your stocks are located on to whatever currency you *would* use if you were to buy the stock. This feature is only for tracking; it has nothing to do with whether you plan to actually buy your selected stocks.

3. **Under the Ticker Symbols banner, enter the stock symbols you want listed in your portfolio.**

   Put a space between all your symbols. If you don't know a stock symbol, use the look up symbol link. You can also use the alphabetical listing link, but the list is gigantic. It's easier to search for the company specifically if you know its name.

4. **Click the check boxes next to any indices you want to appear in your portfolio.**

   You may choose as many indices as you like. If the one(s) you want aren't on the short list, click the More U.S. Indices and More International Indices links.

5. **Under the Basic Features banner, check the boxes if you'd like your stocks listed alphabetically and if you want a small-type display.**

   If you deliberately entered your stock symbols in the order you'd like them to appear, ignore the alphabetical option. The small font is useful if you choose any display option other than Basic. All the other options contain more information than can fit into most browser windows. (Although that depends on your screen size, screen resolution, and how wide you keep your windows.) I routinely use small fonts.

6. **Using the drop-down menu, choose a profile view.**

The views determine how much information is stuffed into your portfolio. The views correspond to the quote views you get when ordering a stock quote from the Yahoo! Finance home page. Basic view contains the least information, and is good for quickly getting the gist of your portfolio's activity. The views get more detailed as you move down the list. Don't agonize over this decision; you can change views on the Portfolio page, and also return to this page to edit your configuration at any time.

7. **Click the Finished button.**

Your portfolio is displayed (see Figure 9-9). To edit your options, look above the Portfolio banner, next to your currently displayed portfolio name, to find the edit link; click it to return to the Edit your portfolio page.

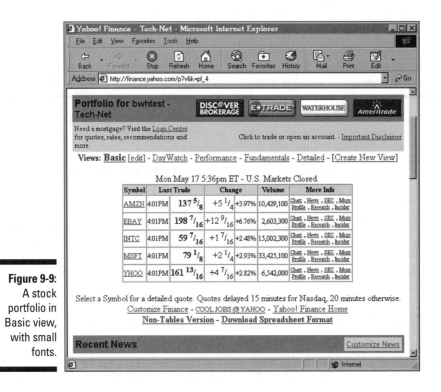

Figure 9-9:
A stock portfolio in Basic view, with small fonts.

Note the Create New View link on the Portfolio page (refer to Figure 9-9). Use this link if you're unsatisfied with the preset views available for your stocks. You might be particularly interested in each stock's P/E Ratio and Volume, but have interest also in the dividend information. The Edit your portfolio views page (see Figure 9-10) lets you customize what information your portfolio displays for each stock. Even better, you can use your personalized view when calling up individual quotes from the Yahoo! Finance home page. All in all, it's one kickin' feature. Here's how to use it:

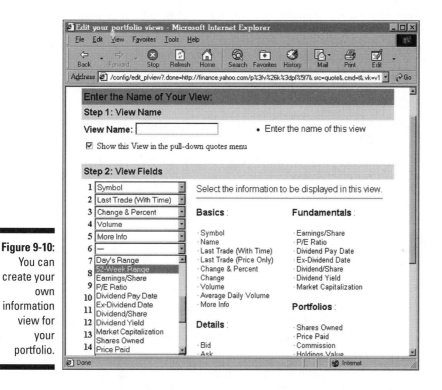

Figure 9-10:
You can create your own information view for your portfolio.

1. **On the Edit your portfolio views page, name your new view in the View Name field.**

2. **If necessary, click to insert a check next to "Show this View in the pull-down quotes menu."**

   There is no reason to uncheck this box, which is checked by default when you first display this page.

3. **Use the drop-down menus next to each numbered field to select what information is divulged for your stocks.**

   When you drop down the menus, use the right-hand scroll bars to see the entire list of options.

4. **Click the Accept Changes button.**

Your portfolio is displayed in its new view. You may still change views easily, using the Views links directly above the portfolio. To change to another portfolio, you use the links above the Portfolio banner.

Setting up a trading portfolio

Things can get more complicated than the simple portfolio just described. Whether you actually own stocks or want to pretend you do for trading practice, Yahoo! Finance lets you add Buy and Sell information into your portfolio. Here's how to proceed:

1. **On the Yahoo! Finance home page, click the edit link next to any portfolio you want to alter.**

If you're starting from scratch, use the Create New Portfolio link on the Yahoo! Finance home page.

2. **On the Edit your portfolio page, scroll down to the Step 4: Advanced Features (Optional) banner.**

If you're starting a new portfolio, fill in the information under the first three steps on this page, as described in the preceding section. See Figure 9-11, which shows the advanced features.

3. **Click to check the boxes next to the information features you want included in your portfolio.**

4. **Click the Enter More Info button.**

Do not click the Finished button at this point. Checking the boxes only tells Yahoo! what fields to include in the portfolio; you still must enter basic information in those fields for the portfolio to do its work.

5. **On the Edit your portfolio details page (see Figure 9-12), type share, price, date, commission, and limit details for each stock in your portfolio, and add whatever notes you want to appear.**

6. **Click the Finished button.**

Your new portfolio appears. To see the share, price, and gain or loss figures, you must be in Performance view. Click the Performance link if that is not your default view. Click the edit link to return to the Edit your portfolio page, where you can make Performance your default view. Figure 9-13 shows a Performance portfolio.

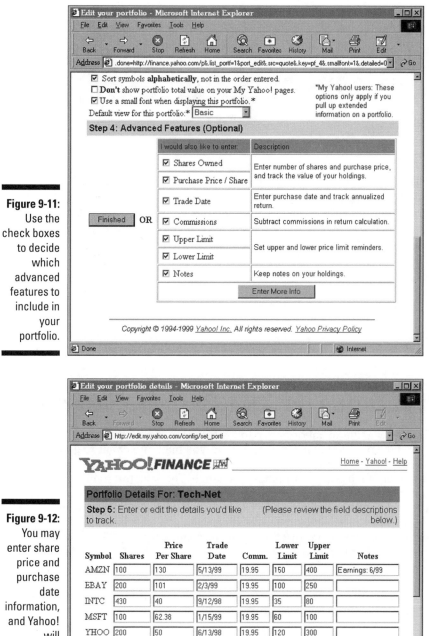

Figure 9-11:
Use the
check boxes
to decide
which
advanced
features to
include in
your
portfolio.

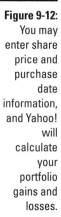

Figure 9-12:
You may
enter share
price and
purchase
date
information,
and Yahoo!
will
calculate
your
portfolio
gains and
losses.

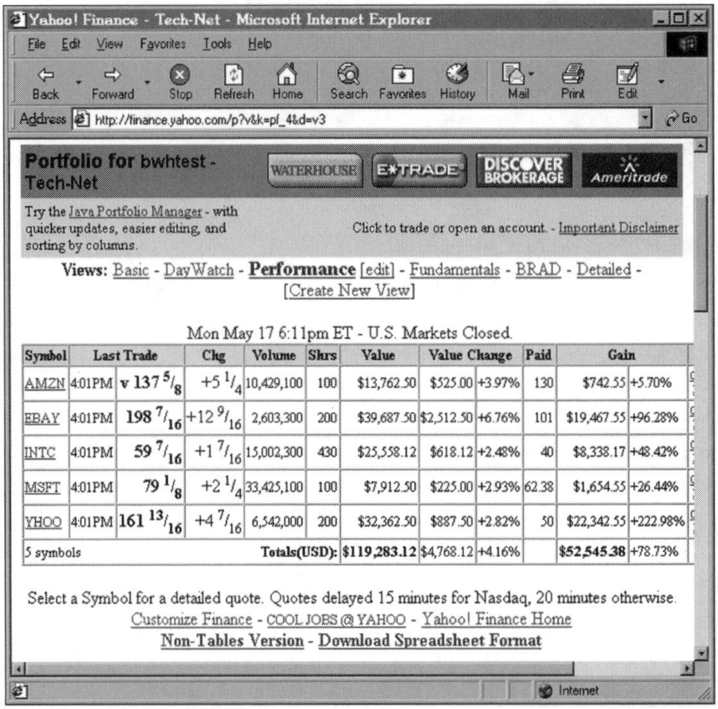

Figure 9-13:
An
expanded
portfolio
with share,
price, and
capital gain
figures.

The figure shows a browser window titled "Yahoo! Finance - Tech-Net - Microsoft Internet Explorer" with address http://finance.yahoo.com/p?v&k=pf_4&d=v3

Portfolio for bwhtest - Tech-Net

Try the Java Portfolio Manager - with quicker updates, easier editing, and sorting by columns.

Click to trade or open an account. - Important Disclaimer

Views: Basic - DayWatch - **Performance** [edit] - Fundamentals - BRAD - Detailed - [Create New View]

Mon May 17 6:11pm ET - U.S. Markets Closed.

Symbol	Last Trade		Chg	Volume	Shrs	Value	Value Change		Paid	Gain	
AMZN	4:01PM	v 137 5/8	+5 1/4	10,429,100	100	$13,762.50	$525.00	+3.97%	130	$742.55	+5.70%
EBAY	4:01PM	198 7/16	+12 9/16	2,603,300	200	$39,687.50	$2,512.50	+6.76%	101	$19,467.55	+96.28%
INTC	4:01PM	59 7/16	+1 7/16	15,002,300	430	$25,558.12	$618.12	+2.48%	40	$8,338.17	+48.42%
MSFT	4:01PM	79 1/8	+2 1/4	33,425,100	100	$7,912.50	$225.00	+2.93%	62.38	$1,654.55	+26.44%
YHOO	4:01PM	161 13/16	+4 7/16	6,542,000	200	$32,362.50	$887.50	+2.82%	50	$22,342.55	+222.98%
5 symbols				Totals(USD):		$119,283.12	$4,768.12	+4.16%		$52,545.38	+78.73%

Select a Symbol for a detailed quote. Quotes delayed 15 minutes for Nasdaq, 20 minutes otherwise.
Customize Finance - COOL JOBS @ YAHOO - Yahoo! Finance Home
Non-Tables Version - **Download Spreadsheet Format**

Introducing the Java Portfolio Manager

The Java version of Yahoo!'s portfolios makes management much easier than in the Web-page version. Once you try it, you might not want to go back to the relatively cumbersome system of surfing to the Edit your portfolio Web page every time you want to make a change. The Java program is far more interactive, allowing you to add and delete stocks, update prices, change portfolios, and change portfolio views without using your Web browser at all.

You may use the Java Portfolio Manager on any Windows 95, Windows 98, Windows NT, Macintosh, or UNIX computer that supports Java applets. Here's how to start it:

1. **On the Yahoo! Finance home page or any Portfolio page, click the Java Portfolio Manager link.**

   A window pops open while the Java program is automatically downloaded into your computer.

2. **When the start JPM button appears, click it.**

   The Java program appears on your screen (see Figure 9-14). It's as easy as that.

Figure 9-14:
The Java
Portfolio
Manager is
far more
interactive
than Web
portfolios.

Symbol	Last Trade		Chg	Volume	Shrs	Value	Value Change	Paid
AMZN	4:01PM	137.62	+5.25	10,429,100	100.0	$13,762.50	$525.00 +3.97%	130
EBAY	4:01PM	198.44	+12.56	2,603,300	200.0	$39,687.50	$2,512.50 +6.76%	101
INTC	4:01PM	59.44	+1.44	15,002,300	430.0	$25,558.13	$618.12 +2.48%	40
MSFT	4:01PM	79.12	+2.25	33,425,100	100.0	$7,912.50	$225.00 +2.93%	62.38
YHOO	4:01PM	161.81	+4.44	6,542,000	200.0	$32,362.50	$887.50 +2.82%	50
Totals:						$119,283.13	$4,768.13 +4.16%	

In the Java Portfolio Manager, the following features make it easy to manage your stock listing:

✔ Click the drop-down Portfolio menu to select one of your portfolios.

✔ Click the View drop-down menu to select a portfolio view.

✔ Click any stock name and drag it to a new position in the list to alter the order of stocks.

✔ Click any stock name and drag it to the trash can icon to delete it from the list.

✔ Click the Update button to get new prices. (Stock prices are delayed at least fifteen minutes.)

✔ To insert a new stock into your list, type its stock symbol in the Add Symbol field, and then click the Add Symbol button.

✔ Click any column header to sort the list according to that column's data. Click it again to reverse the order.

Changes made in the Java Portfolio Manager affect your portfolios as they appear in the Yahoo! Finance Web pages. The two methods of managing your stocks — Web and Java — are linked, and all changes made in one mode appear in the other mode.

Do not close the Java Portfolio Manager download window while the Java program is running. That's the window in which you clicked the start JPM button to launch the Java Manager. If you close that window (even though it is not the program window itself), the Java Portfolio Manager closes also.

Playing the Investment Challenge

Stock trading can be fun — that's the premise behind Yahoo!'s investment game. The basic rules are simple. You start out with a portfolio of 100,000 dollars in imaginary cash. You may spend that cash buying stocks costing at least five dollars on the New York Stock Exchange, American Stock Exchange, or Nasdaq stock exchange. Each contest lasts one month, by the calendar, and you may enter at any time during the month. The cash prizes are substantial, and the game is phenomenally popular.

Here's how to enter:

1. **On the Yahoo! Finance home page, under The Investment Challenge, click the Enter link.**

2. **On the Investment Challenge Registration page, use the drop-down menu to choose one of your Yahoo! IDs.**

3. **Select the default portfolio view you want to see in your Investment Challenge portfolio, and select whether or not to view small fonts.**

4. **Furnish information about yourself in all the fields.**

   Yahoo! needs much more information about your location than the service usually asks during interactive-feature registrations. This detail is required because you are entering a contest with cash prizes.

5. **Answer the Tie Breaker Question.**

   Guess the level of the Dow Jones Industrial Average on the date listed, in case your portfolio results tie with another winner's.

6. **Click the Enter Investment Challenge button.**

After you are registered in the Investment Challenge, the Investment Challenge portfolio appears in your portfolio list just like any other you create. Click the Trade link on your Investment Challenge portfolio page to buy or sell stocks using your treasure chest of fantasy money.

The Investment Challenge is not meant as a test of real-world investment expertise. The contest runs in one-month bursts, and winners take a bold, aggressive, daring approach to stock buying that they probably wouldn't use with real money. Doing well relies on successful market timing, which most professionals agree is impossible to sustain in the real stock market. In other words, winners are usually lucky in these investing games. I suggest having fun with it, going for broke, and trying again next month if you don't win.

Chapter 10

In Search of Pop Culture

· ·

In This Chapter

▶ Discovering Yahoo! Music

▶ Trying out the new Yahoo! Radio

▶ Reading about Movie news

▶ Finding movie showtimes for your town or city

▶ Getting local TV listings and searching for shows

· ·

*I*n this chapter, I combine three related areas of the Yahoo! service: music, movies, and TV. Yahoo! assembles news and programming information about these entertainment fields in a mostly coherent, easily navigable format. This chapter steps you through the main features of each section.

Yahoo! Music

Yahoo! Music is extremely oriented toward rock and pop. The recent addition of Yahoo! Radio to the lineup broadens the focus somewhat, but when it comes to information content, the hit scene is where Yahoo! is at. You can see for yourself at the Yahoo! Music home page (see Figure 10-1), which is called Rock & Pop Music Home. This page presents a mix of news, reviews, charts, live Internet events, a search engine, and chances to exercise your credit card in the service of music CD acquisition.

To see the Yahoo! Music home page, click the <u>Music</u> link near the bottom of the main Yahoo! home page, or go directly to the following URL:

```
rock.yahoo.com
```

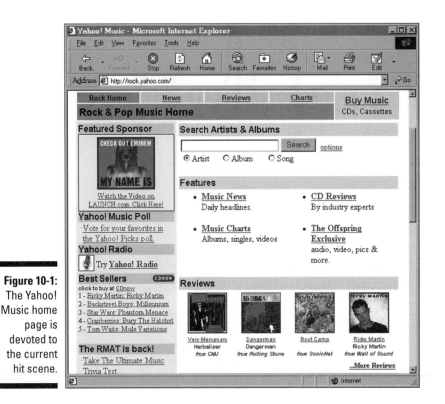

Figure 10-1:
The Yahoo!
Music home
page is
devoted to
the current
hit scene.

The newsy stuff

Music might be a language unto itself, but a lot of words are used to describe it. Many of those words can be found at Yahoo! Music. To read the latest headlines about the music business, scroll down to the Headlines section of the music home page. For a greater selection, click the Music News link. Figure 10-2 shows what the Music news page looks like. Each headline is accompanied by a story summary; click the headline to read more.

Yahoo! Music provides new stories from a handful of Internet publications, including CMJ, Launch, Rolling Stone, SonicNet, and Wall of Sound. The news page displays timely stories from any or all of these sources. (Clicking the headline link keeps you within Yahoo! Music.) Notice that just beneath the News banner is a menu of links to the sources themselves. In fact, you don't go to the source site when you click one of those links, but you do go to another Yahoo! Music news page featuring stories only from that source.

Music reviews are provided by the same sources as the news stories. For a general selection of reviews, just click the Reviews link (near the top of the page) or the CD Reviews link (under the Features banner) on the Yahoo!

Music home page (both links go to the same place). Under the Latest Reviews banner, you can get to reviews by just one of the sources by clicking that source's link on the Latest Reviews page.

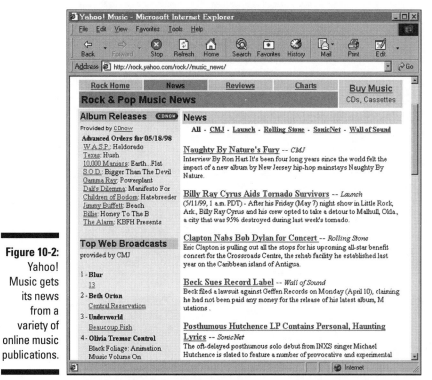

Figure 10-2:
Yahoo!
Music gets
its news
from a
variety of
online music
publications.

Charts are organized pretty much the same way as news and CD reviews. Three sources are used for the sales charts: Billboard Magazine, CMJ, and Rick Dees Online. Each source carries its own charts and compiles those charts using its own methods. Billboard and CMJ each feature nine music charts, ranging from Top 40 hits to blues albums to Internet retail bestsellers.

One of the best features of the Yahoo! Music charts is the way chart entries link to artist information in the Yahoo! Musicfinder database. Musicfinder is the source of search results in Yahoo! Music, which I describe in the next section. For an example of how this works, look at Figures 10-3 and 10-4. Figure 10-3 shows the Billboard Top 40 music chart, with Sarah McLachlan perched in the number one spot. Her name, along with most of the others, is a hyperlink. A click of that link takes you to Figure 10-4, the Musicfinder page for the popular singer and tour organizer. I describe Musicfinder features more fully in the next section on searching.

| Yahoo! Music - Microsoft Internet Explorer | | | | | | | | | | _ □ × |

File Edit View Favorites Tools Help

| ← Back | → Forward | ✕ Stop | ↻ Refresh | ⌂ Home | 🔍 Search | ⭐ Favorites | 🕘 History | ✉ Mail | 🖨 Print | Edit |

Address http://rock.yahoo.com/rock/music_charts/billboard/chart.html?s=n/billboard/chart/adult_top_40   ⏵Go

Rock Home	News	Reviews	Charts	**Buy Music**
Rock & Pop Music Charts				CDs, Cassettes

Back to: <u>Charts</u> - <u>Billboard Charts Only</u>

Adult Top 40

This week	Last week	Artist Title	Weeks on chart	Peak Position
1	1	<u>Sarah McLachlan</u> Angel	26	1
2	2	<u>'N Sync</u> (God Must Have Spent) A Little More Time On You	20	2
3	4	<u>Phil Collins</u> You'll Be In My Heart	4	3
4	3	<u>Cher</u> Believe	12	3
5	6	<u>Sixpence None The Richer</u> Kiss Me	8	5
6	5	<u>Shania Twain</u> From This Moment On	36	1
7	8	<u>Monica</u> Angel Of Mine	16	6
8	7	**Elton John & LeAnn Rimes** Written In The Stars	18	2

| | | 🌐 Internet |

Figure 10-3:
The Billboard Top 40 music chart. Most of the artists link to Yahoo! Musicfinder.

Searching for music

In Yahoo! Music, searching has two results: information about recording artists (and their work) and invitations to buy CDs. The best place to begin a search is right on the Yahoo! Music home page. As you can see in Figure 10-1, the search form is front and center on the page. Proceed thusly:

1. **Using the radio buttons below the keyword entry form, select whether you're searching for an artist, an album, or a song.**

2. **In the keyword field, type your keywords.**

3. **Click the Search button.**

The <u>options</u> link next to the Search button leads to a directory page for finding artists by browsing rather than by searching. That page has a search form, too, but the only extra option it provides is the addition of an All radio button for searching artists, albums, and songs simultaneously.

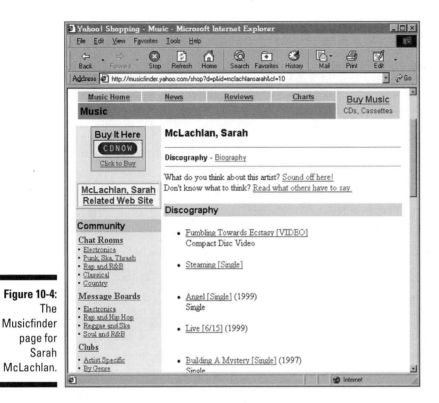

Figure 10-4:
The
Musicfinder
page for
Sarah
McLachlan.

When you search for a music artist, the search results display all hits that relate in any way to your keyword(s). The search engine assumes that you might have entered an incomplete artist name, and delivers extensions of that name if they exist. For example, searching on *sting* displays not only the ex-Police lead singer, but also Paul Stinga, the Blue Stingrays, and other names. If you find your match, click it to see the artist information page, which is part of Yahoo! Musicfinder. The artist information page has two parts: Discography and Biography. You see the Discography page first with a link to the Biography page.

Just about every item on the Discography page is a link for a page of album (or single) information. These album pages contain some good information packed into a small space, such as the song list, review excerpts, and album notes. If you're interested in buying the album, click the Check Prices & Buy link near the top of each album page. That link displays a price comparison among various online CD retailers. I describe the music shopping experience in greater detail in the next section.

Searching for an album or a song sidesteps the artist information page, but otherwise is identical to searching for an artist. The search results skip right to links of album or song names, but you can always click the artist's name in parentheses to see that artist's info page.

In a buying mood

Like any self-respecting online service, Yahoo! provides plenty of ways to spend money online. Yahoo! Music is sponsored by CDNow, the online music retailer, and many of the ads on the search results pages (see the preceding section on searching) link to CDNow purchase pages for the album you searched for. Yahoo! Music also contains an entire Music Shopping section. To see the home page for that area, just click the Buy Music link on the Yahoo! Music home page. (See Figure 10-5 for the Music Shopping home page.)

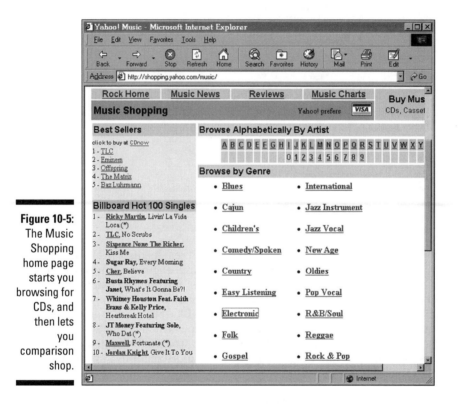

Figure 10-5: The Music Shopping home page starts you browsing for CDs, and then lets you comparison shop.

The Music Shopping home page is basically the top of a music CD directory. Click any genre or take the alphabetical route with the letter links above the genres. Either way, you eventually end up with an artist page listing all available albums for that group or artist. This is where things get interesting. Click any album to display the comparison shopping page (see Figure 10-6). On this page, the retail outlets carrying that CD are listed by price, enabling you to snap up the best bargain without visiting each store and searching for the CD.

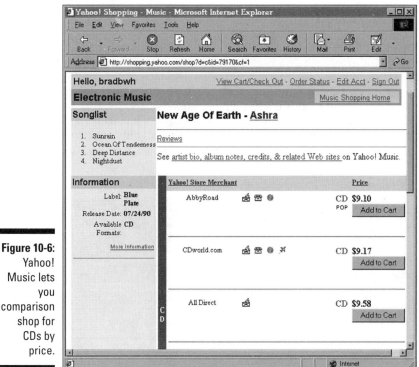

Figure 10-6:
Yahoo!
Music lets
you
comparison
shop for
CDs by
price.

It's important to keep in mind that Yahoo! Music compares prices among the CD stores that have online shops within Yahoo! Shopping but no other online music stores. Fortunately, Yahoo! Shopping has a good selection of stores. But it's like comparing prices in a single mall. You might be accustomed to buying from other stores on the Net, but if you went to one of them you'd lose the convenience of the price comparison feature. Yahoo! Music currently hosts online shops for Tower Records, Cdworld.com, Compact Disc Connection, and a few others. So the selection is good, but if you insist on buying all your entertainment from Amazon.com or CDNow, you must take the initiative to price the CD at those sites. My own price comparisons, broadened to include other online stores, indicate that the prices for music CDs at Yahoo! Shopping are excellent, routinely saving as much as $2.50 for the same album at Amazon.com or CDNow. But if you insist on getting the best price every time, shop around yourself.

When it comes to buying, just click the Add to Cart button. All of Yahoo! Shopping uses the same online shopping cart screen (see Chapter 21). You may settle on a single product or continue shopping and adding things from other stores to the cart.

Real events

If you scroll down to the bottom of the Yahoo! Music home page, you see a listing of Today's Music Net Events. These events cover the gamut from net-casted concerts to audio news from the music industry, Internet radio shows to music chat sessions and celebrity interviews. Any scheduled Internet occurrence related to music might appear in Music Net Events. The selection on the home page is slim; click the <u>More Net Events</u> link to see a complete listing for the day. Figure 10-7 shows the listing, and indicates the range of events you can find. Note the date links above the listings, and use them if you want to plan your Net Event week.

Figure 10-7: Net Events listings are for scheduled Internet radio shows, concerts, and sometimes celebrity chat sessions.

(Screenshot: Yahoo! Net Events :Entertainment :Music — Microsoft Internet Explorer)

Address: http://events.yahoo.com/Entertainment/Music/

Today's Picks
(US Eastern/Pacific times)
- Former Mafia Boss Bill Bonanno, 10:00pm/7:00pm on Yahoo! Chat <u>add</u>
- Growing Flowers, 4:00pm/1:00pm on Martha Stewart Living <u>add</u>
- Living to 100, 2:00pm/11:00am on drkoop.com <u>add</u>

Inside Yahoo!
- Y! Calendar - your own personal organizer.
- Y! Chat - welcome to the party.
- Y! Full Coverage - current events.
- Y! Internet Live - today's highlights from Y!-Life.
- Y! Local Events - events in your backyard.
- Y! Movie Showtimes - see what's playing.
- Y! TV Coverage - check your local listings

Programs on Tue, May 11 1: 16 ET-PT- GMT

Mon 10 | **Tue 11** | Wed 12 | Thu 13 | Fri 14 | Sat 15

7:00am Neil Chase "7~9" - popular music radio program from Hong Kong. RealPlayer. *NeilChase.com*. <u>add</u>

9:00am Radio Free World - spinning eclectic world music, cool jazz, hip-hop, new age, techno, and more. RealPlayer. <u>add</u>

12:00pm Koolout - get down with hard to find soul and funk classics. RealPlayer. *Pseudo*. <u>add</u>

12:00pm Morning Becomes Eclectic - progressive pop, international, jazz, and classical music show with in-studio inverviews and live performances; hosted by Nic Harcourt. *KCRW*. <u>add</u>

12:00pm The Static Channel - a music and culture show featuring rock and roll, swing, punk, metal, glam and more. RealPlayer. *Pseudo Online*. <u>add</u>

1:00pm Music with Jay Pearce - spins some of the finest adult album alternative music on the planet. RealPlayer. *93.5 The Web*. <u>add</u>

1:00pm The Louisiana Music Spotlight - a series of shows featuring interviews with Louisiana artists. Each show features the interview as well as the artist's music. RealPlayer. *louisianaradio.com*. <u>add</u>

2:00pm Digital Dialectic - live musical performances from virtual recording artists and friends. Web Chat. *virtualrecordings.com*. <u>add</u>

3:00pm Radio Free World - spinning eclectic world music, cool jazz, hip-hop, new age, techno, and more. RealPlayer. <u>add</u>

5:00pm Scene Heard - music critics Robert Wilonsky and Zac Crain

The links to specific events take you out of Yahoo! to the host site for the event. All audio shows require some kind of streaming audio plug-in for your browser — RealPlayer in most cases.

Note the <u>add</u> links after each Net Event listing. Clicking an <u>add</u> link places the event on your Yahoo! Calendar. It doesn't e-mail you a reminder, but if you look at your calendar, a listing for the event jogs your memory.

If you are hosting a music-related event, you can submit it to Music Net Events and possibly get listed on the schedule. To add an event, follow these steps:

1. **Scroll to the bottom of the Yahoo! Music home page, and click the <u>Add Event</u> link.**

   The Add to Yahoo! Net Events page appears (see Figure 10-8).

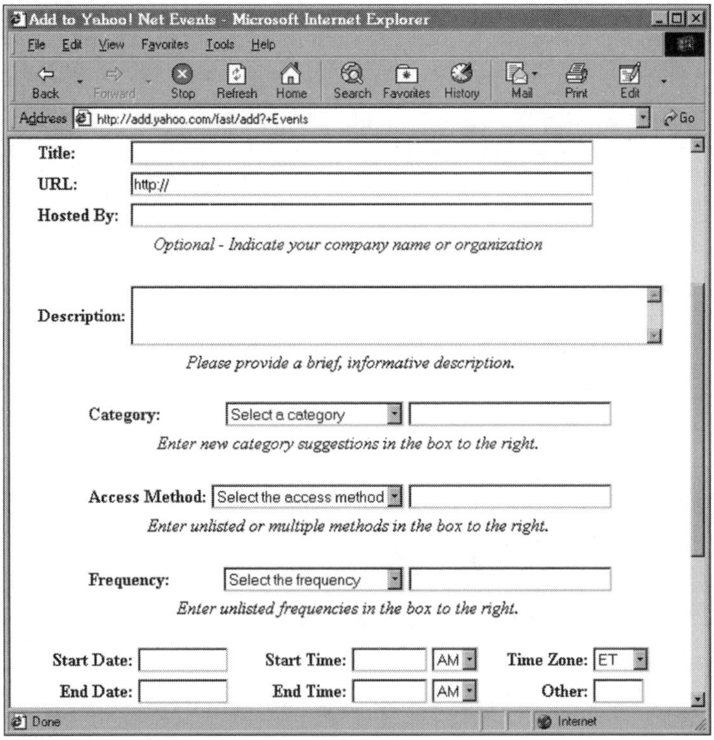

Figure 10-8: Filling in the forms lets you submit a scheduled event to Yahoo!'s Net Events directory.

2. **Fill in all the forms describing the nature and scheduling of your event.**

3. **Click the Submit button.**

Net Events is for scheduled events only, and Yahoo! will discard any submissions of regular Web sites. Naturally, your site is the hosting Web address for the event, but the submission must be for a live, real-time broadcast, chat, or interactive feature that occurs at a specified time.

Listening to Yahoo! Radio

Yahoo! has recently added a radio player to its music lineup. You need the RealPlayer browser plug-in to listen to it. If your computer is so equipped, follow these steps to begin listening:

1. **On the Yahoo! Music home page, click the <u>Yahoo! Radio</u> link in the left sidebar.**

   A small browser window pops open — this is the radio itself. (See Figure 10-9.) The first time you open Yahoo! Radio, it tests your system to see whether you have the RealPlayer plug-in. If you do, you soon hear a spoken introduction. If you don't have RealPlayer, you can get it (it's a free download) at this URL:

   ```
   www.real.com
   ```

Figure 10-9: Yahoo! Radio. Click a music button or choose a channel from the drop-down menu.

2. **Click any channel button, or select a channel from the drop-down menu.**

   After a few seconds, the selected channel begins playing.

3. **Use the on-screen volume-control slider next to the microphone picture to adjust the listening level.**

   You may also use the volume-control knob on your computer speakers.

4. **To stop the radio, click the Stop button below the volume slider.**

The Yahoo! Radio window displays the song, artist, album, and channel you're listening to.

Beneath the music buttons in the Yahoo! Radio window is an ARTIST INFO button. Clicking it opens a new browser window displaying the currently playing artist's information page in Yahoo! Music. If a song really catches your ear, it's a simple matter to swing over to Yahoo! Music Shopping (mentioned previously) with your main browser window, and exercise your credit card.

Listening to Yahoo! Radio (or any streaming audio programming) might make it slower or more difficult to browse the Web when the music is playing, depending on your connection speed. If you use a telephone modem (28.8K, 33.6K, or 56K), you might run into difficulties — either the music stream is interrupted intermittently or Web pages load into your browser more slowly. If the slowdown gets too intense, just turn off Yahoo! Radio. Cable modem and DSL users shouldn't have any problem.

Yahoo! Goes to the Movies

When it comes to movies, Yahoo! tells you where to go. Wait — that doesn't sound right. It's easy to find movie showtimes for your local area (or any local area) — that's my point. The Yahoo! Movies section also presents a good deal of information about films currently in theaters or on video.

The place to start, naturally, is the Yahoo! Movies home page. Click the <u>Movies</u> link under Other Guides near the bottom of the main Yahoo! home page, or go directly to this URL:

```
movies.yahoo.com
```

The Movies home page (see Figure 10-10) throws a mix of information onto your screen. News headlines about the film industry rub elbows with top box-office lists and upcoming video releases.

Movie news is handled in typical Yahoo! fashion. Headlines with story summaries are linked to full stories on another Yahoo! page. Yahoo! gets its movie news from four sources: Reuters/Variety; Hollywood Reporter; a bunch of wire services such as PR Newswire and Business Wire; and E! Online. Scroll down the Movies home page to the Movie News section. There, you have a few top headlines, with a <u>More</u> link beneath them. In addition, you may use any of the source links above the headlines (see Figure 10-10) to view stories from only that source.

Yahoo! provides a directory of movie-related Net Events, as with music (see the preceding section in this chapter). Unlike music, scheduled, streaming movie content is rare on the Internet, so most of the movie Net Events listings are chat sessions about films or online interviews with actors. As with the music Net Events listings, the <u>add</u> link puts the event on your Yahoo! Calendar. Unlike music Net Events, there is no invitation to submit a movie Net Event to the directory.

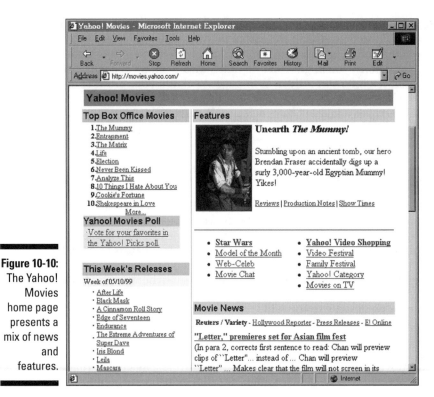

Figure 10-10:
The Yahoo!
Movies
home page
presents a
mix of news
and
features.

Despite what I said about the lack of streaming movie content over the Web, you *can* find a few unscheduled, ongoing movie stations. Yahoo! Movies lists a few of them on the Net Events page. Here's how to find the listing:

1. **Scroll down the Yahoo! Movies home page, until you get to the Net Events section.**

2. **Click the <u>More</u> link.**

   The Net Events page appears.

3. **Scroll down to the Audio/Video Channels section.**

   A handful of movie channels are listed, some of which play films continuously and even create a chatting space for watching and talking with others. A high-speed Internet connection (ISDN, DSL, or cable modem) makes these channels work better than with telephone modems.

Getting the gist

Most of us like to have some idea of what a movie is about before forking over the bucks for greasy popcorn while watching it. Yahoo! Movies helps the cause of foreknowledge by providing concise movie information pages for most current theater releases. Yahoo! doesn't have a search engine for films, sorry to say. But you can lock your eyeballs onto information about top-grossing movies by clicking titles in the Top Box Office Movies list on the Yahoo! Movies home page (see Figure 10-11). Furthermore, when you check your local listings (see the next section), just about every listed movie is linked to its information page.

Figure 10-11 shows the Movie Info page for *The Mummy,* a gentle, pastoral movie honoring history and the sacredness of ancestry. The film's synopsis is front and center on these information pages, and the rating and length are in the left-hand sidebar. That might be enough to send you running for the theater (or away from it), but there's more:

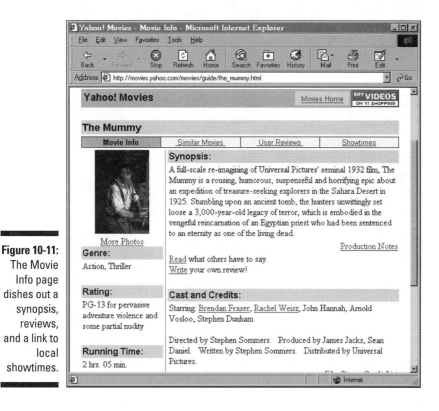

Figure 10-11:
The Movie Info page dishes out a synopsis, reviews, and a link to local showtimes.

✓ **Similar Movies.** Yahoo! collects films that are similar to each other, either in plot or by virtue of sharing actors, and places them on a separate page. This is a good idea, and helps locate videos that bear some relationship to a theater movie you just watched. As you can see in Figure 10-12, you can also check out similar classic movies.

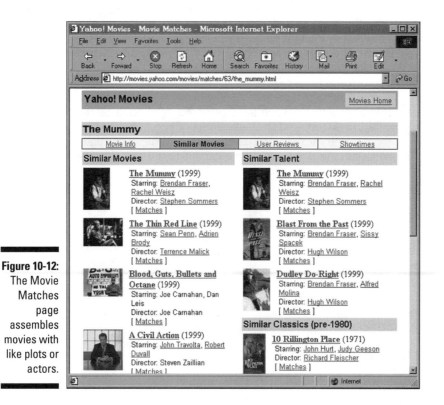

Figure 10-12:
The Movie Matches page assembles movies with like plots or actors.

✓ **User Reviews.** This link drops you into the Yahoo! message board for the movie, where you can enjoy Yahoo! members debating (sometimes raucously) the merits of the film.

✓ **Showtimes.** This link takes you to an abbreviated version of your local movie showtimes listing, presenting the showtimes for just the movie you're investigating. You must have entered a zip code for your local area, as described in the next section.

For career biographies of a film's starring cast, scroll to the bottom of the Movie Info page and click the <u>Film Bios</u> link.

Leaving the house

This might be hard to believe (at least, it is for me), but every once in a great while it's a good idea to stand up from the computer, walk out the door, and stare at a screen in some other dark room. It's called a movie theater. Yahoo! Movies helps you break away from your monitor by listing showtimes for your local theaters.

For the showtimes feature to work, Yahoo! needs to know (approximately) where you live. Here's how to proceed:

1. **On the Yahoo! Movies home page, use the Enter Your Location form near the top of the page to type your zip code or city/state location.**

   If you have already entered the information in a previous session and are signed into Yahoo! under one of your IDs, just click the <u>Take me to my listings</u> link.

2. **Click the Showtimes button.**

   Figure 10-13 illustrates the Showtimes page.

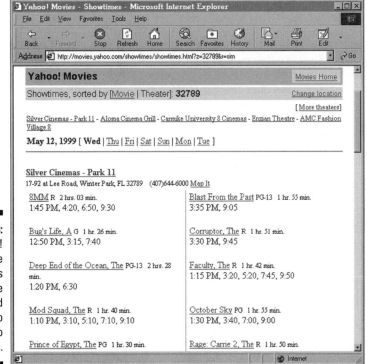

Figure 10-13:
Yahoo!
Movie
Showtimes
links to the
real world
and to
Movie Info
pages.

Use the title links in the Showtimes page to view Movie Info pages (see the preceding section). Note that you can view upcoming showtimes a week in advance — very helpful considering most theaters change their film lineup and times every Friday. Scroll down the page to see the theaters assigned to the zip code or city/state you entered, and click the <u>More theaters</u> link to expand the geographical radius.

In the Enter Your Location form, you may enter a different zip code or city/state location than the permanent location associated with your Yahoo! ID. (You may have entered that permanent location when creating your My Yahoo! page, which I describe in Chapter 2.) You can view as many locations as you want without changing your permanent setting. After viewing showtimes for an alternate location, just go back to the Yahoo! Movies home page and click the <u>Take me to my listings</u> link to see your home-town showtimes.

The Showtimes page defaults to the Theater listing, where you can see all the movies playing at each theater. You can change the page's organization to the Movie listing, in which you can see all the theaters showing each movie. Just click the <u>Movie</u> or <u>Theater</u> link to switch back and forth.

Staying home

If you can tear yourself away from the computer but can't bear the thought of leaving the house, Yahoo! Movies caters to your sorry state by dishing up a shopping directory for videos. The Video Shopping area works just like the shopping directory for music, described in the preceding section. Get your credit card out and click the <u>Yahoo! Video Shopping</u> link on the Yahoo! Movies home page, or go directly to the following URL:

```
shopping.yahoo.com/video
```

Yahoo! Couch Potato

Yahoo! TV is primarily about program listings. It's a great listing and program search system, too. Get to the Yahoo! TV home page by going directly to this URL:

```
tv.yahoo.com
```

Yahoo! TV skips the news coverage found in the music and movies sections. As you can see in Figure 10-14, the main portion of the Yahoo! TV home page is taken up with entry forms for the program guide, pushing news headlines out of the picture entirely.

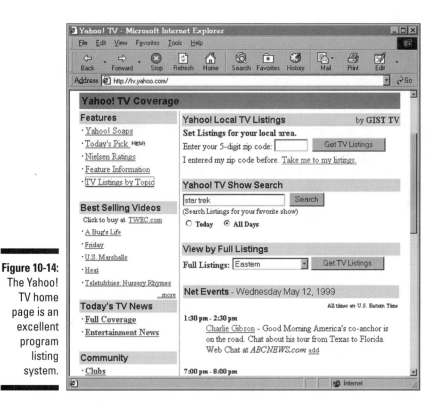

Figure 10-14:
The Yahoo!
TV home
page is an
excellent
program
listing
system.

Four types of TV listings are available in Yahoo!:

- ✓ **Local TV Listings.** By entering your zip code, Yahoo! can find out what's playing on your tube, both on broadcast channels and through your local cable.

- ✓ **TV Show Search.** By entering keywords or show titles, you can see a schedule of broadcasts for that show in your local listings database.

- ✓ **View by Full Listings.** These listings disregard locality and display all cable and broadcast network listings, leaving out local programming.

- ✓ **Listings by Topic.** This section invites you to choose a *type* of program from a directory, and then shows you all programs of that type within any three-hour time period.

Getting local listings

The best place to start is Local TV Listings. The Local TV Listings form is where you teach Yahoo! where you live and what cable service (if any) you use. After you've trained Yahoo! TV, you can add your listings to your My Yahoo! page (see Chapter 2). Just follow these steps:

1. **Type your zip code into the form.**

2. **Click the Get TV Listings button.**

   A page appears asking you to select what kind of television setup you have. (See Figure 10-15.)

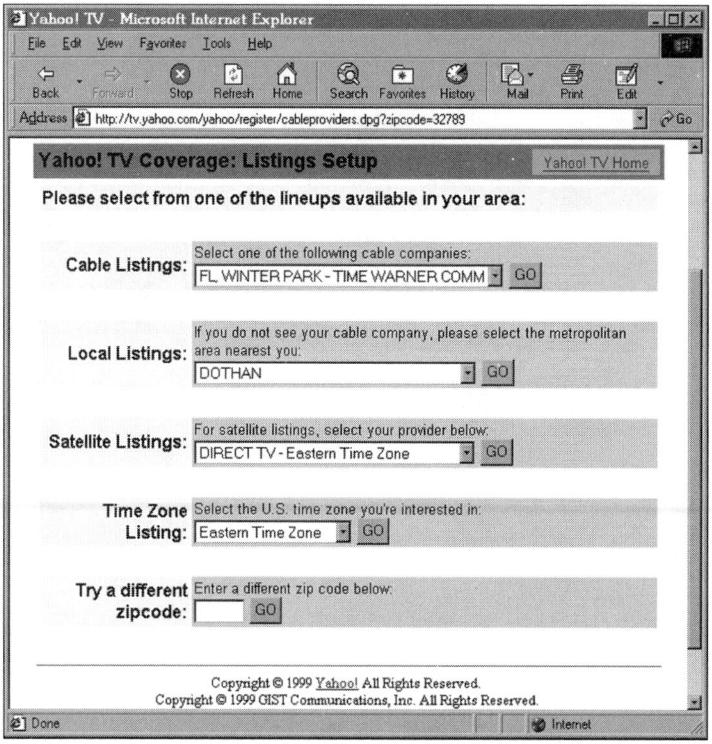

Figure 10-15:
Teaching
Yahoo! TV
what kind of
television
setup you
have.

3. **Choose the cable company, satellite company, or local metropolitan area you use at home for television reception.**

   You may also use this page to switch area codes or get general cable and network listings for a United States time zone.

4. **After selecting your TV system, click the GO button next to the drop-down menu you used.**

5. **On the next page, click the finish button to lock in your settings.**

   You may always change your TV setup by repeating these steps. Like the movie listings described previously in this chapter, Yahoo! TV remembers your original setting when you enter a new zip code. The Take me to my listings link always displays listings for your original zip code location.

Figure 10-16 illustrates the TV Listings grid for local cable in central Florida. The illustration doesn't show it, but different types of programming are conveniently color-coded. Use the drop-down menus to select the date and time you want to peruse. (The grid always shows a three-hour window of programming.) You may also use the drop-down menus to narrow in on specific categories of programming or a single channel.

Most show titles on the grid are links. Click any show link to see a brief description of the episode, movie, sporting event, or whatever it is. As a bonus, the resulting page provides links to show-related sites.

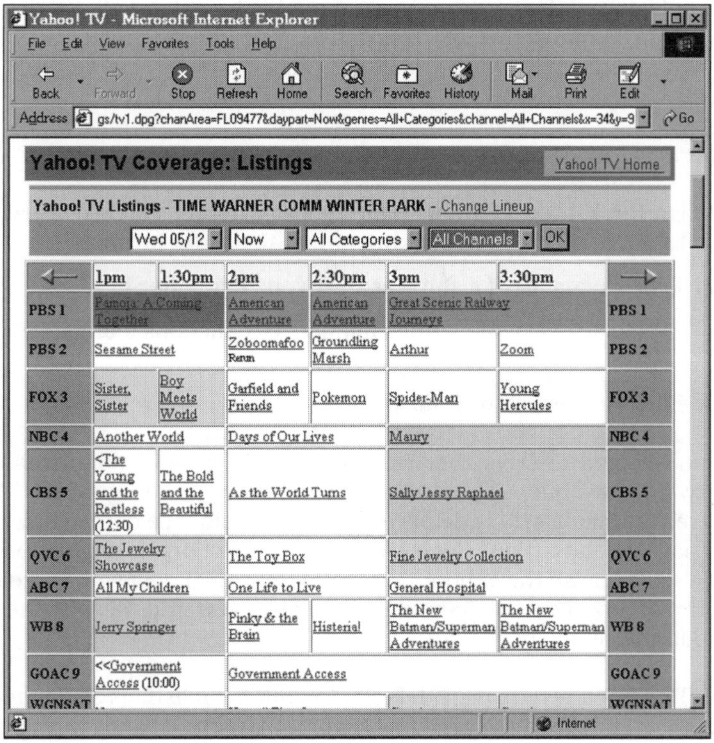

Figure 10-16:
The TV Listings grid. Use the drop-down menus to define your view.

When working with the Listings grid, keep in mind that each day's programming begins at 6:00 a.m. — not at midnight. So if you're looking to see what's on at 2:00 on a Tuesday morning, you need to look at Monday night's listings.

Searching for a show

You can search for a show's broadcast times in Yahoo! TV. I use this feature to find every syndicated rerun of all the Star Trek shows, but my hope is that you have a more elevated television pursuit. You might use the feature to find wrestling shows, for example.

The search engine uses keywords, and you don't need to know the exact title of the show. My search for Star Trek, for example, delivers good results when using the keyword *trek*. Searching on actors doesn't work well, though — names deliver results only when the name is part of the show's title. For example, I used the keyword *stewart*, hoping to match with Patrick Stewart, a lead actor in one of the Star Trek shows. The returned matches were only The Daily Show With Jon Stewart and Martha Stewart Living, and only one of those takes place in outer space. (Guess which one.)

Searching for a show is easy:

1. **On the Yahoo! TV home page, select whether you are searching for today or all days by clicking one of the radio buttons.**

2. **Type the name of a show as best you remember it.**

   Typing an exact show title eliminates extraneous matches to your keywords.

3. **Click the Search button.**

If you selected All Days, the Listings page that shows your search results is awkwardly laid out — the weak link of Yahoo! TV (see Figure 10-17). An entirely new mini-grid is displayed for each incidence of the show, breaking the page up and making it very long. This way of organizing the page is required because the Yahoo! TV software can deal only with three-hour blocks of time. Each three-hour segment is a new grid. Despite the unsightly layout, the search results are useful.

The TV search results page defaults to your local listings as defined by your zip code entry. (See the previous section.) Use the <u>Change Lineup</u> link to switch localities.

Getting a quick picture

The Full Listings feature is not too aptly named because the listings are not as full as the Local TV Listings. Use Full Listings to glimpse an overview of what's playing for just about anyone with basic cable service or a TV that picks up network broadcasts. Here's what you do:

1. **On the Yahoo! TV home page, use the drop-down menu under View by Full Listings to select a U.S. time zone.**

2. **Click the Get TV Listings button.**

The resulting grid works just the same as the Local TV Listings grid, but local programs are not included.

Game shows only

Sometimes you just want to know what movies, or science fiction shows, or sports events are on the tube. At those moments, you need the Listings by Topic feature. You choose a type of program, and then the Listings grid displays only those shows. Here's how to use the feature:

1. **On the Yahoo! TV home page, click the <u>TV Listings by Topic</u> link in the left-hand sidebar.**

2. **On the TV Coverage By Topic page, click any topic or show type.**

In the resulting Listings grid (see Figure 10-18), portions of the grid are blank, with only the selected show types filled in.

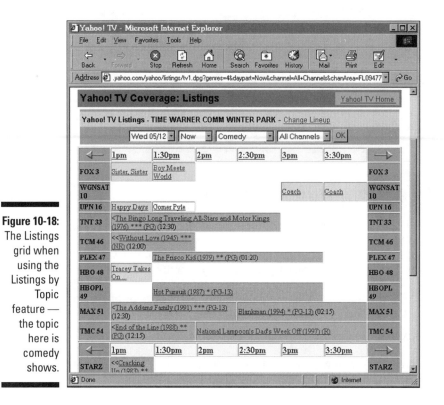

Figure 10-18: The Listings grid when using the Listings by Topic feature — the topic here is comedy shows.

Once again, as with other listing features, the grid defaults to your local zip code, assuming you've entered it previously. Use the <u>Change Lineup</u> link to change location.

Part IV
Meeting the Yahoo! Community

The 5th Wave   By Rich Tennant

IT WAS ACTUALLY ON THE WEB ONE NIGHT THAT
CAPT. AHAB CAUGHT UP WITH HIS OBSESSION.

In this part...

Community is the life of any online service. The Yahoo! Community is vast and vibrant, and Yahoo! provides a number of ways to connect with others. The following five chapters make up the largest part of the book, and explain how to use Yahoo! Chat, the message boards, the extraordinary Yahoo! Messenger, Yahoo! Clubs, and the e-mail and phone search engine.

Chapter 11

Introducing Yourself to Yahoo! Chat

In This Chapter

▶ Reviewing the appeal of real-time chatting

▶ Navigating the Yahoo! Chat home page

▶ Comparing the features of HTML and Java chat

▶ Switching rooms and creating rooms

Chatting has been on the cyberspace activity list for many years — since long before the Web was around. Online services such as CompuServe and Prodigy provided virtual meeting rooms where people could talk through their keyboards in real time. Those early rooms were a nice alternative to discussions on message boards, which tend to be more literate, but also much more prolonged. Those ancient chat rooms, however, didn't have nearly the range of features found in modern virtual rooms. Besides, only members of the online service could use them. In Yahoo! Chat, anyone from the general population of approximately 70 million Internet users can easily join the party.

And what a party it is! People gather to talk about almost everything under the sun, and you can create your own chat room for special gatherings. Yahoo! makes it easy to see which of your online friends are currently chatting and also to view the Yahoo! Profile of any member in any room you enter. Yahoo! Chat is an incredible way to meet people, and this chapter explains all the features that are at your command.

Ups and Downs of Chatting

America Online really made online chatting popular, and when the Web brought millions more people into the virtual realm, chatting took off as a worldwide phenomenon. Why is chatting so popular? Many reasons exist, but in my experience observing people interacting in this fashion, the most common appeals are these:

✔ **Instant party.** No matter what your schedule, chatting is there for you. It is truly a 24-hour, 7-day gathering.

✔ **Global reach.** You're liable to meet people from almost anywhere in a chat room. Log on just before bed for a quick chat, and you're likely to talk with someone wasting time in an office in Australia. Log on from your American office, and you might meet someone in England kicking back in the evening.

✔ **Kindred spirits.** Most chat rooms are topical or try to be, anyway. When you find one whose participants meet to discuss a subject you care about, it's a gathering of like minds without regard to geography or time zones.

✔ **Appearance is secondary.** Like the famous cartoon says: On the Internet, nobody knows you're a dog. (Said by one mutt to another, and originally published in *The New Yorker.*) When chatting, as with message-board conversations, words and ideas come through first, without the physical clues that can distract us from a person's character when interacting face to face. Of course, quite a lot of chat-room content isn't very profound, to say the least. But as with any experience, you get out of it what you put into it.

✔ **Humor.** Chatting is fun partly because it's so funny. A lot of wit floats around chat rooms, and humor tends to come packaged in a concise form because everyone is typing short, single sentences. The result is a chat-room cultural mood of caustic, punchy humor.

✔ **Speed talk.** In a busy chat room, a fast typist who thinks quickly can have a multitasking blast, engaging in multiple conversations, public and private. Popular chat rooms are bustling places, and the sheer freneticism of their energy is part of the appeal.

✔ **Prowling.** I can't leave this item off any list of chatting's allure because flirting and cybersex are ragingly popular chatting pursuits. Sex is a major currency of chatting — flirting is the small change and cyber affairs are the large bills. But don't be put off if that's not your cup of tea. Yahoo! provides a distinct adult area for provocative chatting, and so many rooms are available to choose from that anyone can find the desired mood.

If chatting has a major downside, it's identity confusion. Almost everyone uses a chatting alias (or three or four), and you never have a guarantee that chatting partners bears any resemblance to the person they say they are. To put it plainly, men sometimes pretend to be women, and vice versa. People can pretend about their age when asked. Online identity can be slippery. Chat-room scandals that spill into the offline world are highly publicized, but it should be remembered that scandals are exceptions, not the rule. If you proceed with sensible caution, there's no reason not to make good, honest, and fun connections in public and private chat rooms.

Internet users must have a Java-compatible browser to use the Java Yahoo! Chat program. However, earlier versions of browsers without Java implementation can use the HTML chatting program. (I describe the differences between the two, and how to access both, later in this chapter.) America Online members who are using the AOL browser must have version 3.0 or later of the AOL program.

Yahoo! Chat Home Page

Yahoo! Chat is available to anyone with a Yahoo! ID (see Chapter 1). The place to begin your chatting experience is the Yahoo! Chat home page, which serves as a combination room menu and event guide. (See Figure 11-1.) Get there by clicking the Chat link on the Yahoo! home page, or go directly to this URL:

```
http://chat.yahoo.com
```

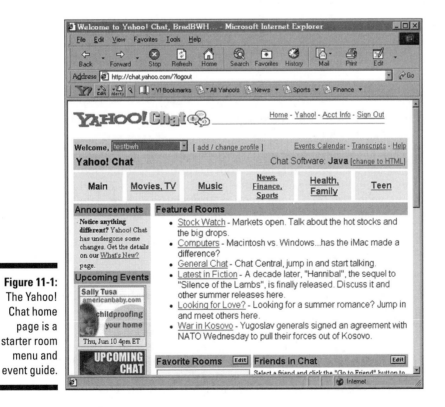

Figure 11-1: The Yahoo! Chat home page is a starter room menu and event guide.

Near the top of the Chat home page is a starter menu of chatting channel links, each leading to a selection of rooms. These rooms represent the very tip of the iceberg. It's a way to get started, but once inside the Yahoo! chat empire you have your choice of hundreds of rooms, some of them created by other users. And you can make your own room.

Beneath the channel links are the Featured Rooms, which change depending on the time of day and what's going on in the news. The Featured Rooms are always open, and set to automatically generate extra "spillover" rooms to handle large numbers of chatters. So when you select one of those rooms (StockWatch, for example) and enter the chat area, you might be deposited in the third version of the StockWatch room (StockWatch:3). From there you can navigate to other rooms, as I explain later in this chapter.

If you want to see a complete list of Yahoo! Chat rooms, click the <u>Complete Room List</u> link on the home page (scroll down to see the link). It's a good way to gain a quick overview of permanent chat rooms. User rooms, however, aren't on this list. User rooms provide some of the most interesting (and less crowded) chatting experiences on Yahoo!, so if you want to sample them, follow the procedure I describe later in this chapter.

The UPCOMING EVENTS section of the home page advertises upcoming celebrity chats. Celebrity chats are a different and less social experience than free-for-all personal chatting. Still fun, though, in their own way. These formal chats are moderated, and the software controls who can speak at any moment. Time to get started! Here's what to do first:

1. **On the Yahoo! Chat home page, use the upper drop-down menu to select a Yahoo! ID.**

   This menu contains all your IDs, if you have created more than one. Frankly, it's a good idea to have an ID (or two) just for chatting. Because everyone's ID is the changeable part of a Yahoo! e-mail address, it's a simple matter for anyone to roam through the chat area collecting e-mail addresses. If you chat often enough, you're bound to get some spam. Why not isolate it in its own e-mail box? Furthermore, it makes sense to create a Yahoo! Profile for your chatting ID that contains absolutely no personal information. Click the <u>Create/Edit Your Profiles</u> to do this, and refer to Chapter 1 for details about the process.

2. **Use the Chat Software: links to choose Java chatting or HTML chatting.**

   The default selection is Java and is the best bet for anyone using a fairly modern computer, Windows 95 or later, and version 3.0 or later of the Explorer or Navigator browsers. The next sections explain the pros and cons of each system. The simple story is that Java chatting is smoother and has more features but takes longer to load into your computer and occasionally crashes. Both methods have the same rooms available and allow you to navigate from room to room and to create rooms.

3. Click a room link, or click a channel link followed by a room link.

Start anywhere you want. You can move around once you get inside. If you click a room from the more extensive Complete Room List, you're logged into the Java version of Yahoo! Chat (see Figure 11-2).

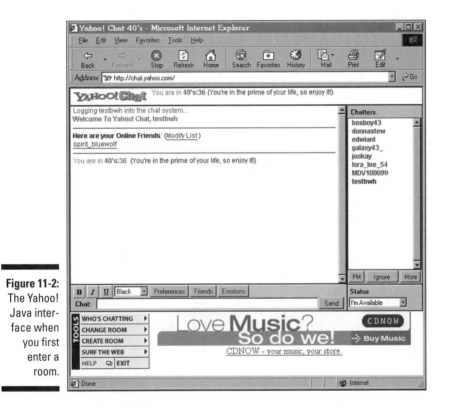

Figure 11-2:
The Yahoo! Java interface when you first enter a room.

Chatting and Messenger — joined at the hip

While you're using the Java chat program, Yahoo! Chat is closely integrated with Yahoo! Messenger (see Chapter 13). When you first enter a chat room in Java, the screen tells you which Messenger friends are currently online. They can also see you come online if their pagers are active, just as if you had booted your pager instead of logging into a chat room. Don't be surprised if a pager message from one of those friends pops up in a separate window. By the same token, you can talk with any friend by clicking that ID and typing in the window that appears.

After you're in a chat room, you may stick around there and meet people or roam around the Yahoo! Chat landscape looking for the perfect room. The next two sections detail the features of HTML and Java chatting. The section after that explains how to find other rooms in either program.

Down to Basics with HTML Chat

On the Internet at large, HTML chatting is generally considered to be primitive, compared to Java chatting, but the HTML Yahoo! Chat program is pretty good. The biggest difference between HTML chatting and Java chatting lies in how smoothly the chatting streams onto your screen. With Java chat, the discussions flow seamlessly onto your main chat window. With HTML chat, the window must be updated (called *refreshing*) to see new lines of talk. The HTML program refreshes the window automatically every twenty seconds or so (and whenever you send a line of chat into the room). You can also click a Refresh button if you want more frequent updates. (Figure 11-3 shows an HTML chat room in action.)

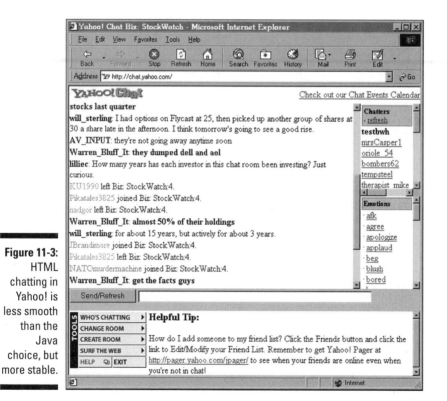

Figure 11-3:
HTML
chatting in
Yahoo! is
less smooth
than the
Java
choice, but
more stable.

HTML Yahoo! Chat has fewer features than the Java version, but loads a little faster every time you enter a room and is more stable. (That means it doesn't crash your browser, which the Java chat program does every once in a while.) Both chatting systems access the same rooms. However, the HTML program does not hook into the Yahoo! Messenger the way the Java program does (see the next section for details on that snazzy feature).

If no chatting appears on your screen for several seconds after entering an HTML chat room, just click the Send/Refresh button, and the chat should appear. Or, if you don't feel like reaching for the mouse, just wait about twenty seconds for the automatic refresh.

You can participate in HTML chatting by typing a line in the text-entry field, and then clicking the Send/Refresh button. (Using your keyboard's Enter key sends the line into the room also and is more convenient than clicking the on-screen button.)

Decisions, decisions — HTML or Java?

You might think that Yahoo! is creating unnecessary confusion by providing two chat interfaces, HTML and Java. Especially because Yahoo! itself seems to want you to use the Java interface — in the drop-down selection menu on the home page, Java is described as "best choice." So what gives? Why would anyone use the HTML version of Yahoo! Chat? Why is it even there?

In fact, there are good reasons to choose HTML chatting sometimes — and for some people, all the time. In particular, older Web browsers and computers cannot accept Java applets (small programs written in the Java language), so people using older systems should definitely try HTML if Java chatting isn't working. That situation alone justifies the presence of the HTML system because it means no one is excluded from the popular chat realm of Yahoo!.

Under normal conditions, with a fairly modern computer, most people probably should choose Java chatting. Java is easier, smoother, and has more features. If you fit into any of the following situations, however, HTML is preferable:

✔ If you use Windows 3.1 with any browser.

✔ If you use a Macintosh computer to run Internet Explorer or a version of Navigator before version 3.0.

✔ If you access the Internet through WebTV .

✔ If you use an America Online version before version 3.0 to access the Internet (probably on Windows 3.1).

✔ If you are accessing the Internet from behind a firewall, as is often the case with corporate office connections. (By the way, it's time to stop chatting and get back to work.)

✔ If you have many Yahoo! Messenger friends and want to avoid the distraction of being paged while chatting.

Fortunately, it's easy to try both HTML and Java chatting. Whichever you're using, click the EXIT button to leave the chat room, and then enter the chatting area again from the Yahoo! Chat home page after selecting the other method from the drop-down menu.

Meeting new friends in HTML chat

In the upper-right portion of the HTML chat window (see Figure 11-3) is a scrollable list of the current occupants of the chat room. This list doesn't renew automatically, so use the <u>refresh</u> link every once in a while to stay up to date. You may chat with any other room participant in the following fashion:

1. **Click any name in the Chatters list.**

   The names are standard hyperlinks. Don't double-click or right-click. After you click, the text-entry field is changed to an Instant Message (IM) field, directed at the person privately.

2. **Type something (coherent, preferably) and click the Send IM button.**

   Your message appears on the chosen person's screen, and no one else's.

When the text entry field is changed to an Instant Message field, your chosen person's name appears next to the Send IM button as a hyperlink. Click that name to see a Yahoo! Profile of that ID (see Chapter 1), which appears in a new browser window.

After sending a private Instant Message, the text field automatically reverts to a public-chat text entry field. You need to click the person's name again to send another private line. If you want to revert the field before you send a private line, click the <u>Back</u> link (not to be confused with your browser's Back button).

When you send a private Instant Message, the following appears in your main chat window: "You tell *person*" where *person* is the ID you're chatting with. Your sent message follows — it appears only on your and the other person's screens. Private responses appear as "*person* (private)" followed by the return message.

You must refresh the Chatters list when you change rooms in HTML chat. Well, you don't have to, but my point is that it doesn't update to the new room by itself. If you can't see a <u>refresh</u> link, use the scroll bar to reach the top of the Chatters list.

Getting verplunkt in HTML

Who knew chatting was such an emotional experience? <sniff> It's a beautiful thing. <sob> I love you, man! Sorry, I don't know what came over me. I'm better now. You can use emotions when chatting as I just did, but Yahoo! Chat gives you fancier ways. The Emotions list is positioned to the right of the main chat window, and offers about 30 emotional selections. Some aren't emotions so much as actions, and a few are unexpectedly entertaining. (The HTML emotions are different than the Java ones.)

You express an emotion by clicking it — it's as simple as that. Clicking any emotion link sends the emotion to the public chat space, preceded by your name. For example, clicking <u>applaud</u> sends this to the chat window:

```
yourname applauds
```

The applaud emotion is predictable, but some of the others are idiosyncratic, to say the least. Part of the fun is guessing at their meaning, and then being startled by what appears. But one person's fun is another person's embarrassment.

When you're ready to leave HTML chat or change rooms, use the EXIT and CHANGE ROOM buttons beneath the main chat window, as described in a later section of this chapter. You may EXIT to the Yahoo! Chat home page and switch to Java chat, or change rooms while remaining in HTML chat. You may fix yourself a sandwich. Who am I to dictate your life?

When you exit an HTML chat room using the EXIT button, you are returned to the Yahoo! Chat home page, and your chat software drop-down menu is returned to the default "Java — best choice" selection. If you want to try another room in HTML mode, you must reset that selection. Your Yahoo! ID is also reset if you choose a different ID from the drop-down menu.

In HTML chatting, all private discussions you are pursuing come to an end when you leave the chat area using the EXIT button or change rooms using the CHANGE ROOM button. If you're tired of talking in the main chat window, but still want to chat privately with an individual in the room, you must stay in the room. This differs from Java chat, which allows private discussions to follow you from room to room.

Going Upscale with Java Chat

Yahoo!'s Java chat interface presents comfy rooms with lots of features. Chatting in this environment is sort of like visiting a friend's great apartment — the bar is stocked and he has a new home theater system. Improvements have been steady and productive for the past few years, and now Yahoo! can be proud of one of the slickest, most entertaining and workable text-chatting atmospheres on the Net. Figure 11-4 shows a Java chat room in action. You might want to refer to it as I describe the features, or even log onto a room online and follow along that way.

Participating in a Java chat room is as easy as typing a line in the Chat text-entry field, and pressing the Enter key. (You can also use the on-screen Send button, but it's less convenient when you're chatting quickly and sending many lines.) Later in this section, I describe features that change how your text lines appear in the public room.

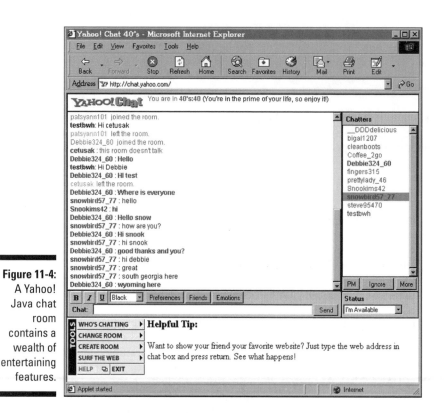

Figure 11-4:
A Yahoo!
Java chat
room
contains a
wealth of
entertaining
features.

Going private in Java

To the right of the main chat window is a narrower Chatters window that lists everyone in the room. Beneath the Chatters window are three buttons: PM (Private Message), Ignore, and More. Those buttons, together with a few other options, let you control and direct the flow of chatter and learn more about your fellow chatters.

Probably the most used function in the Chatters window is the Private Message button, which enables personal, side-of-the-room talking. You can engage in as many private chats, simultaneously, as you like. This type of interaction is extremely popular in Yahoo!. It's not too unusual to enter a room with 15 people in it, and see nothing whatsoever in the main chat window — everyone is talking privately, and the PM windows are flying around behind the scenes.

It's perfectly acceptable to approach strangers with private greetings but be polite. And remember that no one is obligated to talk with anyone else. If you don't receive a response to a private overture (fairly common), don't be offended and don't persist unless you know the person. A silent person might have his or her hands full with other windows or might not understand Yahoo! Chat features well enough to reply. Just find someone else. The most sensible approach is to chat publicly for a while; you'll find a natural opportunity to extend a conversation in private mode.

To begin a private chat, just proceed as follows:

1. **Click any name in the Chatters window.**

2. **With that name highlighted, click the PM button beneath the Chatters window.**

   A small PM window pops open (see Figure 11-5). You may also pop that window open by double-clicking any name in the Chatters window.

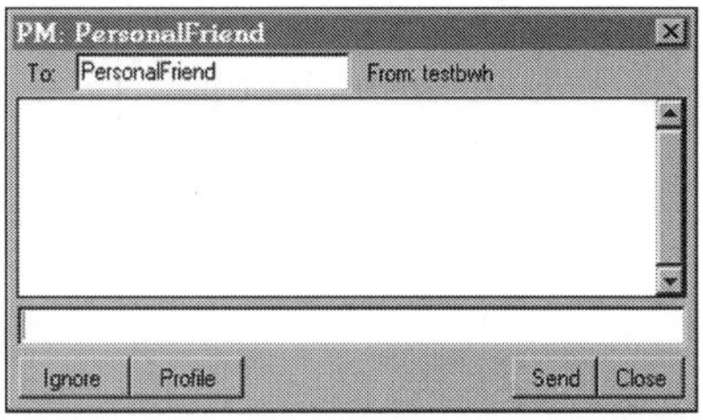

Figure 11-5:
The Private
Message
(PM)
window.

3. **In the text entry form near the bottom of the window, type a message.**

   You may type as long a message as you want, but it's polite to keep it very brief.

4. **Click the Send button, or use the Enter key of your keyboard.**

   Sending the message causes an identical window to pop open on the recipient's screen, with your words in the main, central portion. Your PM window stays open, with your words appearing in the main portion. If the person responds, the incoming line appears beneath your line, and you have a conversation going.

After you've established that private connection, it's an independent, autonomous stream of chatting. By that I mean the PM window stays open even if you move to another chat room. You may continue your private conversation as you move from room to room, for as long as you stay within Java chat.

More people things

Stay on that Chatters window because you can do more with it. First, note one cool feature that appears when you run your mouse cursor over the names in the Chatters window (don't click, just position the cursor over a name). A small pop-up message indicates how long, in minutes and seconds, that person has been idle — in other words, how long since that person typed anything in the main chat window. Also, if that person has changed his or her status (see the following section), that info appears.

The preceding section describes how to talk privately with a fellow chatter. A menu of options relate to other people in a chat room. Try this:

1. **Click any name in the Chatters window.**

   The name becomes highlighted. Be careful not to double-click — that just opens up a Private Message window.

2. **Click the More button below the Chatters window.**

   The Select Action window pops open (see Figure 11-6). You can also make it appear by right-clicking any name in the Chatters window.

Figure 11-6:
Select
Action
relates to
other
chatters.

Here's what you can do with that Select Action window:

- ✔ **Click the Private Message button.** This is the third of three ways to open a Private Message window (see the preceding section).

- ✔ **Click the View Profile button.** This button opens a browser window displaying the Yahoo! Profile (see Chapter 1) for the selected ID.

- ✔ **Click the Invite button.** This function is unrelated to the name you've highlighted. The Invite button sends an on-screen invitation to another Yahoo! member to join you in your current chat room. Needless to say, all the names in the Chatters list *are already* in your current chat room, so the button might seem pointless. However, you may change the ID that appears in the Select Action window, substituting the ID of an acquaintance who isn't in the room. (Invites appear on the other person's screen as small windows with Yes and No buttons.)

✔ **Click the Add as Friend button.** This action places the currently selected ID in your Chat Friends list. If you don't have a group of friends called Chat Friends, Yahoo! automatically creates one for you. This way, new additions aren't mixed in with other Groups you might have already created. (See Chapter 13 for details about creating lists and Groups of Friends through Yahoo! Messenger.)

✔ **Check the Highlight box.** When the Highlight box is checked, the selected person's contributions to the main chat window are highlighted in bolder type, on your screen only.

✔ **Check the Ignore box.** When the Ignore box is checked, the selected person's contributions to the main chat window do not appear at all, on your screen only.

If you've checked either Highlight or Ignore (they can both be checked, but that's pointless because they conflict), click the OK button to put the changes in action.

You can do a quick Ignore on someone by using the Ignore button below the Chatters window. Just highlight a name and click the Ignore button. From then on, the Ignore button becomes an Ignore Off button when that person's ID is highlighted, so you can admit the person's chat back to your screen at any time.

Where are you?

In Figure 11-6, check out the Status menu below the Chatters window. The Status options are in a drop-down menu, and when you select one, your chosen status appears once in the main chat window. These messages provide some preset explanations as to why you're being rude and not talking in the chat room. They are hooked into Yahoo! Messenger, and some are more appropriate to Messenger interaction than chat room socializing. However, the Be Right Back and On The Phone selections are good to use when your chat session is interrupted — in an environment where no one can see anyone else, it's polite to explain extended silences.

Just click once on any option in the drop-down Status menu, and your status appears (once) in the main chat window, next to your name. Because chat text is continually scrolling upward, you might want to repeat the action if your phone call (or whatever) lasts a while. Note that your status also appears when you run your mouse cursor over your ID in the Chatters window.

Your status automatically reverts to I'm Available when you type anything into the main chat space.

Color your words

Yahoo! chat rooms are colorful places, mostly because any participant can distinguish his or her text lines by using colors and altered typefaces. Look at Figure 11-4 again and note the left-hand options above the Chat text entry field. If you use a word processor, these items might be familiar. You can use them to change the appearance of your text in the main chat window. Here's how:

- ✔ Use the **B** button to make your words appear in **bold type.**
- ✔ Use the *I* button to make your words appear in *italics.*
- ✔ Use the <u>U</u> button to make your words appear <u>underlined</u>.
- ✔ Use the drop-down color menu to select a color for your words.

These selections are not only fun but also useful because they distinguish your "appearance" in the main chat window from everyone else's. Because multiple conversations are usually going on at once, it helps when the person you're talking to has a distinctive look.

One thing you don't want to do in a chat room (or on a message board, for that matter), is use all capital letters. In cyberspace, all caps SOUNDS LIKE SHOUTING! From time to time, everyone accidentally hits the Caps Lock key of the keyboard, and if that happens to you you'll probably get a polite reminder to lower your voice. Heed the reminder and hit the Caps Lock key again to turn them off, before people start shouting back at you. Another piece of chat protocol to remember: Use the underline feature only occasionally, for emphasis.

Customizing the chat room

A number of options are available for adjusting what the main chat window looks like. These options are invaluable in creating a better chat experience, and well worth finding out about. See the Preferences button above the text entry field? That's where these features reside. Click it to open the Preferences window (see Figure 11-7), where you find these choices:

- ✔ **Font** and **Size.** This is where you set the typeface and font size of all the lines scrolling up the main chat window. Don't confuse this with the color, bold, italic, and underline setting for *your* lines, as described in the preceding section. Use Display Options for selecting the typeface and font size for *everyone's* words. Individual choices about color, boldness, italics, and underlining will still appear on your screen. If you prefer large type, choose a larger Size from the drop-down menu. If you prefer squeezing as much chat as possible in the window, choose a smaller font size.

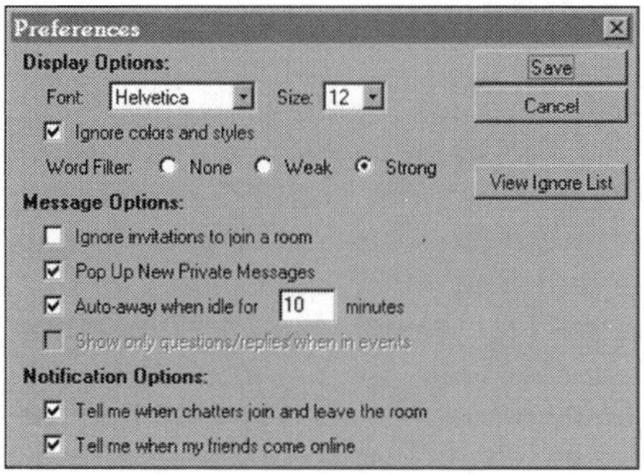

Figure 11-7:
The
Preferences
Window,
where you
can change
the way
chat
appears on
your screen.

Figure 11-7: The Preferences Window, where you can change the way chat appears on your screen.

✔ **Ignore colors and styles.** Check this box to make everyone's text look the same in the main chat window. Your selected Display Options still have effect.

✔ **Word Filter.** Yahoo! maintains a database of words generally considered obscene or offensive. Yahoo! doesn't divulge the contents of its lists, but you can apply a general filter to words by selecting Weak or Strong. Use None if your language sensibility is robust.

✔ **Ignore invitations to join a room.** Checking this box suppresses pop-up invitations. Anyone inviting you receives a messages that you're not accepting invitations.

✔ **Pop Up New Private Messages.** If you don't want to miss any whispers from fellow chatters, check this box to ensure that new Private Message windows are displayed on top of your chat window where you can't miss them.

✔ **Auto-away when idle.** You may select this to make your status change if you don't say anything for a while. This feature is good for talkative chatters, and not so good for people who like to listen quietly. Verbose chatters can leave their computers for a few minutes without having to remember to manually change their status. Silent types, however, will find their status unexpectedly changing even while they're happily (and demurely) watching the action — and may not receive any Private Messages if Auto-away kicks in.

✔ **Tell me when chatters join and leave the room.** This option is checked by default, but you might uncheck it when visiting high-traffic rooms. Busy rooms with lots of talk and plenty of people coming and going are hard to keep up with when the screen fills up with notices of arrivals and departures. Sometimes, the text can scroll so quickly upward to accommodate the chatter and the notices that it's hard to read. Slow things down and clear away the clutter by getting rid of the announcements.

✔ **Tell me when my friends come online.** This is a nice feature if you're waiting for someone in your Friends list to log on.

Keeping track of friends

Yahoo! has a buddy system called Friends that links people to each other through the Yahoo! Messenger (see Chapter 1). Because the Messenger and Yahoo! Chat are an integrated set of features, your Friends can find you in the chat realm even if they are using only the Messenger, and you can likewise contact them from either program. The only requirement is that both sides of the conversation be logged into *either* Yahoo! Messenger *or* Yahoo! Chat.

When you're in a Java chat room, you can adjust your Friends list and access your Friends by using the Friends button just above the text entry field. Clicking it displays a message in the main chat window, notifying you who among your designated Friends is online (through Chat or Messenger), and linking you to your Friends list. You can do two things at this point:

✔ Click the ID of any friend who is online to open a Private Message window and talk to that person. Your friend need not be in the chat room with you or even in Yahoo! Chat — but if your friend isn't in Yahoo! Chat, he or she must be using Yahoo! Messenger. (That person's name wouldn't appear if he or she weren't available for a private chat.)

✔ Click the Edit your Friend List link to open a new browser window showing your groups of friends. Whatever adjustments you make on this page are saved for your Messenger settings and your Chat settings.

A final warning

In this chapter, I mentioned sex in chatting a few times. Although Yahoo! Chat provides a demarcated space for rooms with sexually explicit themes, there is really no way to confine human nature or Internet trends. And the truth is, chatting culture has a broad sexual component and a widespread pornographic element.

When you search for new rooms (as I explain how to do in the following section), especially the User Rooms, do not suffer the misunderstanding that if you stay out of the Adult Rooms section you are ensuring a chaste experience. Flirting within rooms and placing sexual titles on rooms are rampant. It's never hard to leave a room, and I've never had much trouble finding fun, normal conversations. But if your ears burn easily, be forewarned about chatting in general. Even more importantly, if you have kids, beware of taking them into any general, unregulated chat environment.

Emoting, Java style

The same range of emotional declarations is available in Java chat as in HTML chat. (See the HTML section for a rundown of specific selections and what they display on the screen.) Just click the Emotions button above the text entry field to pop open a windowed list of all options. You must double-click any emotion to display it in the main chat window, but that's all you need to do. No typing is required.

Tools of the Chat Trade

Beneath the main chat window in both the HTML and Java rooms is a TOOLS box with several buttons that help you navigate among rooms and people. These buttons work identically in both chat systems, so I've grouped the explanation about them in this section.

Finding individual chatters

You can search for, or browse among, all Yahoo! IDs currently chatting in all the rooms. Just follow these steps:

1. **Click the WHO'S CHATTING button in the bottom-left panel.**

2. **Click a letter in the displayed alphabet, or type a Yahoo! ID in the search entry form and click the Search button.**

   Going the alphabet route lets you browse among all current chatters. (See Figure 11-8.) This option has little point unless you don't quite remember a person's ID but do remember its first letter. Otherwise, you're rummaging through a gigantic list of screen aliases. Use the search entry form if you know a person's ID and want to see whether he or she is chatting.

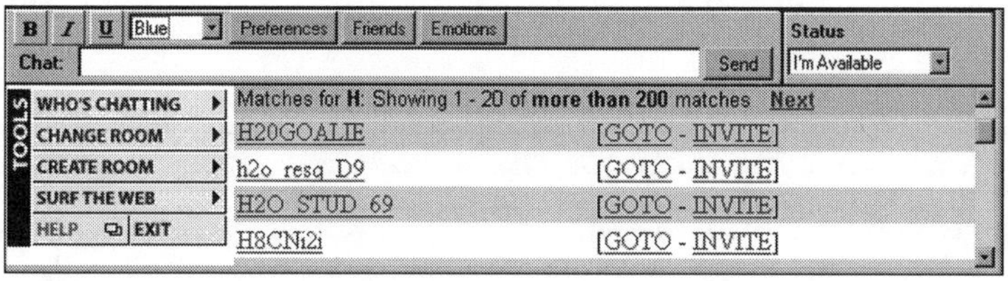

Figure 11-8: Browsing among current chatters, beneath the main chat window.

3. **In the list of names, click a name, the <u>GOTO</u> link, or the <u>INVITE</u> link.**

   Clicking a name opens a new browser window and shows you that person's Yahoo! Profile. The <u>GOTO</u> link shifts you into the chat room that person is currently occupying.

   The <u>INVITE</u> link sends an invitation to join your current room. It could be a room you created or any room at all. In HTML chat, the invitation appears on the person's main chat screen with a <u>Yes</u> link that, if clicked, shifts that person into your room. In Java chat, the invitation appears as a pop-up box with Yes and No buttons.

After you get into the same room with someone (either that person's current room through GOTO or your own through an accepted INVITE), you may pursue further conversation on the main chat screen or with a private message.

Finding new rooms

Chat room surfing is just as much fun as Web surfing. Yahoo! has what you might call house rooms, provided by the service and always open, and User Rooms, which anyone can create.

You can't search for a room by name, unfortunately, but you may browse among all created rooms:

1. **Click the CHANGE ROOM button in the bottom panel.**

   The CATEGORIES window appears.

2. **Click any category.**

   The ROOMS window appears.

3. **Select either Yahoo! Rooms or User Rooms.**

   Unsurprisingly, Yahoo! rooms are created by the service and remain open all the time. (See Figure 11-9.) Any room on this list might overflow into replicated rooms if there's a big crowd. User rooms are temporary (and don't overflow), but any that appear on the list are currently open. User rooms are often more interesting than Yahoo! rooms, are less crowded, and are dedicated to quirkier topics.

Figure 11-9:
Browsing
through
chat rooms.

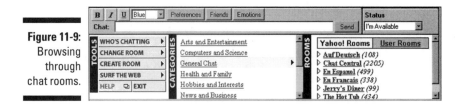

4. In the ROOMS window, click any room.

You're automatically shifted into that room, and your Chatters list changes to list the people in that room.

In the ROOMS window, individual rooms are listed by order of popularity, with the busiest rooms at the top of the list. This is good to remember, because if you specifically want a more intimate chat in a less crowded room, you should scroll down toward the bottom of the list.

In the CATEGORIES window, you might notice an Adult link. That's where the sex-oriented rooms are stored. There's no getting around it — explicit sex is one of the most popular topics in Yahoo! Chat. Clicking the Adult link displays a warning and states the age requirement of 18 years or older to enter the area. However, there is no software block or verification routine in place to stop someone of any age from entering. So, parents, beware.

When you enter the Adult Chat area, the function of the CHANGE ROOM button changes. The CATEGORIES window is eliminated, and the whole lower panel is dedicated to the Adult Chat category. The extra space is used to display Yahoo! Rooms and User Rooms at the same time.

Making your own space

Throwing together your own room is uniquely satisfying, and a good way to provide a space into which you can invite others. Here's how to get started:

1. Click the CREATE ROOM button in the bottom panel.

2. In the CREATE ROOM window, enter a room name and a welcome message.

It's a good idea to keep the room name fairly short, or it won't fit well in the User Rooms list. (Three or four words usually fit without trouble.) The welcome message appears in the main chat window when people enter your room.

3. Select whether your room will be Public, Private, or Secured.

Public rooms are open to anyone to enter at any time. Private rooms are not listed in the User Rooms list, but people can still enter them by using the GOTO link next to anyone who is in your private room. Secured rooms also do not appear in the User Rooms list, and no one can enter them unless you invite them with the Invite feature. (See Figure 11-10.)

4. Click the Create my room button.

Figure 11-10:
Creating
your own
room.

Surfing from Yahoo! Chat

The SURF THE WEB feature in the bottom panel of the Chat window would be a good idea if the bottom panel were resizable or somewhat larger to begin with. Have you ever surfed the Web with a browser that's about one inch tall? Now is your chance to give it a try. It's not the most gratifying experience in the world, I can tell you that. However, here's a method for improving things:

1. Click the SURF THE WEB button in the bottom panel.

2. Click one of the Related Features options.

The Related Features are simply locations in the Yahoo! service — the financial section, the news section, the movie section, and so forth. You may even search the main Yahoo! index from this panel by clicking Yahoo! Search.

3. Right-click any Related Features link, and select Open in New Window.

Ah, that's better. Now you can spread out a little. Yahoo! should code the links to open new browser windows automatically, but because they didn't, the only way to cope is to open that new window yourself. Now the SURF THE WEB button opens a convenient bookmark list of Yahoo! features. Just remember the right-click trick.

Chapter 12

The Thread of Discussion: Yahoo! Message Boards

In This Chapter

▶ Browsing through the directory of message boards

▶ Using the Yahoo! Messages search engine to find topics

▶ Joining in by posting your own messages

▶ Creating a new message thread

*M*essage boards have a curious but profound appeal. I have a long-standing affection for them, as message-board communities were the first aspect of cyberspace I became addicted to, long before the Web. A good messaging community provides a unique forum for human acquaintance in a few ways:

✔ Message board discussions transpire outside of real time. You might post a message during your lunch hour, which someone might reply to while you're in an afternoon meeting. A few more people might chip in while you're commuting home, and by the time you log on in the evening, you have five messages to reply to. Yet the cumulative effect somehow blends together into a coherent, flowing discussion.

✔ Friendships on message boards develop independent of physical proximity and time-zone differences. As a result, you might find yourself meeting people from all over the world, as if they were neighbors. Message boards emphasize that in cyberspace, everyone is a neighbor.

✔ Message-board discussions tend to be deeper than chat-room discussions.

✔ Getting to know someone in a message discussion eliminates the physical clues by which we tend to judge each other in person. On the board, people get to know each other from the inside out. Ideas and their articulation become paramount.

Yahoo! message boards are popular. As I describe in this chapter, the underlying software that manages message *threads* is not as advanced as in some other discussion forums. However, the simple interface keeps pages moving quickly, which is important when you're reading lots of messages, each on its own page. This chapter explains how the boards work for those who prefer to read only and for those who want to post a message or create a new thread topic.

Getting in the Fray

Yahoo! Messages is organized in typical directory style — similarly to the Yahoo! directory, as you might expect. Instead of directory pages to Web sites, browsing yields directory pages to Yahoo!-created message boards with user-created message topics on them.

Browsing for a discussion

The place to start is the Yahoo! Messages home page (see Figure 12-1). Click the Message Boards link near the bottom of the Yahoo! home page, or go directly to the message section with this URL:

```
messages.yahoo.com
```

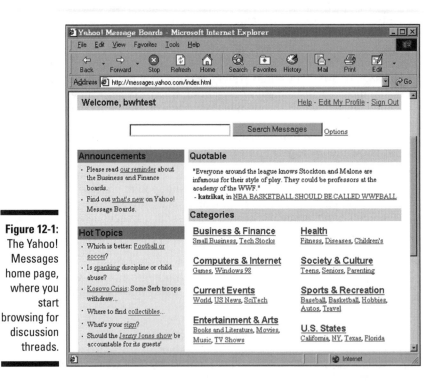

Figure 12-1:
The Yahoo!
Messages
home page,
where you
start
browsing for
discussion
threads.

The main part of the Messages home page is the Categories directory, which contains links to every message board in Yahoo! and every discussion thread on those boards. The following steps drill into the Health section of the directory, by way of illustrating how it is designed:

1. **On the Yahoo! Messages home page, click the <u>Health</u> directory category.**

   The Health directory page appears (see Figure 12-2). Note that each sub-category link has a short description. Actually, the descriptions are sometimes missing in other categories — chalk that up to carelessness at Yahoo!. Each subcategory represents a Yahoo!-created message board, on which users can create discussion topics, also called *threads*. You can't create a message board (a subcategory in the directory). Some categories, such as Business & Finance, have many more levels than the Health category. When in a deep category, just keep drilling down — you eventually see discussion threads.

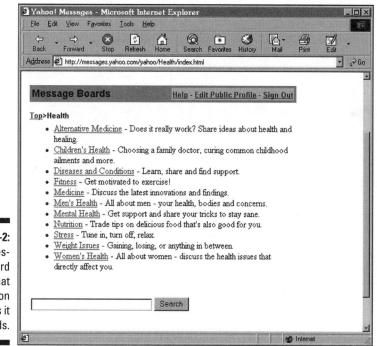

Figure 12-2:
Click a mes-
sage board
to see what
discussion
threads it
holds.

2. **Click any subcategory link (<u>Fitness</u> for this example).**

   The Fitness message board appears (see Figure 12-3). Note that you may list discussion topics in one of three views. The page loads to a default view of Most Recent, meaning that the threads, which have messages posted to them most recently are grouped at the top. The Most Popular view is likely to be similar, but not necessarily — it prioritizes threads by how many message are posted to them. The Alphabetical list is useful if you're looking for a particular topic you've seen before.

3. **Click any discussion thread (topic) to see its messages.**

   The message page appears (see Figure 12-4).

4. **Read the original message of the thread, reply to it, or browse other messages in the thread.**

   I explain replying to messages and creating original messages (new threads) later in this chapter. In Figure 12-4, notice that the thread, which at the time of this screen shot contained 110 messages, lists those messages in reverse order — most recent first, from number 110 backwards.

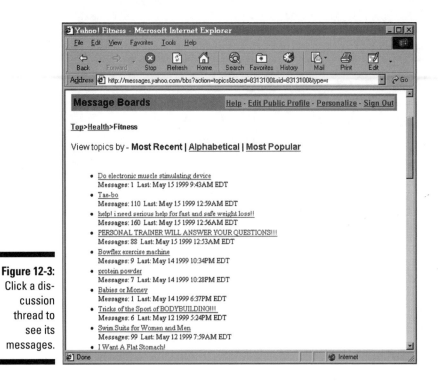

Figure 12-3:
Click a discussion thread to see its messages.

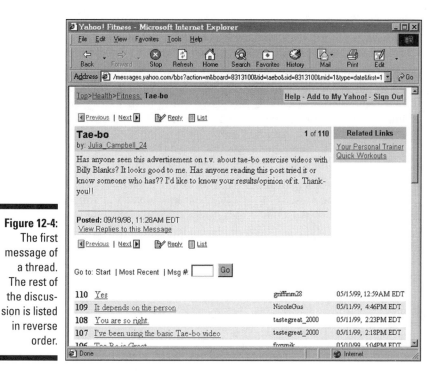

Figure 12-4:
The first
message of
a thread.
The rest of
the discus-
sion is listed
in reverse
order.

All the navigation options are available when viewing any message in any discussion thread — not only when viewing the originating message, as in
Figure 12-4.

Navigating a message thread

Unlike Usenet newsgroup readers such as Outlook Express and Netscape
Messenger, Yahoo! Messages does not use a *graphical threading* system.
Dedicated messaging programs like those two arrange discussion thread
using indents to show visually which message are responses to which other
messages. Such a system is convenient because you can tell at a glance how
the discussion is flowing and who is responding to whom. Other well-known
and popular message-board systems, such as America Online and Yahoo!,
work more like a traditional cork message board, on which everyone posts
messages and hopes for the best. Yahoo! Messages provides certain features
that help you make sense of the message thread structure.

The following options are available on every message page:

✔ **View the next message.** You can move chronologically through the message thread, viewing each message. Just keep clicking the Next link or
  the arrow next to it.

✔ **List messages in order.** Normally, thread messages are listed in reverse order, with more recent postings near the top. You can see a chronological list of messages by clicking the <u>List</u> link.

✔ **View replies to any message.** In any thread, multiple discussions spring up as people respond to different messages. You can sort out the various conversations by using the <u>View Replies to this Message</u> link. (If the link is not present beneath any message, that's because nobody has replied to that message.) As you can see in Figure 12-5, the link delivers a list of replies, from which you link to see the actual replies, one at a time. The replies might have their own replies.

✔ **View the author's profile.** The author of the message is linked immediately below the message title. Click that link to see the Yahoo! Profile for that ID.

✔ **Reply to the message.** Using the <u>Reply</u> link gets you started on a reply to the message. I discuss replying to and creating message threads later in this chapter.

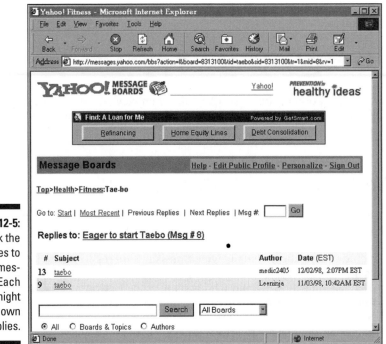

Figure 12-5:
Track the replies to any message. Each reply might have its own replies.

Following discussion threads is all the trickier in Yahoo! because a response does not necessarily have the same message title as the original message. In fact, because the Reply feature asks for a title rather than supplying the original title, in most cases responses *are* titled differently. For this reason, using the <u>View Replies to this Message</u> link frequently really helps you follow along. Remember, though, that when you use it on a topic's original message (message number 1), all messages in the thread are listed, because every message is a response to the number 1 message, however many times removed.

Message boards can be just as unruly as chat rooms. In fact, I've noticed much more hostility in Yahoo! Messages than in Yahoo! Chat. You're more likely to run into sexual language and erotic flirting in a chat room, but the boards are full of irascibility over the most trivial subjects. You might have trouble believing (but I hope are at least somewhat entertained) by the level of ire vented on the message boards when people argue over a new movie. If you feel moved to report outright abuse, racism, or some other socially unacceptable message-board behavior to Yahoo!, use the following URL:

```
add.yahoo.com/fast/help/mb/cgi_feedback
```

Cut to the chase

Browsing is a good way to get acquainted with the overall scope of Yahoo! Messages, but when it comes to finding a specific topic, thank goodness for search engines. The Yahoo! search engine is woven throughout the Yahoo! Messages sections and is accessible from virtually any page you're on.

Message searching works similarly to directory searching (see Chapter 5). You type one or more keywords, and the search engine returns matches that lead to message boards or individual messages or both.

You may begin a message search from any part of Yahoo! Messages. For illustration, the following steps walk you through a search beginning on the Yahoo! Messages home page.

1. **On the Yahoo! Messages home page (refer to Figure 12-1), type one or more keywords into the search field above the directory categories.**

2. **Click the Search Messages button.**

The search engine looks for matches to your keyword(s) in message titles, author IDs, and message texts. Because the engine doesn't automatically treat multiple keywords as an unbreakable phrase, and because matches can occur in the text, title, or author ID, you might get more results (and less relevant results) than you want.

To force the search engine to recognize your keywords as a phrase, place quotation marks around the words. An example is the keyword phrase *call options*. Without the quotation marks, the keywords match with every instance of *call* and *options* in every message and title in the system. Using *"call options"* narrows the results beautifully, returning matches to discussions about investment strategies using call options.

Figure 12-6 shows a typical results page in Yahoo! Messages. Two types of keyword matches are available:

- ✔ **Board Matches.** Board Matches occur when one of your keywords matches a message board (subcategory) title. A Board Match indicates that your search query is solidly matched to a broad subject with many possibly relevant discussion threads.

- ✔ **Message Matches.** Message Matches occur when at least one of your keywords matches within a message, a message title, or an author ID.

Board Matches and Message Matches provide a similar distinction that Category Matches and Site Matches do in the main Yahoo! directory.

Figure 12-6:
A search might return Board Matches and Message Matches.

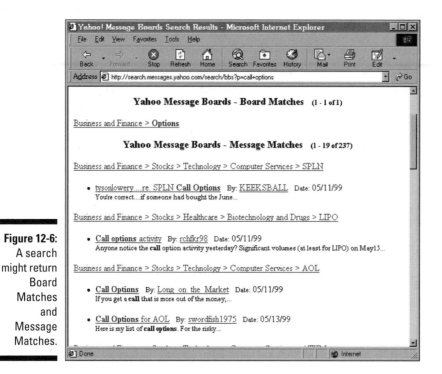

To gain access to more advanced search options, click the Options link next to the Search Messages button on the Yahoo! Messages home page. Figure 12-7 illustrates the extra search options, which take the form of radio buttons. Simply click the radio button next to the message element you'd like to search. Here are a few hints for using these options:

✔ There is no point using the All option. If you want to search everything, stick to the main keyword entry form on the Yahoo! Messages home page.

✔ Use the Titles option when you want to narrow in quickly on extremely relevant messages. When used with a keyword phrase or a name, such as *"sean connery"*, the Titles option provides a laser-quick way of getting to discussions on well-defined topics.

✔ Use the Message Text option when you have time to pore over lots of results. Narrow your hits by using more keywords or enclosing a phrase in quotes.

✔ Use the Authors option when you know someone's ID (or part of the ID), and you're looking for that person's messages.

Every message board page has a new search form at the bottom. Figure 12-8 illustrates the drop-down menu associated with these search forms. The extra menu lets you select whether you're searching all of Yahoo! Messages or just the message board you're currently viewing. Use the Only in this Board option to keep your search narrowed and on topic.

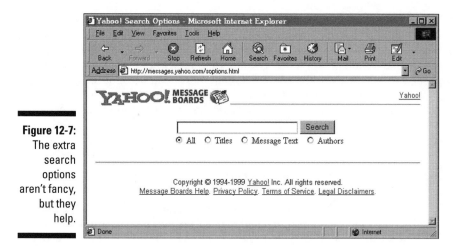

Figure 12-7:
The extra search options aren't fancy, but they help.

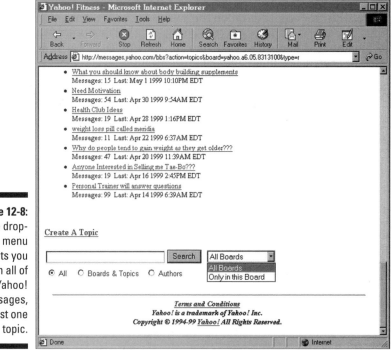

Join in the Fun

It's not necessary to ever post a message, and many people enjoy message boards in *lurker mode* — silently reading threads without speaking up in a message. However, even the most steadfast lurker can be tempted out of the closet with a provocative discussion or an opinion that just must be expressed. This section explains how to post a message and create a new topic (thread).

Adding your two cents

As I explain in a previous section, every message has a <u>Reply</u> link attached to it. Clicking that link takes you to a series of forms you use to formulate a reply, title it, and post it on the message board. (See Figure 12-9.) Proceed as follows:

1. **Select an identity from among your Yahoo! profiles.**

   See Chapter 1 for instructions on creating a Yahoo! Profile. If you have created only one, you may either use it as your public profile on the message boards or create a specialized one for messaging. Click the <u>EDIT or ADD identities</u> link to create a new profile.

2. **Scroll down the page and enter a title for your message.**

   It helps other visitors to the thread if you make your title similar to, identical to, or at least vaguely reminiscent of the title of the message you're responding to. Unfortunately, the original title is nowhere to be found on this page. At any rate, keep the title fairly short.

3. **Type your message.**

   Yahoo! Messages accepts URLs as part of messages, and turns them into live links that anyone can use. So feel free to add a link to your Web page beneath your signature, or link readers to a Web site that's relevant to your message.

   To see what your message looks like before committing it to the message board, click Preview before Posting. From that page, you may edit your message or go ahead and post it.

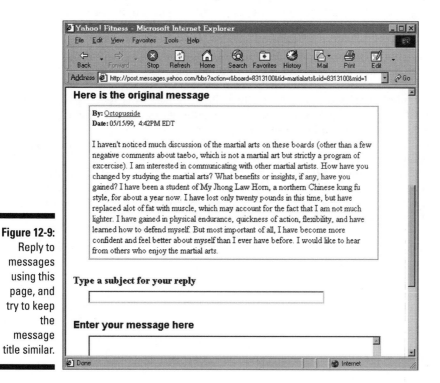

Figure 12-9:
Reply to messages using this page, and try to keep the message title similar.

4. Click the Post Message button.

Notice that the message you're replying to is placed on this page, but it doesn't appear in your message unless you manually copy and paste portions of it into the "Enter your message here" field.

Starting up a conversation

The next level of active participation after replying to messages is creating new message threads. You may create the first message of a new thread on most boards that are at the bottom of their directory levels. This means, for example, that you *cannot* create a new thread at the directory level where all the major league baseball teams are listed. Yahoo! has sensibly created a board for each team, and users cannot create duplicate or irrelevant boards at that level. However, you *may* create a new thread on the board of your favorite team. The upshot is that you can create a thread on the message board, but you can't create the message board itself.

Figure 12-10 shows a bottom-page view of the New York Mets baseball message board. The <u>Create A Topic</u> link is for starting a new thread. It leads to a page virtually identical to the Reply page, but without any reference to an original message because you are creating the thread's first message. Just choose your profile, as before, and then type a title and your message. Click the Create Topic button when you're finished, or the Preview before Posting button to see what you did before committing it to the board.

You might notice that not every thread board uses the <u>Create A Topic</u> link. That's because each board has a certain amount of room, though Yahoo! does not divulge how much or how the space is measured. You may create a topic wherever that link exists. If there's no link, you're out of luck for the time being, pure and simple. A recent upgrade of the entire Yahoo! Message system has improved what used to be a somewhat frustrating situation. When you can't create a new thread, simply start a new topic using the Reply feature and create a very different message title. That method gets the discussion going just as well.

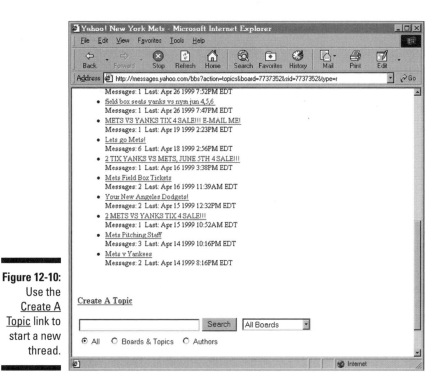

Figure 12-10:
Use the
Create A
Topic link to
start a new
thread.

What is e-mail verification, and why do we need it?

You must be a registered Yahoo! user to post a message. That simply means you must own a Yahoo! ID (see Chapter 1). Yahoo! puts you through an extra step before you post your first message by requiring e-mail verification of your *true* identity. This extra step was added to tighten security in a realm where identity is fluid, at best. If someone posts material that is flagrantly illegal, Yahoo! (and legal authorities) have a handle on tracking the real person down. So, for the sake of security, everyone must proceed through the e-mail verification procedure — but only once.

When you attempt to post your first message, Yahoo! displays a screen asking for your non-Yahoo! e-mail address. That's the one that comes with your online access account. It could be an address from America Online, or AT&T, or Earthlink, or whatever provider you use. No sooner do you enter an address than Yahoo! sends a verification note to *that* address, with instructions for proceeding. In most cases, you simply click a link to another Web page, type your Yahoo! password, and you're verified.

Chapter 13

Your Messenger Is Knocking

. . . .

In This Chapter

▶ Exploring Java Messenger

▶ Downloading and launching Yahoo! Messenger

▶ Finding and chatting with friends

▶ Using Messenger as a Yahoo! control center

▶ Searching Yahoo! with Messenger

. . . .

*L*et me state it right up front. Yahoo! Messenger is one of the great features of cyberspace. For Yahoo! users, it's an invaluable gadget that centralizes much of the Yahoo! experience. Messenger is small and doesn't take much screen space, but this powerful little module keeps you in contact with friends, lets you search the Web, delivers e-mail alerts, tracks your stock portfolio, updates sports scores, and integrates beautifully with your browser.

Yahoo! has designed Messenger to stay running all the time, and while that might seem like a corporate attempt to keep the Yahoo! logo on your screen, I've found that it's exactly what works best for me. It's the first thing I boot up when I go online, and I never turn it off.

The Double Life of a Messenger

Yahoo! provides two working versions of Messenger. One is a Java applet that you can activate from the Yahoo! Messenger Web page. The other, more complete version is a distinct program that must be downloaded and installed on your computer's hard drive. The full version has far more features, and you should definitely choose it to get the full Messenger experience. Both versions are available from the following URL:

```
messenger.yahoo.com
```

Both versions of Yahoo! Messenger are free. The full, downloadable version contains conferencing and voice chat; hooks into My Yahoo! and Yahoo! Finance, News, Sports, E-mail, Personals, and Web directory; and a search engine that can rummage through just about any portion of the whole service.

The Java version of Messenger is convenient as a tester and for computer systems that can't run the full version (including Macintosh, UNIX, and Windows 3.*x*). The Java applet is somewhat less stable than its full-featured counterpart, causing occasional browser crashes.

With Yahoo! Messenger, you can

- ✔ Chat with individuals or small groups outside Yahoo! Chat, while integrating some features into Yahoo! Chat when you go into chat rooms.

- ✔ Create groups of friends (called, amazingly, Friends) and set up alerts for when your friends connect through Yahoo! Messenger or Yahoo! Chat.

- ✔ Work in tandem with your browser to quickly link to news stories, financial information, Yahoo! E-mail, search results, and many other portions of Yahoo!.

- ✔ Talk — really talk, with your voice (if you have a microphone and speakers attached to your computer) — with people all over the world, free of charge.

One thing Yahoo! Messenger cannot do that some other chatting products can do is to send computer files to chat partners. This feature is planned for the future.

Trying Java Messenger

If you like the idea of voice chatting or any of the other features of Yahoo! Messenger, go straight for the full version. But if you use a Macintosh computer or want to give a slim version of Messenger a quick whirl, follow these steps to try the Java version:

1. **On the Yahoo! home page, click the <u>Yahoo! Messenger</u> link.**

2. **Click the <u>Java™ Edition</u> link.**

   Although the link is recommended for Macintosh and UNIX users, anyone can try it, no matter what computer you use. Allow a minute or two for the Java applet to download and install in your computer. You don't need to do anything. Java Messenger (Figure 13-1) pops open when it's ready.

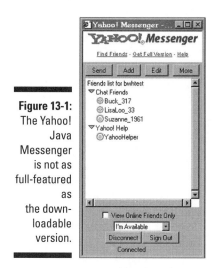

Figure 13-1:
The Yahoo!
Java
Messenger
is not as
full-featured
as
the down-
loadable
version.

3. **Wait for Java Messenger to connect.**

The Connected signal appears with a green light at the bottom of Messenger. Your Friends list appears in the main window, and Messenger determines who is currently online, indicating online status with a yellow smiling face.

As you can see in Figure 13-1, Java Messenger has a row of four menu buttons across the top. Here's how to use them:

✔ **Send.** The Send button initiates an Instant Message — also called a Private Message (PM), especially in Yahoo! Chat, where people routinely talk about "PMing" each other. The easiest way to use Send is to high-light a friend's ID, and then click the button. Your selected friend's ID is inserted in the To field. You may also simply double-click any Friend name to open an Instant Message window.

✔ **Add.** If you meet a new friend online, use the Add button to add the ID to one of your Friend groups. Figure 13-2 shows the Add a friend/group window. Fill in the ID in the top field, and then use the drop-down menu to select which group you'd like the ID in. (It's okay if you have just one group, but you may create a new group by typing its name in the field next to the drop-down menu.) Select one of your identities (you may have just one, which is perfectly fine), and include a short message to the person in Step 4 of the window if you'd like.

Figure 13-2:
Use the Add
button to get
this window,
where you
add a new
friend in
Java
Messenger.

> **Add a friend / group**
>
> Step 1 - Enter your friend's Yahoo! ID:
> Yahoo! ID: [   ]
>
> Step 2 - Select the group to add your
> friend to or type a new name in the box:
> [Chat Friends ▾] [Chat Friends   ]
>
> Step 3 - Select one of your own identities:
> Your ID: [bwhtest ▾]
>
> Step 4 - You can include a short message with this request (optional).
> [   ]
>
> [Add] [Cancel] [Help]

✔ **Edit.** The Edit button pops open an Edit Menu window with five action buttons. With three of those buttons — Friends/Groups, My Profiles, and Account/Password — your browser displays Yahoo! pages that let you modify your settings. The Ignore list opens a small window in which you type the IDs of any people (friends or foes) you *don't* want to hear from. Instant Messages from those IDs don't reach you, and the sender gets a message to that effect. The Preferences button opens a tiny window in which you determine whether alerts of various kinds get your attention by playing a sound, displaying a dialog box, both, or neither.

✔ **More.** The More button opens a menu window with some interesting action buttons. The View a Profile button lets you select a Yahoo! ID whose profile you'd like to see, and then opens that profile in a browser window. Search Profiles sends your browser to the Search Profiles page in Yahoo!. Invite a Friend hijacks your browser also, displaying a page from which you can send a form letter to any e-mail address, inviting the recipient to download the Yahoo! Messenger. The Start a Chat Room button is the coolest (see Figure 13-3), enabling you to create a free-floating chat room through Messenger and invite members of your Friends group into the room.

Figure 13-3:
Create a
free-floating
group chat
room with
the Start a
Chat Room
window.

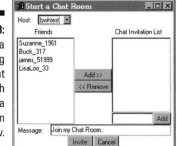

> **Start a Chat Room**
>
> Host: [bwhtest ▾]
>
> Friends   Chat Invitation List
> Suzanne_1961
> Buck_317
> james_51999
> LisaLoo_33
>   [Add >>]
>   [<< Remove]
>
>   [   ] [Add]
> Message: [Join my Chat Room.   ]
>   [Invite] [Cancel]

When you add a friend to one of your groups, that friend is added no matter how you access Yahoo! chatting functions. You may be in a chat room or using either Java Messenger or the installed Messenger, and your friends will remain the same no matter from which area you added them.

Near the bottom of Java Messenger, a check box forces Messenger to display only Friend IDs that are currently logged on. Check it if you have lots of online friends, and the long list is cumbersome in the little window. Use the drop-down menu to indicate whether you're available for a chat, temporarily busy, not at home, on the phone, or any of the other choices. Your selection appears next to your name on other Friends lists that include your ID — except if you choose the default I'm Available, in which case your name simply appears, unadorned by any message.

When you're ready to disconnect from Java Messenger, click the Disconnect button. Doing so withdraws your Messenger connection, but leaves you logged on to the Internet. It *does not* disconnect your modem. The Sign Out button is for signing off your Yahoo! ID. If you do sign out, you'll need to sign in again before using other Yahoo! interactive features.

Getting the Full Messenger Experience

The free, downloadable Yahoo! Messenger program is built for Windows 95, Windows 98, and Windows NT. Your computer must be running one of those operating systems to use Messenger. Mac users and early Windows (pre-95) users can have fun with the Java version of Messenger (see the preceding section).

Downloading Messenger and connecting to Yahoo! through it isn't very hard and is definitely worth it. The file is less than one megabyte — far smaller than many program downloads. The download takes a few minutes through a 28.8K modem and is even faster through speedier modems. Just follow these steps to get started:

1. **On the Yahoo! home page, click the <u>Yahoo! Messenger</u> link.**

2. **Click the <u>Download for Windows 95/NT/98</u> link.**

   The Windows File Download window appears.

3. **Select Save this program to disk, and click the OK button.**

   The Save As window appears.

4. **Select where on your hard drive you want to place the file.**

   Saving the file to your desktop makes it easy to find in the next step, but use whatever download location you're comfortable with.

5. **When the download is complete, find the file (called ymsgrie.exe or ymsgrie!.exe) and double-click it.**

   Double-clicking the file begins the installation procedure.

6. **Follow the instructions that appear on your screen.**

7. **When installation is complete, click Yahoo! Messenger in your Start menu to launch the program.**

   When Messenger launches (see Figure 13-4), it automatically attempts to connect with Yahoo!. If you're already logged on to the Internet, Messenger recognizes that and simply connects with the Yahoo! server and begins locating any Friends you've assigned to your ID.

Figure 13-4:
Yahoo!
Messenger
as it first
appears
after logging
on. Friends
who are
online are
listed.

 Messenger starts as a small window, but can be resized to any dimension you like. It's convenient to keep it compact for viewing online friends and chatting, but when using the information features described in this section, widening the window is helpful.

 When Yahoo! Messenger first launches and connects, it lists any Friends who are online. Offline friends are not listed. However, you can change this display to include all friends, with a lit-up icon to distinguish those who are connected. Just pull down the Messenger menu, and select Show All Friends.

Training Messenger

You can make Messenger behave properly when you turn on your computer, and appear the way you want while you're using it. Just follow these steps:

1. **Pull down the Edit menu, and select Preferences.**

   The Preferences window appears.

2. **Click the General tab.**

On the General tab of the Preferences dialog box, seven check boxes are related to basic operating selections (see Figure 13-5). Use the check boxes to do the following:

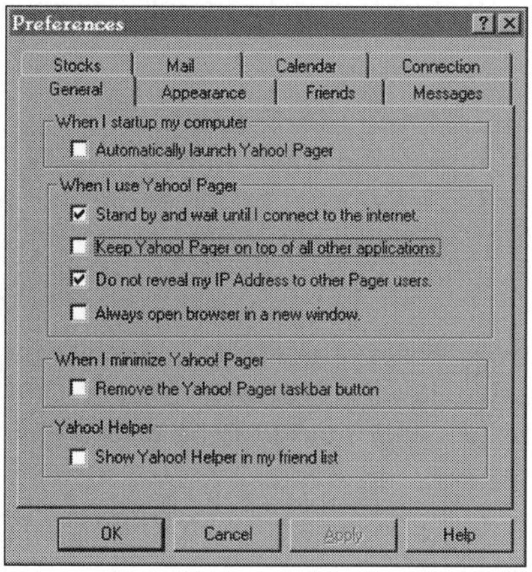

Figure 13-5:
General
Preferences
determine
how
Messenger
behaves
when
started.

✔ **Automatically launch Yahoo! Messenger.** Checking this selection puts Messenger in your startup folder, from which it boots automatically when you turn on your computer and load Windows.

✔ **Stand by and wait until I connect to the Internet.** Whether you set Messenger to launch automatically or not, this setting determines whether Messenger attempts to connect with Yahoo! even if your computer is not yet online. Check the box to put the brakes on, forcing Messenger to wait until you manually connect with the Internet.

✔ **Keep Yahoo! Messenger on top of all other applications.** Check this box if you want Messenger to be visible on your screen at all times. You may find running in this mode inconvenient, because it blocks your view of other on-screen windows, but you may uncheck it at any time.

✔ **Do not reveal my IP Address to other Messenger users.** For most people, it's a good idea to check this box for security reasons. The IP address reveals your exact log-on path to the Internet.

✔ **Always open browser in a new window.** I like to check this box. When Messenger uses your browser for something — getting news stories or sports scores, for example — this selection ensures that a fresh browser pops open so that you don't lose whatever you're looking at in the current browser window.

✔ **Remove the Yahoo! Messenger taskbar button.** This selection takes effect when you minimize the Messenger window. I prefer showing Messenger in the taskbar at all times, so I leave it unchecked.

✔ **Show Yahoo! Helper in my friend list.** Yahoo! Helper is an automated Help feature that accepts and responds to Instant Messages. If you use it often, it makes sense to keep it visible as a "friend."

If you not sure what you did and want to start again from scratch, click Cancel to close the Preferences window, and then open it again and begin anew. When you've made your selections, click the Apply button, and then click OK.

Five of the other Preferences tabs ask you to select an audio sound to play when certain things happen. I've found that the sounds are useful for getting my attention, and they eliminate the need for me to keep Messenger visible on my screen. I often like to know when friends come online and log off, and when something comes into my Yahoo! e-mail box. Here's how it works:

✔ **Flash the taskbar "tray" icon.** This is the most inconspicuous type of alert, because you see it only when you happen to glance at the Windows tray. (The tray is the right-hand portion of the Windows taskbar with the tiny icons.)

✔ **Display a dialog box.** The dialog box is a tiny window that appears atop your screen, in active mode. If you're working in another application (such as typing a book chapter in a word processor), you might be surprised to get jolted out of one window and placed in another. Still, I keep this function selected so that I know what the alert is about.

✔ **Play a sound.** This feature is great. Default sounds download with the Messenger package and are loaded into all the alerts. You may audition the sounds by clicking the ear button, and select new ones to audition by using the Browse button.

Use the preceding selections to get notified when friends come and go (Friends tab in the Preferences window); when you receive an Instant Message (Messages tab); when it's time for an event listed on your Yahoo! Calendar (Calendar tab); when you receive something in your Yahoo! e-mail box (Mail tab); and when you receive a stock alert (Stocks tab).

Making friends and chatting

Yahoo! Messenger began as a chat module, pure and simple. It was a social program. Information pieces have been added to Messenger, but many people still use it primarily as a way of meeting people online and chatting with them.

Friends are at the heart of Yahoo! Messenger. You may use Messenger to
search for new friends and of course to get to know current friends better. All
four buttons beneath the menu bar (refer to Figure 13-4) contain functions
related to friends and communication. Some of those functions are dupli-
cated when you right-click a friend's name. Furthermore, the Messenger
menu puts all the functions in one place. In other words, Yahoo! Messenger
tries to make it as easy and intuitive as possible to talk to people.

The following sections explore the two basic social functions in Yahoo!
Messenger — finding and talking to friends.

Finding and adding friends

If you're completely new to Yahoo!, the best way to begin meeting people is
to participate in Yahoo! Chat, which I explain in Chapter 11. From there, it's
easy to throw a new friend directly into your Friends list. However, that
process is somewhat hit-or-miss if you're looking for friends who share particular interests. Another way is to use the Friends button on Messenger:

1. With Yahoo! Messenger connected, click the Friends button.

Messenger appropriates your browser and displays the Member
Directory Search page (see Figure 13-6).

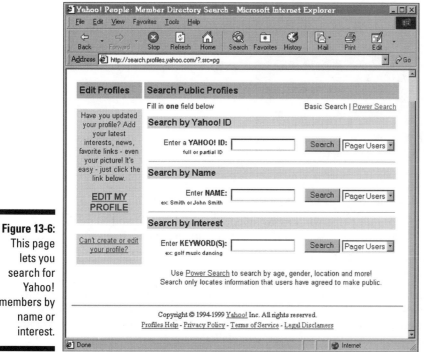

Figure 13-6:
This page
lets you
search for
Yahoo!
members by
name or
interest.

2. **Below the Search by Interest banner, type one or more keywords.**

3. **Using the drop-down menu, select whether to limit your search to Messenger users or to search the entire Yahoo! membership.**

   In this case, because you're interested in chatting through Messenger, it makes sense to limit the search. (See Chapter 1 for a more detailed exploration of searching for Yahoo! members.)

4. **Click the Search button.**

   The Member Directory Search Results page appears.

5. **Click the Yahoo! ID of any member to see a Profile.**

6. **When you see a Profile of someone you'd like to add as a friend, make a note of the Yahoo! ID.**

   You need to make a note because there's no one-click way of putting an ID into your Friends list from the Member Directory Search pages.

7. **In Yahoo! Messenger, click the Add button.**

   The Add a Friend/Group window appears (see Figure 13-7).

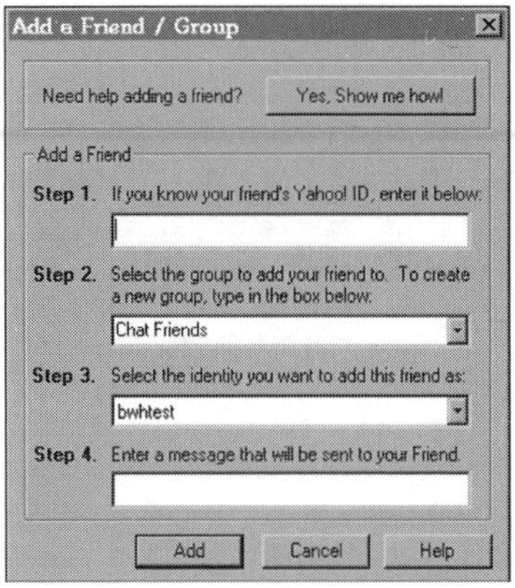

Figure 13-7:
The Add a
Friend/Group
window.

8. **In the Step 1 field, type the ID you wrote down.**

   Complete this window by selecting which group and ID you're adding the name to. Step 4 is particularly important because you're adding a stranger to your Friends list. A small note breaks the ice.

Of course, you may use the Add button to include friends in your group after meeting them in some other fashion. You can also encourage friends you know outside Yahoo! to get Messenger and join the party. Just click the Friends button, select "Invite a friend to get Messenger," fill out the Web page that appears in your browser, and click the Invite Friend button. If your friend takes you up on the offer, he or she will need to download Messenger and install it, or use Java Messenger.

The time is bound to come when you want to remove a friend from your group. It's not necessarily an insult (though if a fellow Trekker called you a Denubian slime devil, you should dump that person immediately) — sometimes a Friend link goes unused because the other person is rarely online. Whatever reason motivates the removal of a friend, it's easily accomplished:

1. **When Yahoo! Messenger is connected, right-click the name of any friend.**

   If Messenger is set to display only friends who are currently connected, pull down the Messenger menu and select Show All Friends.

2. **Right-click the ID you intend to remove from your group.**

3. **Click the Delete Friend selection.**

   A small window opens, asking whether you're sure you want to delete this person. Be sure! Yahoo! IDs are often obscure, and it can be hard to find someone again.

4. **Click the OK button.**

   After a second, the deleted name disappears from your list of friends.

Chatting with friends

You can chat with other Messenger users in four ways:

- ✔ **Online text chatting.** This is traditional chatting, using an Instant Message window to trade lines of typed text with another connected user.

- ✔ **Offline text chatting.** You may send an Instant Message to anyone on your Friends list, even if that person is not presently connected. If your friend is unconnected, the message is stored until he or she next connects Messenger.

- ✔ **Online voice chatting.** Yahoo! added real-time voice chatting to Messenger in May, 1999. To use this feature, both participants must be using a version of Messenger released after that time. Not sure whether your Messenger is recent enough? Pull down the Messenger menu. If one of the selections is Start a Voice Chat, you're in business. If not, download a new Messenger (it's free), as described previously in this chapter.

- ✔ **Online group chatting (text or voice).** You can pull more than one friend into a chat, which is then called a Conference. Conferences operate in both text and voice mode simultaneously. It is outrageously cool.

The most typical way of beginning a Messenger chat is to send an Instant Message to a connected friend. You can do this in five ways, which reveals how important chatting is to the Messenger lineup of features. I'm spelling out the five methods because it's important to find the most comfortable way to begin chatting:

- Double-click any friend's name. (The friend can be connected or unconnected, but don't expect an instant response if he or she is not online.)

- Right-click a friend's name.

- Click a friend's name and use the Ctrl+S keyboard combination.

- Click a friend's name, click the Messages button, and click the Send Instant Message selection.

- Click a friend's name, pull down the Edit menu, and click the Send a Message selection.

Whichever way you open an Instant Message window, Figure 13-8 illustrates what it looks like. The Instant Message window is easy enough to use — at the most basic level, you just type a message and click the Send button. The full-featured Messenger incorporates some fancy text perks, though, that are missing from Java Messenger:

- The floppy disk icon is for saving a chat to your hard drive. The save should be performed after a chat is complete, before you close the Instant Message window. Yahoo! Messenger *does not* save the chat as it proceeds — in other words, you can't save it at the beginning and end up with the whole chat later, unless you save it again at the end.

- The printer icon lets you print a chat session.

- Click the color palette icon to choose a color for your text. Colored text appears colored both on your screen and the other person's.

- Use the **Bold**, *Italic*, and Underline icons to change your text. You may use any or all of these in combination with text color.

Figure 13-8:
The Instant
Message
Window,
where text
chats
transpire.

When you first send an Instant Message, the window disappears from your screen. This might be disconcerting if you're accustomed to chat systems that leave the window open. You can change this default setting in the Preferences window (Ctrl+P) under the Messages tab. Just click the check box next to Keep message window open, then click the Apply button, and then click the OK button. I also find it useful, under the same Messages tab, to set the Enter key to send the message rather than insert a carriage return.

Most chatting involves a series of short lines — rambling dissertations are unusual, and besides, Yahoo! automatically wraps long lines of text to the recipient's window size. So carriage returns aren't necessary unless you chat in verse.

Begin a voice chat by following these steps:

1. **When Yahoo! Messenger is connected, click the Messages button.**

   Alternatively, you may right-click any friend's name.

2. **Click the Start a Voice Chat or Start a Conference selection.**

3. **In the Invite Friends to a Voice Chat (or Invite Friends to a Conference) window, click the name of the friend you want to invite.**

   Only connected friends are listed in this window. If you'd like to invite a Yahoo! ID not on your Friends list, type the ID in the Add field and click the Add button.

4. **Click the Add>> button.**

5. **When you have selected and added everyone you want in the chat, click the Invite button.**

   Everyone on your list receives an invitation window, and clicks a Yes button to accept or a No button to decline (nothing personal, it's just that the last time you spent four hours talking about your ingrown toenail).

When you send your invitation, a new window opens on your screen (see Figure 13-9). The Voice Chat window is where you manage voice and conference chats. Notice that all the Instant Message features are incorporated near the bottom of the window. Conveniently, text chatting is fully available during voice chats. It's especially convenient because the voice feature works for only one person at a time.

Conferences and voice chats — two sides of a coin

Starting a conference or voice chat is a two-step process in which you first invite a person (or more than one) into a conference window, and then proceed with the chat or conference in that window. A conference is a group chat, and a voice chat can transpire between two or more people. So they are almost the same thing; they happen in the same window, and the voice feature is always available in conferences. Accordingly, it doesn't matter whether you start things off with the Start a Conference or Start a Voice Chat feature — they both lead to the same result, which is a specialized chat window with two or more people talking through a mix of text and voice.

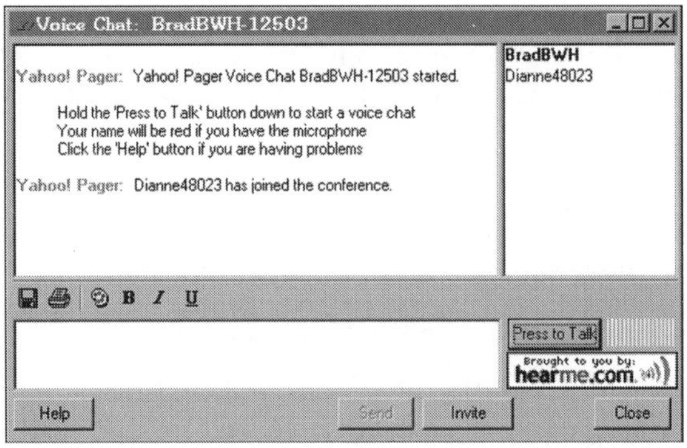

Figure 13-9:
The Voice
Chat
window,
where you
can use text
and micro-
phone
chatting.

When you want to talk in a voice chat, click and hold the Press to Talk button, and speak into your microphone. Your partner (or all your partners in a conference) hears your words almost as you speak them — the transmission speed is about as fast as a phone call. People chatting from far-off points of the globe experience a slight delay.

Only one person can use the Press to Talk button at a time. When a person is speaking, that ID is highlighted in the list of people attending. This system gets a bit frustrating in a group chat, but works well enough one-to-one. Remember that you can continue typing while people are speaking into their microphones.

The Messenger Control Center

Although many people are satisfied with Yahoo! Messenger as a social tool, it's far more than just a mobile chat room. Five tabs at the bottom, plus a hidden search engine, unlock its information resources. The tabs are not identified with text, but divulge their identities when you run your mouse cursor over them. Here's what those five tabs do:

✔ **Friends.** The left tab opens the window described in most of the previous sections of this chapter. This is where your Friends groups appear and where you initiate Instant Messages and voice chat sessions.

✔ **Stocks.** The Stocks tab, second from the left, displays the stock prices you selected in the Stock Portfolios of My Yahoo!. (It doesn't display the more advanced portfolios from Yahoo! Finance.) If you haven't created a stock portfolio in My Yahoo!, this tab displays a simple default selection of stock prices. To adjust your portfolio, visit your My Yahoo! page and click the Edit button in the Portfolios module (see Chapter 2).

✔ **News.** As with the Stocks tab, the News section links to your settings in My Yahoo! and displays the same headline links. In this tab, an Edit button is provided for making alterations, which get applied to both My Yahoo! and Yahoo! Messenger. When you click a headline link in Messenger, your browser displays the full story.

✔ **Sports.** Again, the Sports tab follows your My Yahoo! settings. An Edit button lets you change those settings, hooking into your browser window. An added twist in this tab is that clicking anywhere in the main window space connects your browser to Yahoo! Sports. It's a nice feature, though unexpected and startling at first. This feature might be added to the Stock and News tabs by the time you read this.

✔ **Alerts.** The right-hand tab provides a recap of what's happening in your account. The list notifies you of new e-mail that's arrived at your Yahoo! address, new messages in your Yahoo! Personals mailbox, alerts from your Yahoo! Calendar settings, stock alerts if you've established alert parameters in your My Yahoo! portfolio, and a Friends Online summary. (See Figure 13-10.)

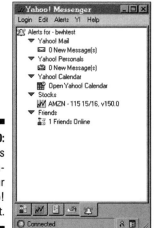

Figure 13-10:
The Alerts tab summarizes your Yahoo! account.

Note the small magnifying glass icon in the lower-right corner of Messenger. Clicking that icon reveals the hidden keyword entry form for searching. More convenient even than searching within Yahoo!'s Web pages, this powerful search engine can be told to rummage around in almost any portion of the entire Yahoo! service.

To conduct a Messenger search, follow these steps:

1. **With Messenger connected, click the magnifying glass icon to reveal the keyword entry form.**

2. **Click the small arrow next to the keyword form to pop open a menu list.**

3. **From the menu, select any item.**

4. **Click your mouse in the keyword entry field, and type one or more keywords.**

5. **Press the Enter key of your keyboard.**

   Messenger takes control of your browser and displays the search results in a browser window.

Chapter 14

Virtual Treehouses: Yahoo! Clubs

● ●

In This Chapter

▶ Browsing and searching for Yahoo! clubs

▶ Joining someone else's club and uploading pictures

▶ Creating and configuring your own club

● ●

*I*magine creating your own Web site, dedicated to a subject of interest —
perhaps music, movies, sports, genealogy, current events, or meeting
people. Now imagine the site complete with a message board for posted discussions and a chat room for real-time talking. Creating a feature-rich site like
that, from scratch, would take more knowledge and skill than most people
have time to acquire.

Yahoo! clubs are an alternative to building a site from scratch. Think of clubs
as site-building kits. Just follow the easy instructions and all the features get
plugged in automatically, arranged in the site as neatly as a sectional couch.
Yahoo! offers a simple trade: You get ease in exchange for customization. In
other words, all Yahoo! clubs look pretty much the same (see Figure 14-1), so
you're not going to make a personal visual statement, but setting them up is a
snap and they work well.

Although Yahoo! clubs are great for enterprising people who want their own
site, you don't need to be ambitious to enjoy them. They're also great for visiting and joining. Clubs are meeting places for people with a shared interest.

This chapter goes into detail about how to search for Yahoo! clubs, use the
their features, and create your own club.

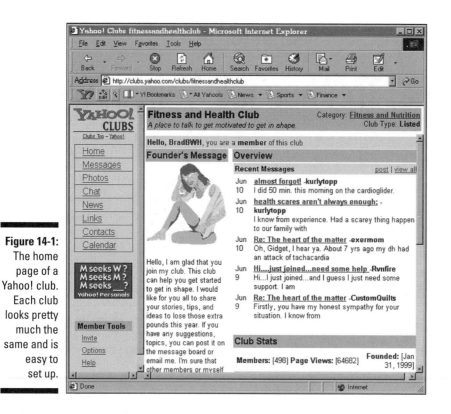

Figure 14-1:
The home
page of a
Yahoo! club.
Each club
looks pretty
much the
same and is
easy to
set up.

Finding and Joining Clubs

You can get started with Yahoo! clubs by proceeding directly to the Yahoo! Clubs directory at the following URL. Browse among the clubs, visit any in the directory, and join clubs you might want to return to later.

```
clubs.yahoo.com
```

Feel free to poke around the directory and explore individual clubs. You might get the hang of it quickly, through trial and error. The following sections walk you through browsing, searching, and joining clubs.

Club hopping

The Yahoo! Clubs directory and search engine work similarly to the main Yahoo! Web directory described in Chapter 4. On the main directory page, you see 16 main directory topics, each listed with a handful of subcategory links. (See Figure 14-2 for a partial view of the directory page.) Click any directory link to begin drilling down to a topic of interest.

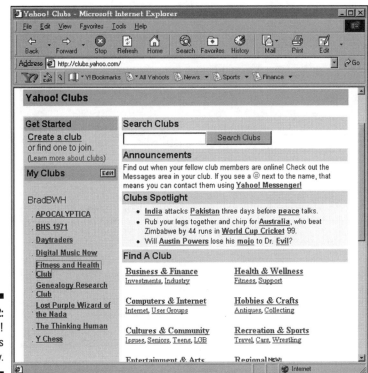

Figure 14-2:
The Yahoo!
Clubs
directory.

If you join any Yahoo! Clubs, those clubs are listed in the left-hand sidebar of the main Yahoo! Clubs directory. It makes it easy to reach your clubs, though you might also want to create bookmarks for them in your browser, which makes it even easier.

Each page of the Yahoo! Clubs directory presents links to individual clubs, and — in all but the lowest directory levels — subcategory links leading to other clubs in more specific topics. The second-level directory pages list the most popular clubs (by membership count) in *all* the subcategories of that directory topic. Figure 14-3 illustrates how the listing is arranged. The figure shows the Computers & Internet directory category. First come the links to subcategories, then the most popular clubs for the whole Computers & Internet category.

Lower subcategories continue to list the most popular clubs, but only within the subcategory. In many cases, too many clubs exist to list them all on one page, so you need to use the A-Z Index link to sort through them all.

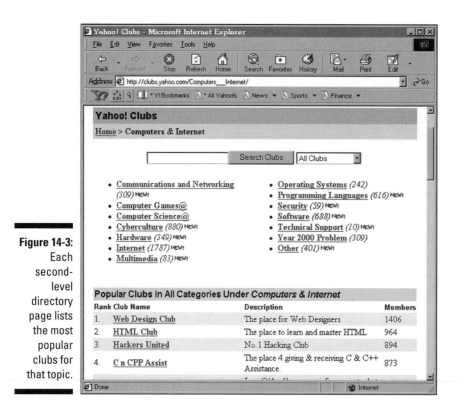

Figure 14-3:
Each second-level directory page lists the most popular clubs for that topic.

Popularity breeds popularity, especially when Yahoo! places the high-membership clubs so visibly in the directory. The result of this system is that the clubs with big memberships tend to get even bigger, while less visible clubs remain anonymous. How does a club get more members in the first place? In many cases, a club gets members simply by being one of the first clubs in a certain subcategory. If you want to find hidden gems (worth searching for in many cases), you need to take the path less traveled. Dig down into the directory using the A-Z Index link, or by simply exploring lower directory levels. Best of all, use keywords to search the directory.

Finding the right club

At any time while browsing, you may crank your investigation to the next level by searching the Yahoo! Clubs directory with keywords. The process is nearly identical to searching the main Yahoo! Web directory, described in Chapter 5. Just follow these steps:

1. **On any Yahoo! Clubs directory page, type a keyword (or more than one) in the keyword entry form.**

2. **If you're in any directory page except the top one, use the drop-down menu to select whether to search All Clubs or In This Category.**

3. **Click the Search Clubs button.**

Just as in the main Yahoo! Web directory, your search results might contain both Category Matches and Site Matches (called Clubs Site Matches in this directory). This arrangement occurs when you search with broad keywords, especially single keywords. Figure 14-4 shows a Clubs Search Results page for a search on the keyword *mp3*, a digital music format. The Category Match links you to the subcategory directory page for MP3 clubs, where you can browse all relevant clubs whether or not they contain the term *mp3* in their club name. The Clubs Site Matches list represents all clubs with *mp3* in their names.

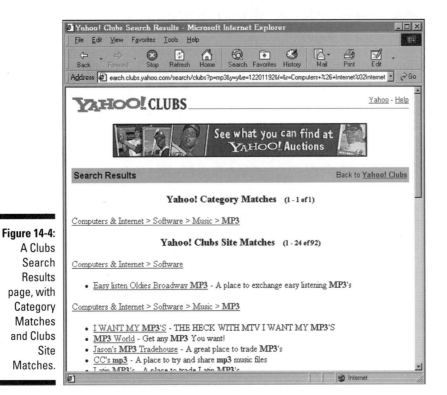

Figure 14-4:
A Clubs Search Results page, with Category Matches and Clubs Site Matches.

Joining in

As you find interesting clubs, you might want to join up with some of them. Yahoo! places no limit on the number of clubs you can join. However, your patience might have a limit as you begin receiving e-mail communications from all your new clubs. Fortunately, it's easy to get out of clubs (I describe how a bit later on).

You can explore any club to some extent without joining. But until you're a member, you can't do the following:

- ✔ View member-uploaded photos (and upload your own)
- ✔ Post messages on the message board
- ✔ Place items on the calendar
- ✔ Be included in the club's member listing
- ✔ View the News page

So limited observation is possible as a nonmember, but participation requires membership. Joining is easy. On the home page of any club you visit, do the following:

1. **Click the <u>Join this club</u> link (upper-right corner of the page).**

   The Join *Clubname* page appears.

2. **Select the Yahoo! ID you'd like to use in this club.**

   If you have just one Yahoo! ID, it's an easy choice.

3. **Type a comment if you'd like one to appear next to your name in the member list.**

4. **You may review the Terms of Service agreement at this time by clicking that link.**

   I discuss the Terms of Service later in this chapter. It's a standard legal document, and you don't need to review it every time you join a club.

5. **Click the Yes! I Accept button.**

   You just joined! The next thing you see is the club home page, and all club features are now available to you.

You must have a Yahoo! ID to join a club. Chapter 1 describes how to make an ID.

Being an Active Member

After you join a club (which takes about ten seconds; see the preceding section), all its features are open to you. The clubs are very interactive. Yahoo! clubs all contain the same basic features, which are linked in the left-hand sidebar. The following sections walk you through the various rooms and hallways of your new club.

Welcome home

The first page a visitor or member sees when visiting the club is its home page. This is where you find the purpose of the club according to the Founder's Message. Here's what else you find on the home page:

- In the Overview section, several of the most recently posted messages are linked. You may read any one of them or click the view all link to — you guessed it — see a complete list of messages. The post link is a shortcut to putting something up on the message board. Use the post link to start a new discussion topic. If you're responding to someone else's message, use the Reply function on the message screen.

- Under Club Stats, you see how many members the club has, and how many page views the club has displayed to all members. (A questionably useful statistic.) It also gives the date the club was founded, for those of an historical bent. A daily log of the past few days shows how busy the club has been.

- The Contact section contains an e-mail link for contacting the club founders. The link displays a page with a text entry form for typing a message, and a Send Mail button. The e-mail is automatically addressed to the club founders — you don't need to look up an address.

- The Chat Room section displays how many members (if any) are currently logged on to the chat room. The enter link takes you there.

- The left-hand navigation bar has all the main club links. It provides the easiest way to access the message board, chat room, photo area, News page, and other standard features.

Notice the links under Member Tools. They give you a few more things to do:

- **Invite.** Click this link for a fill-in form that allows you to send a standard club invitation to any e-mail address.

- **Options.** Options are always good, but these particular options don't have much to do with your presence in the club. Clicking the Options link opens up the following possibilities: sending an e-mail to the club founders, editing the list of clubs you've joined, editing your Yahoo! Profile (see Chapter 1), or searching the database of Yahoo! Profiles (see Chapter 1 again).

✔ **Help.** Clicking the <u>Help</u> link delivers some pages of explanation about how everything works. Obviously, considering the immortal quality of the prose you're holding in your hand right now, you don't need the Help section.

✔ **Sign Out.** Talk about a negative Member Tool. Use this link when you want to quit your Yahoo! ID. Doing so launches you right out of the club, and you need to sign in again (which you can do from many locations in Yahoo!) before visiting any of your clubs as a member.

When you're navigating around a Yahoo! club, you don't need to use your Back button very much, if at all. That's because the main navigation sidebar is enclosed in an autonomous *frame*, and it doesn't change when you click a link. So, for example, you may travel from the Home page to the message board and then to the News page, all without using your Back button to get at the navigation links again. The links stay in place as you're surfing around.

Tacking up a message

The message board is where most club conversations take place. The most recent messages are linked to the main portion of the home page, or you can click the Messages link to see a complete list (see Figure 14-5). The Messages page is full of links. You may, of course, click any message link to see the message. Clicking the Member ID of the message's author pops open a new browser window with that person's Yahoo! Profile displayed.

The messages are displayed in chronological order, with most recent postings at the top. So as you cast your eye down the screen, you're looking back in time, seeing the discussions in reverse order. The messages are not threaded in an indented style as you might be accustomed to from a Usenet newsgroup reader or some other message boards on the Web. Still, you can follow the discussions pretty well by watching the message titles, because replies to messages keep the same title. Also, when viewing any message that has had replies posted to it, you may see those replies by clicking the <u>View Replies to this Message</u> link. (See Figure 14-6.) Create a reply yourself by clicking the <u>Reply</u> link. (I'm not sure you needed me to tell you that.)

Don't be fooled by the <u><-Previous</u> and <u>Next-></u> links. Those links refer to the previous and next messages *chronologically*, not necessarily the parent message and reply to the message you're reading. Usually, many conversations on several topics are transpiring on the message board simultaneously. Always use the <u>View Replies to this Message</u> link to follow a single discussion.

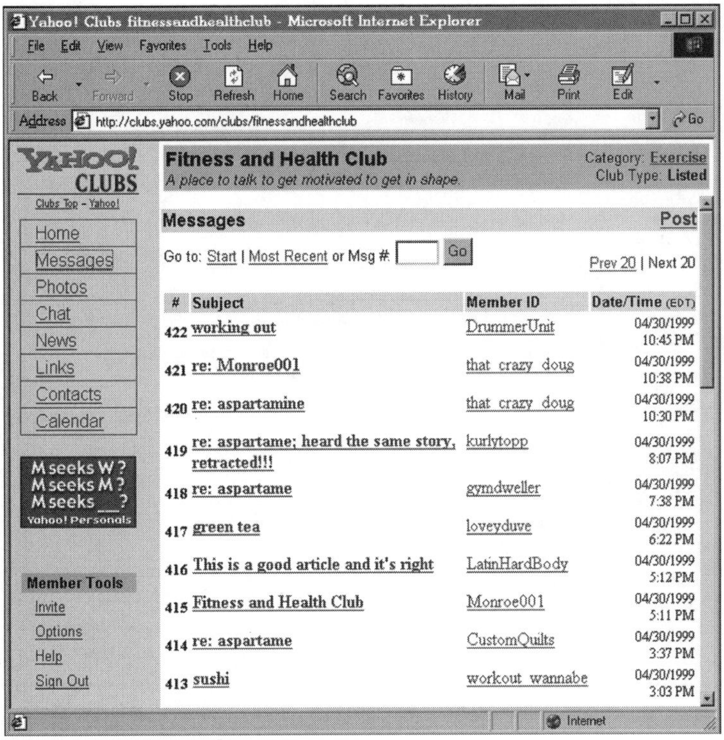

Figure 14-5:
The
Messages
page of a
Yahoo! club.
You can
rummage
for
messages
and view
member
profiles.

Showing yourself off

The Photos section really makes the clubs more personable by encouraging members to upload pictures of themselves or anything that relates to the club's topic of interest. Whether you upload a picture or not, you may browse the photos of other members:

1. **Click the Photos link in the left-hand navigation bar.**

   The Photo Album page is displayed.

2. **Click any of the photo album links.**

   The page for that album is displayed, with links to individual photos.

3. **Click any little camera icon or the name of the photo to see that photo (see Figure 14-7).**

   A new page appears, and in a second or two the photo will appear.

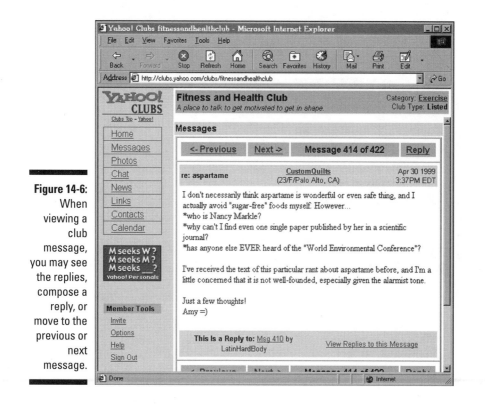

Figure 14-6:
When
viewing a
club
message,
you may see
the replies,
compose a
reply, or
move to the
previous or
next
message.

Members are entitled to create photo albums or upload individual photos into preexisting photo albums. You always have a Default Club Album to upload into. To contribute a picture, you must have one digitized and residing on your computer's hard drive. It helps (very much) to know where on the hard drive the picture is located. Given those requirements, here's what you do:

1. **Click the Add Photo button on any photo page.**

   If you're on the Photo Album page, there is no such button. Use the <u>Add Album</u> link to make a photo album, or click the album to which you'd like to upload your photo, and then click that Add Photo button.

2. **On the Adding a Photo page, click the Browse button to locate your photo.**

   The Browse button opens a file locator, which you can use to look for the picture in your hard drive files. Use the <u>on the web</u> link to use a picture stored somewhere on the Web. Note that linking to someone else's graphic without permission is considered unethical and could even be illegal.

3. **In the Name and Description fields, title your photo and type a short description.**

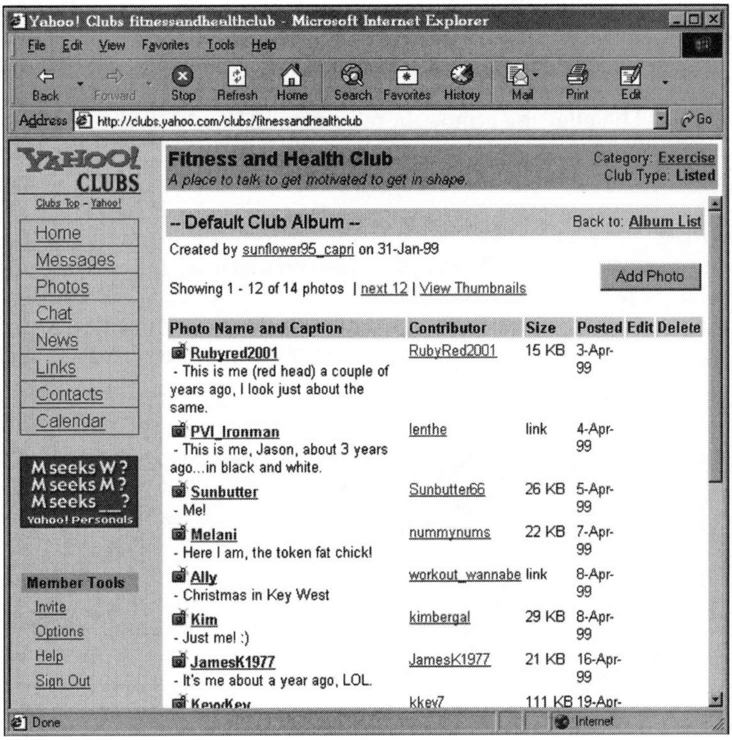

Figure 14-7:
A Yahoo!
club photo
collection.
Click a
camera icon
to see a
picture.

4. **Select whether you want your photo resized, and if so, by how much. Or click the Don't resize selection to leave your photo in its original dimensions.**

   Resizing is a bit tricky. If your photo is very big, you should resize it so that other members don't have their systems tied up by downloading a large graphics file. (Also, club Photo areas are limited in size, so everyone should stay small to make room for others.)

   Yahoo! clubs have three default photo sizes: Large, Medium, and Small. The large size is *very* large (640 pixels for your picture's largest dimension). Fellow members might get a bit upset if you use that size. I recommend Medium or Small. Keep in mind that club photos can't be enlarged, only reduced. So if your picture is already on the small side (no more than four inches wide or long), there's no point in resizing it. (Resizing affects your picture's reproduction in the club, not its size on your hard drive.)

5. **If you are resizing your picture, click the Preview button to see the result.**

6. **Click the Upload button to finish the process.**

Ch-ch-ch-chatting

Talking in real-time with other members is a distinct pleasure of club membership. The chatting atmosphere is usually less "noisy" and the screen is less cluttered than in the main Yahoo! Chat area. (See Chapter 11.) Furthermore, conversations tend to stay on topic better in a club.

In other respects, club chatting is similar to general Yahoo! chatting. If you've tried one, you're likely to get your bearings quickly in the other. The software for the two areas is the same. When you click the <u>Chat</u> link on the home page, your browser downloads the Java chat program (it doesn't take long). After it's in place, you can see who else is in the room and begin chatting (see Figure 14-8).

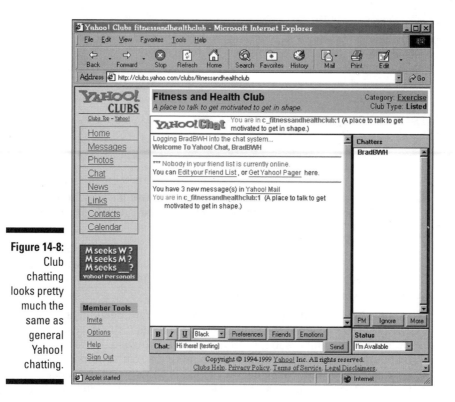

Figure 14-8:
Club
chatting
looks pretty
much the
same as
general
Yahoo!
chatting.

You might come to grips with the chatting interface (the room) fairly quickly through experimentation. Feel free to click buttons, type lines into the room, change the color of your text, send Personal Messages, and so on. If you'd like a detailed walk-through of the Yahoo! Chat program, please refer to Chapter 11, where I hold forth on the subject well into the night.

The Java chat download happens only once — then you can use it repeatedly. As long as you keep your browser open, you may hop in and out of clubs, chatting away, without suffering the delay of downloading the chat program over and over.

No news is bad news

If you click the <u>News</u> link to view the News page, you might notice that it looks similar to a My Yahoo! page. In fact, it is a My Yahoo! page — but in this case, it's a Founder's Yahoo! page because the club's founders have control over what appears on it. They have the same options that you do when you create your own personalized Yahoo! page (which I describe how to do in Chapter 2).

If the News page doesn't contain the content you'd like to see, I suggest writing to the club founders with a request.

Shared links

The Links page is for contributing Web links to sites related to the club topic. Any links you add should be of general club interest — as opposed, say, to your personal Web page (unless your site is relevant to the club).

Clicking any link on the Links page opens a new browser window to display the site, so you don't have to worry about losing your view of the Yahoo! club while you're surfing elsewhere. (Perhaps you weren't really chewing your fingernails over that prospect anyway.)

To add a link, follow these short and simple steps:

1. **On the Links page, click the <u>Add A Link</u> link.**

   The Add A Link page appears.

2. **Type the Web address of the site you're contributing.**

   Note that the *http://* portion of the address is already present, so just add the rest of the URL.

3. **Type a short comment about the site.**

   The comment will appear on the Links page next to the site link.

4. Click the Add Link button.

Your link contribution is added, and the Links page is again displayed. Notice that your link is now at the bottom of the list. (It's at the bottom because it's the most recent, not because it's inferior in any way.) Note also the Edit and Delete icons next to your link. Use the Edit icon if you've made a typing mistake and want to correct it. Use the Delete icon if the whole thing was a horrifying error and you want to remove all the evidence.

Making first contact

The Contacts page is where all the club's members are listed, starting with the founders and moving methodically (and alphabetically) through everyone else. Unfortunately, you can't search for members by Yahoo! ID — a much hoped-for feature for the future. (A future feature creature.) Each member link, if clicked, opens a new browser window with that person's Yahoo! Profile displayed.

You may change the comment associated with your listing (or add a comment if you didn't before) by clicking the Edit My Comments link. You might notice that the page doesn't allow much room for comments, so keep it very short or risk being cut off in mid-profundity.

Mark your calendar

The Calendar is a nifty part of the clubs. Click the Calendar link to see it. Each club founder decides how the calendar is displayed when you first link to it, but you can change it on your screen.

Calendars are used by the founders to schedule club events and mark dates of significance to club interests. However, *any* member can add an event to the calendar. You might think this would be chaotic, and it could be, but my observation is that most members stay away from controlling the calendar, perhaps because they don't realize how much control they have. If that's the case, I might be doing a disservice to club owners everywhere by spilling the beans, but here goes.

Look at Figure 14-9 to see the monthly view of a club calendar. A few dates are marked for club meetings. Note the Add links. Click one of those to add an event to that day. (You can also use the Add Event button to schedule an event for any day.) The calendar works similarly to the general Yahoo! Calendar, which I elucidate in Chapter 20. The main difference here is that you may send e-mail invitations to any event you place on the club calendar (see Figure 14-10). The invitation is a form letter sent to your addressees. The Address Book link connects you with your Yahoo! Address Book, which I describe in Chapter 3.

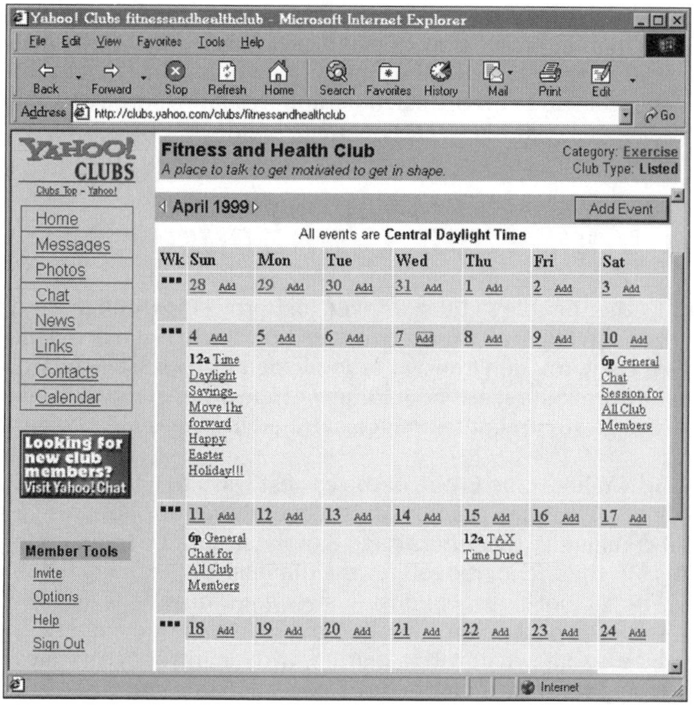

Figure 14-9:
Any club
member can
add events
to the
interactive
calendar.

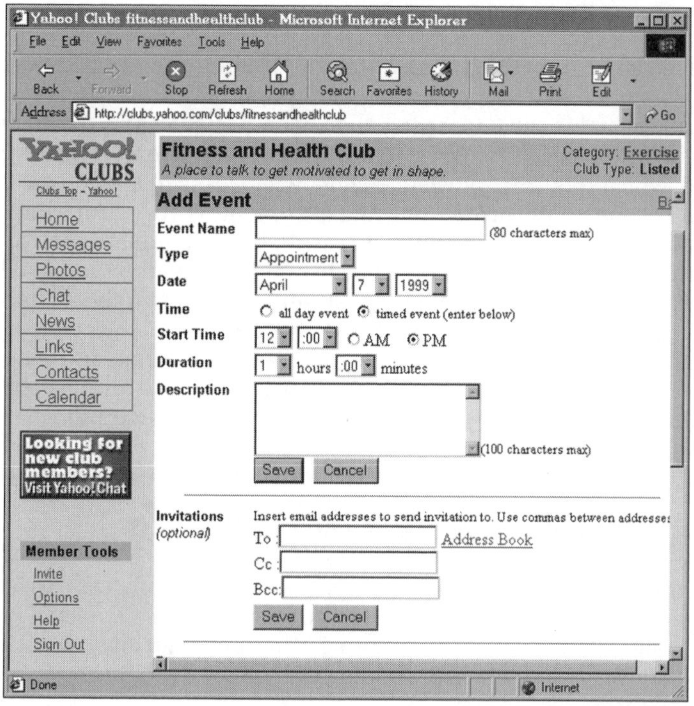

Figure 14-10:
The Add
Event page
provides
date and
time
settings,
plus an
invitation
form.

Be cautious in placing an event on the club calendar. Look through a few weeks or months to see how the club uses this feature. If the membership enjoys celebrating individual birthdays and other personal events, add away along those lines. But if the calendar adheres more strictly to club event scheduling, it's best not to add personal holidays.

Building Your Own Clubhouse

Visiting other people's clubs, or even just browsing through the Yahoo! Clubs directory, can inspire a desire to create your own. Not a problem — Yahoo! makes it easy. You don't design or implement the message board, chat room, uploading procedure, calendar, or any of the other standard club features. Those things are prebuilt and incorporated in your club automatically.

Creating a Yahoo! club is one of the easiest ways to have your own Web site. You get less flexibility than building a cyberhome at GeoCities or some other virtual community that offers page templates and the freedom to add your own HTML code. The tradeoff for the diminished flexibility is the enhanced ease. With Yahoo! clubs, you just answer a few questions and you're in business — your club is online, live, and ready to accept members. You may customize it somewhat, with a picture, with an introductory message, by determining what goes on the News page, and in some other small ways. But basically, Yahoo! clubs are like housing developments — each structure looks pretty much the same.

Let me clarify something in case you're scratching your head over the *HTML code* I mentioned in the preceding paragraph. HTML is HyperText Markup Language, and is the underlying code of all Web pages. You can create a Web page in four basic ways. The most difficult is to write the HTML code by hand, which requires knowledge and a willingness to stay up most of the night correcting mistakes. You can also use an HTML editor, which facilitates the coding process. Next, you may use an online template such as the ones provided by GeoCities and other page-building communities. Finally, and easiest of all, is to plug yourself into a prefab site such as Yahoo! clubs.

This section gets you started with your own Yahoo! club and walks you through the various options at your disposal. I also throw in a few tips about making the club a happy place and promoting it outside Yahoo!.

Starting a simple club quickly

I want to emphasize that starting a Yahoo! club is really easy. Really. Easy. You do have some ways to fancy up the process, but Yahoo! doesn't insist on them, and offers a laser-fast path to getting a club up and live quickly. You can get a very basic club functioning right away by following these steps:

1. **Go to the main Yahoo! Clubs directory at the following URL:**

   `clubs.yahoo.com`

2. **Click the <u>Create a club</u> link.**

   The Create a Club page appears.

3. **Select a subcategory, or select a main category and then a subcategory.**

   This is where you decide where in the directory your club will be listed. You must, in the end, select a subcategory for your club, not a main category. For example, if your club is about music, it's not sufficient to select Entertainment & Arts as your category; you must further select Music as your subcategory.

4. **On the next page, confirm your subcategory and the Yahoo! ID you'd like to use (if you have more than one ID), and then click the Click Here to Continue button.**

   You may use your default `yahoo.com` e-mail address for the ID you're using as the club's founder, or you may use the e-mail address you submitted when creating your Yahoo! ID. If you decide to use your other (non-Yahoo!) e-mail address, click the <u>Change</u> link on this page. Whichever address you select is used to receive e-mail from club members. A link to that address is displayed prominently on the club's main page, so you might get a lot of mail if your club becomes popular.

5. **On the next page, name your club and select whether you want the club listed or unlisted in the Yahoo! Clubs directory.**

   Naming the club is important. Think of a title that conveys the gist of your topic concisely. At the same time, get imaginative. I've noticed that some of the most successful clubs have intriguing names that almost force the casual browser to investigate. (See Chapter 26 for some ideas.) Whether you choose a cryptic title or a plainly descriptive one, keep it short.

   As far as the listing is concerned, most clubs are listed. Usually, you would have no reason to avoid a listing. However, if you're setting up a family club, a work-related club, or any club whose members will all be personally invited to join, select Unlisted.

   You may also enter the geographic location of the club, which would probably be your residence. Unless your club's topic is related to its geographical location, there's not much point in filling it in.

6. **On the same page as Step 5, review the Terms of Service agreement by clicking the <u>Yahoo! Clubs Terms of Service</u> link, and then click the Yes! I accept button.**

   See the "What you're agreeing to" sidebar for a brief, plain-talk summary of the Terms of Service. After you click the acceptance button, your club is created.

The next page gives you a link to the new club, and a link for setting more club options. The club is in the Yahoo! Clubs directory at this point, and you can start inviting friends to join it, using the <u>Invite friends</u> link. (You may access the same invitation page at any time using the link under Member Tools, as described previously in this chapter.)

You need a Yahoo! ID to create a club, or even to participate in them. If you don't currently have one, please perform 74 penitential push-ups. Then go to Chapter 1 where I explain how to create a Yahoo! ID. It's easy.

Customizing your club

Yahoo! clubs all look pretty much the same (which is an advantage when you're club-hopping), but you can do a few things to make yours unique. After you've created the basic club (following the steps in the preceding section), click the <u>Fix it up</u> link to customize your club. The Adjust Club Settings page gives you the following options:

- ✔ **Describe Your Club.** You get only eight words, so make the most of them.

- ✔ **Founder's Message.** This message, usually a few sentences long, appears on the main club page. Use it to expound on the brief club description, or say a few words about yourself, or set up a chat schedule.

- ✔ **Your Home Page Address.** You can fill this in if you have a Web page or site. You don't need to divulge your URL, though. Some people supplement a Web page at another location by using a Yahoo! club because it adds built-in messaging, chat, and calendar features. You might decide to link to your Web page even if it's unrelated to the topic of your club — the option is yours.

- ✔ **Picture URL.** This is where you may place the Web location of a picture, which will appear on the main club page. It's just about the only way you can give your club page a distinctive graphics appearance, but — like the other customization options — it isn't required. You may use a photo of yourself or any graphic you think will enliven your club's subject.

- ✔ **Listed or Unlisted.** By this point, you have already chosen whether to list your club in the Yahoo! Clubs directory or leave it out. This option gives you a chance to reverse your decision.

Note that if you make your club unlisted at this point, you will not be able to list it again in the Yahoo! Clubs directory.

What you're agreeing to

When you create a Yahoo! club, you must click an on-screen button that states your agreement with a Terms of Service document. Every online service has such a document, which protects the service in certain rare confrontations with its members and covers the legal bases. Most people, in their eagerness to start using whatever service is lurking beyond the agreement, blow through the document with barely a glance. There's nothing wrong with that in almost all cases. But just in case you're interested, here's a summary of what you agree to when you create a Yahoo! club.

First, you have to be more than 13 years old to make a club. Furthermore, every other bit of information you submit about yourself has to be true. (In a realm where anonymity and aliases rule, being honest about one's identity is a severe challenge for some people.)

You can't create a hateful club. That means you can't promote anything unlawful, racist, libelous, or infringing on copyright. Yahoo! will indeed pull the plug on any such club. However, I should note that sex-oriented clubs are allowed and represented in the Yahoo! Clubs directory. Part of the Terms of Service acknowledges the adult area and defines it as out of bounds for minors.

You agree to place your club in an appropriate section and not to whine if Yahoo! moves it to another category.

Yahoo! *again* hammers home the fact that some clubs are inappropriate for minors, and admonishes kids to check with their parents before joining any club. If you're creating an adult club, you agree to set an age requirement for membership.

Yahoo! stipulates that the founders of clubs rule their domains, within the broad confines of the Terms of Service. If you want to rule, be a founder, but don't hassle other founders.

One paragraph asserts that while Yahoo! clubs are currently a free service, Yahoo! reserves the right to charge in the future. This doesn't seem likely to me, and even if fees were established, Yahoo! couldn't charge you without your permission.

In the section about uploading photos, Yahoo! *once again* reminds you that some material is bad for minors. (Get the point?) Another point: You must own the rights to any photo you upload. Don't just take one from somewhere on the Web, unless it's from a public domain collection.

Yahoo! spends a few impenetrable paragraphs explaining its privacy policy. The upshot is that, although you supply some personal information to Yahoo! when you create an ID (which you need to create a club), Yahoo! does not divulge that information to other companies or marketers. The only exceptions are when Yahoo! must comply with legal processes.

That's the gist of the Terms of Service, but if you want a really good time, grab some pretzels and read the whole thing in all its legal glory.

The trickiest option is placing a picture on your club page. Keep three points in mind:

✔ You cannot upload the picture to Yahoo!. To the contrary, you point club visitors to your graphic. You must know the URL of the graphic, and when you enter it, Yahoo! automatically creates the code that displays the graphic on your club page.

✔ The process works with the two most common graphic file formats — GIF and JPEG (sometimes called JPG) — but no others. Make sure your picture is in one of those formats before entering the URL. You know the format is correct if the very final portion of the URL is `.gif` or `.jpg`.

✔ The space for the picture on your club page is rather small, to put it generously. Specifically, the picture gets squeezed to a size of 150 pixels high and 150 pixels wide. The closer to that size your picture is, the better it will look. Pictures that exceed one or both of those dimensions will get distorted when they appear on a club page.

After you set all the options you choose to adjust, click the Submit Changes button.

Using the Administrative Tools

As founder of a Yahoo! club, you have awesome power. Perhaps *awesome* is something of an overstatement. At any rate, you have some control over your membership and the settings for club options. This control is located in a series of links called Admin Tools, located in the left-hand sidebar of any club you founded. (Non-founding members can't see the Admin Tools links.)

As a club founder, you can perform four main control tasks:

✔ Remove a member or make him or her a founder

✔ Send e-mail to members

✔ Edit the settings for your club page

✔ Change the settings of your club's calendar

Editing members

The Edit Members page displays a list of your club's founder(s) and members, and provides two actions you can perform on them. Clicking the <u>Delete</u> link removes a member from the club, never to return. Clicking the <u>Make Founder</u> link turns a regular member into a founding member and gives that person access to the Admin Tools.

Think twice before exercising your stunning power to delete a member or make someone a founder. Kicking someone out of your club is permanent, and that Yahoo! ID will never be able to join again. It's stiff punishment, and should probably be used only in cases of severe disruption, such as posting obscene material to your club or harassing other members. Conversely, turning someone into a founder makes that person invulnerable to deletion, so make wise choices. This option is mostly used when a group decides to open a club together — one person creates the club, the others join, and the first person makes them all founders right away.

Sending e-mail

Clicking the Send Email link displays the Send Email to the Club page, where you can contact all your members at once. This is a great feature but should not be overused. If your members start complaining to Yahoo! that you're contacting them too much, your club might get nuked.

This page is easy to use and doesn't require keeping an address book. Just type your e-mail message into the form and click the Send Mail button.

This feature should be used (in moderation) to notify your members of scheduled club events, for periodic updates of your personal news, or to inform your membership of developments in the subject of your club. For example, members of a club about Web animation might be interested to know about a new animated cartoon site. But you can also use the message board for such announcements, and that's probably what your members would prefer.

How much mail is too much mail? Forget about daily circulars to your members — that's way too much in most cases. A weekly bulletin is borderline acceptable to most people. Less frequent communications are acceptable. Remember that your members can't opt in and out of your mailing list. All members are automatically on the list and receive everything you send from the Send Email to the Club page.

One idea that makes greater use of the Send Email administrative tool is to create a club expressly for the purpose of generating a mailing list. For example, you might write a weekly Cool Site tip and desire to distribute it to people by means of an e-mail list. You could create a Weekly Cool Site club, and make it clear that members will receive an e-mail every week. In this case, the message board and chat room are less important features than receiving the weekly e-mail, though of course they can still be used. This idea is a quick, easy, and free way to build a mailing list.

Editing settings

The Edit Settings link provides a continuous opportunity to alter the basic settings you might have adjusted when you created the club. If you didn't set these options at that time, or if you did and you want to change them, it's not a problem. Use the input forms on this page to describe the club in eight words or less, write a brief Founder's message, list your Web page address if you have one, link the club's main page to a picture URL, and de-list your club from the Yahoo! Clubs directory.

Proceed cautiously if you're considering removing your club from the directory. After you Unlist it, you can never list it again. (Another one of those irrevocable decisions so commonplace in life.)

Calendar options

The Calendar page is where you, as a founder, can alter the default settings of the club's interactive calendar. Using the drop-down menus and radio buttons (see Figure 14-11), select the following options:

- ✓ **Default View.** This is where you decide if your calendar will automatically display one week, a month, a day, or a year at a time.

- ✓ **Default Day View.** Your choices here are List and Graphical, referring to how the calendar page is laid out. I prefer Graphical, but try them both and see which looks best to you.

- ✓ **Time Zone.** Select your local time zone from the drop-down menu of global time zones.

- ✓ **Daylight Savings Time.** For most of the United States, it's best to set this option to Automatic. Everyone else should select On or Off.

- ✓ **Working Hours.** This option sets at what hour each calendar day begins and ends.

When you're finished with the settings, click the Save button to see your new calendar. Remember, you can alter these settings at any time.

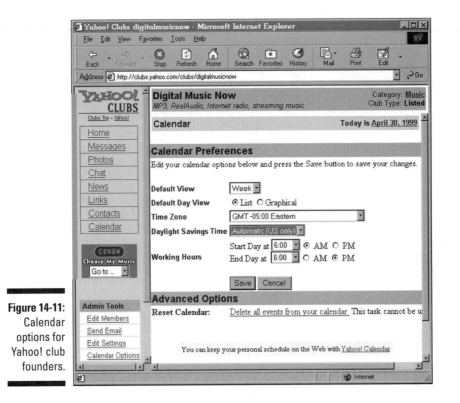

Figure 14-11:
Calendar options for Yahoo! club founders.

Chapter 15

The Great People Quest

The Internet might seem like a galaxy of colorful Web pages (billboard heaven?) but actually it's all about people. What started out as the information highway has a more personal destiny than merely feeding data faster and more overwhelmingly than ever before. Ultimately, the Net will fulfill its potential only if it brings people closer together. It is already stepping into that destiny in a few ways.

E-mail, for all its seeming impersonality, is actually the servant of closer relationships. And I know from personal experience that e-mail has the power to bridge the chasms of time, geography, and neglect. Have you ever thought of tracking down an old friend through e-mail? This chapter explains Yahoo!'s contribution to that goal.

Personal ads also thrive on the Internet. This fact might make the Web seem like nothing more than a digitized meat market. But the truth is that information databasing, when applied to the problem of human loneliness, can improve the human condition. (Didn't think we'd get quite this deep in a *...For Dummies* book, did you? Keep your head — my musings are bound to end soon.) Yahoo! Personals opens up one of the most popular meeting places for people looking for companionship of all sorts. We go there, too, in this chapter. Keep reading to see how your Yahoo! account helps you find old friends and make new ones.

Finding an E-mail Address

To find regular folks, look in the phone book; to find a business, look in the Yellow Pages. To find an e-mail address, what can you do? The Web has several e-mail directories, and one of them is in Yahoo!.

Keeping an e-mail directory is a thorny challenge for a few reasons. First, people increasingly have multiple addresses. Office e-mail, home e-mail, Web-based e-mail. Whereas in the early days of the Internet a single e-mail address defined a person's virtual location — like a street address in the offline world — the contemporary online scene doesn't have a single, irrefutable identifier. People are spread among many addresses.

The second reason e-mail directories are problematic is that even though many people might have a main address, it is liable to be changed fairly often. Every time your long-lost high-school buddy switches Internet providers, the e-mail address changes. Directories try to keep up, but not one of them provides a really stellar, reliable service.

Yahoo! People Search offers e-mail address searching, but from a different angle. The idea is not to attempt a database of all current e-mail addresses. Instead, the service is a registry of information about people who *want to be found*. This idea was originated by a company called Four11, and Yahoo! liked it enough to buy Four11 and recast it as Yahoo! People Search. This directory finds *only* those people who have registered a free listing in the directory. As such, it is not a worthy general-purpose e-mail white pages. People Search is designed to help people find old friends, and invites everyone to include a bit of personal history to help past acquaintances locate them.

 If you've been on the Internet for a while, you might have registered with the old Four11. If you did so before September 1, 1998 — surprise! Your listing no longer exists. Follow the directions in the following section for creating a new listing.

To begin searching for e-mail addresses, click the <u>People Search</u> link on the Yahoo! home page, or go directly to

```
people.yahoo.com
```

Figure 15-1 illustrates the People Search page. Follow these steps:

Figure 15-1:
The People
Search
page, from
which you
can find
e-mail
addresses
and phone
numbers.

1. **On the Yahoo! People Search page, under the Email Search banner, fill in the Name fields.**

   All fields are optional, but the more you know, the easier it is to find someone. Entering only a first name is likely to overwhelm you with results. First and last names combined make things easier. The Domain field is for entering the part of an e-mail address after the @ symbol. America Online members, for example, have aol.com domains. If you know the domain name, typing it narrows your search in a hurry. The Reset button clears all three fields of any text.

2. **Click the Search button.**

   The Email Basic Search Results page appears (see Figure 15-2).

3. **Click any link in the Name column or Email column.**

   Email links open up a window of your default e-mail program, ready to send a note to the selected address. Name links provide as much information about that person as he or she provided to the database (see Figure 15-3).

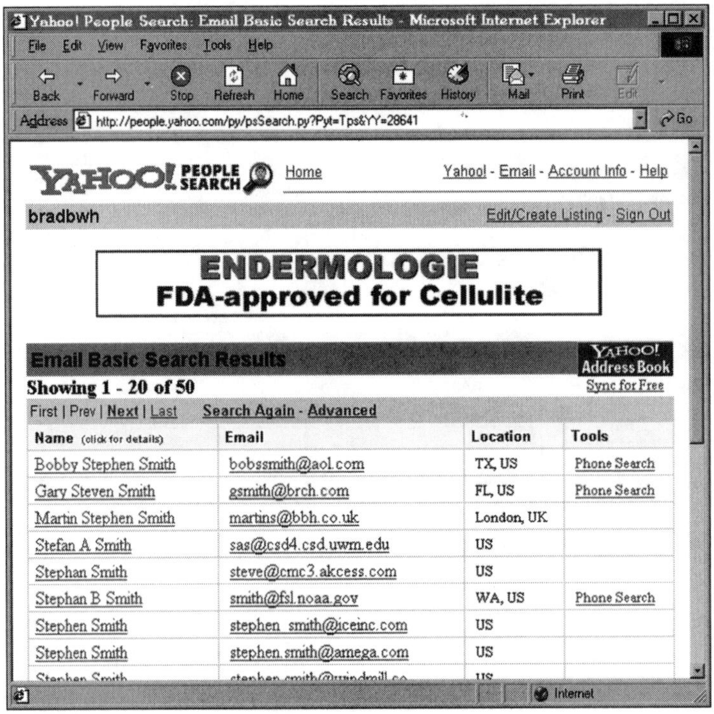

Figure 15-2:
Results of
an e-mail
search.

If you're simply looking for an e-mail address, you can end your search on the Email Basic Search Results page. But if you click a name link to proceed to a person's information page (Figure 15-3), a few conveniences await you:

- Click the Address Book link to add the e-mail address to your Yahoo! Address Book (see Chapter 3 to learn all about Yahoo! Mail).

- Click the Phone Search link (if one exists for the person you've found) in hope of finding your person's phone number. However, the search engine isn't the sharpest knife in the drawer when it comes to this particular function. It gathers the name and state information, disregarding a more detailed address if present, and delivers more phone-number search results than you want. Aren't computers supposed to make things more convenient? Oh well. Try calling directory assistance.

- Click vCard if you have an e-mail program that supports the vCard format. That's about as helpful as mud, right? Here's the story — vCards are just a format for storing address book information. Outlook Express, Netscape Messenger, and other mail programs accept vCard entries, though they use different systems for getting a vCard entry into their address books. Look at your Help files or program documentation for information about vCards. Clicking the vCard link initiates a download of a person's address book information.

✔ The <u>Yellow Pages</u> and <u>Show Map</u> links help you locate the address of your found person — if an address is listed. See Chapter 20 for more about these Yahoo! services. (But feel free to try these links now.)

A somewhat more advanced form of e-mail searching lurks on the other side of the <u>Advanced</u> link on the People Search page. The Advanced Email Search page (see Figure 15-4) invites you to ask for matches to specific aspects of the People Search directory, including an old e-mail address (very handy) and an organization name.

The results of an advanced search depend very much on just how divulging your target person was when registering at People Search or the old Four11. But it's worth a try. Fill in as many of the fields as you can, and then click the Search button full of hope.

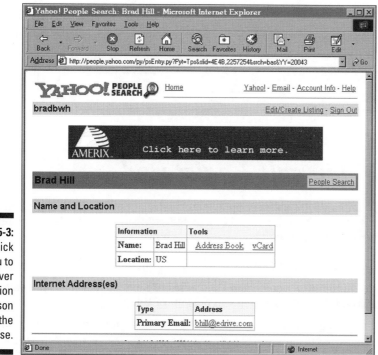

Figure 15-3: One click leads you to whatever information a person added to the database.

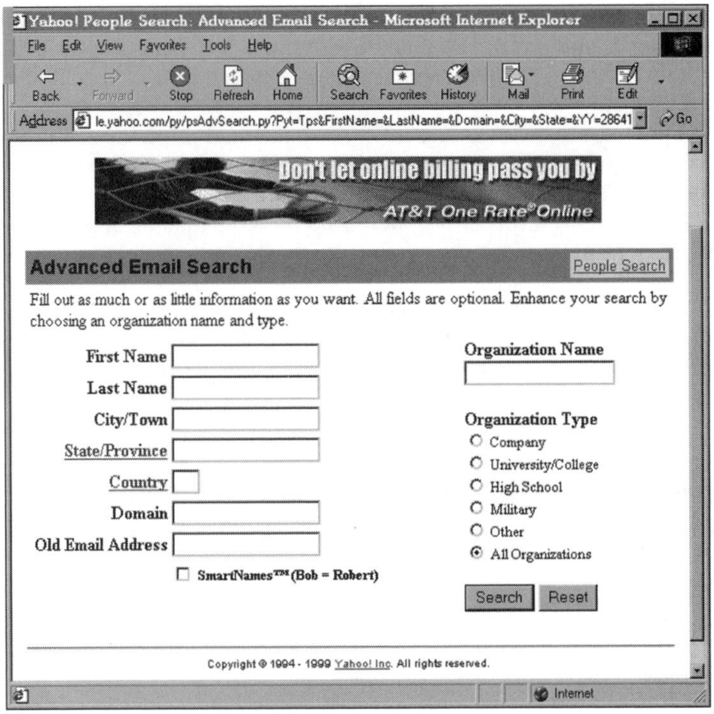

Figure 15-4:
The
Advanced
Email
Search
page.

Getting Yourself Registered

As long as you're using People Search, why not participate in both directions? That is to say, instead of just searching in the database, register yourself so people can find *you*. Here's how:

1. **On the Yahoo! People Search page, click the <u>Edit/Create Listing</u> link.**

2. **On the next page, read the Terms of Service Agreements, and click the I Accept button at the bottom of the page.**

   This agreement is a standard legal morass in which you promise to provide accurate information and absolve Yahoo! of any legal responsibility should you be harmed through the use of People Search. (Like if your keyboard starts biting back at your hands, or if the old college friend you track down makes you pay up, with interest, that 100 dollars you've owed him for 20 years.) One important agreement is that you won't duplicate the listings, or use them for any commercial purposes, such as bulk e-mailings.

3. **On the Create your Yahoo! People Search Listing (could they have thought of a longer page name?), fill in your name and any other info you want to add to the searchable database (see Figure 15-5).**

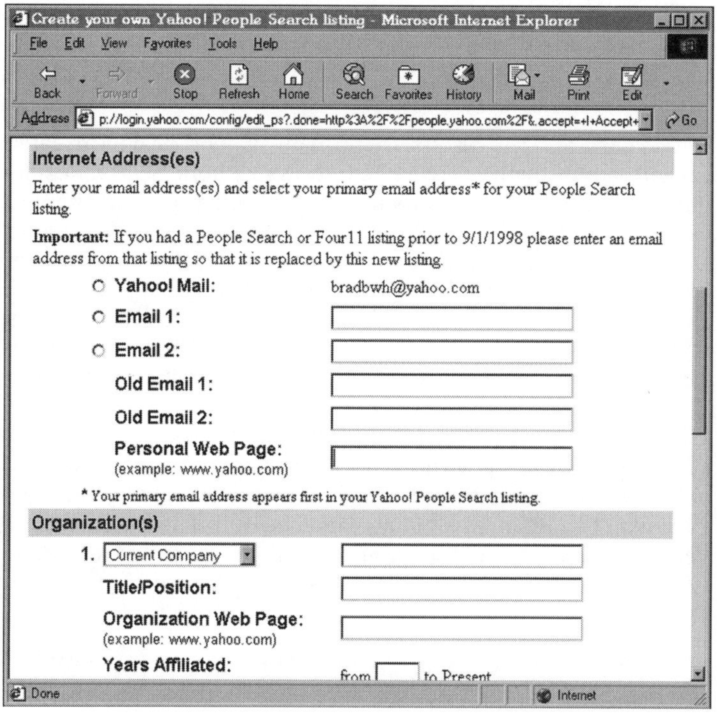

Figure 15-5:
A portion of
the page on
which you
create your
listing in
People
Search.

Text-entry fields are optional, but the more information you plug in, the
easier it is for people to find you. Under the Internet Address(es) banner,
remember that it's not enough to simply fill in addresses — you must
also click the radio button next to any address you want added to the
directory. Filling out the High School and University sections — under
the Organization(s) banner — helps old friends track you down.
Whether that thought inspires you to add the information or leave it out
is up to you.

4. **Click the Finished button at the bottom of the page.**

Looking Up a Phone Number

Yahoo! has a nationwide (United States only) white pages for looking up phone
numbers. This service is separate from the e-mail search, even though you initiate both from the same page. No registration is required — Yahoo! gets its
database information from the phone companies. Here's how to find a number:

1. **On the Yahoo! People Search page, scroll down to the Telephone
   Search area, and enter a name in the Last Name field.**

The Last Name field is the only required field, but the more information you can provide in the other fields, the better.

2. **Click the Search button.**

That was easy, and the results are probably a good deal more satisfying than in the Email Search section. Figure 15-6 shows a Phone Search Results page. You might be wondering what happens when you click a phone-number link. You get a download page for Net2Phone, a free software product that lets you make phone calls over your computer. (The calls aren't free, but the software is.) If you have a Windows computer with speakers and a microphone, you might want to investigate Net2Phone. The download is a no-risk, no-obligation affair, and you can test out the on-screen phone by making real calls to toll-free 800 numbers before opening an account to make toll calls with the program.

The other links on the Phone Search Results page should look familiar — they display a map, show the Yellow Pages section, or throw you into an e-mail search for the selected name. (Chances are very good that the selected person won't show up at all in an e-mail search. The Phone Search section covers everyone with a listed number, but the Email Search section covers only those who have deliberately registered with Yahoo! People Search.)

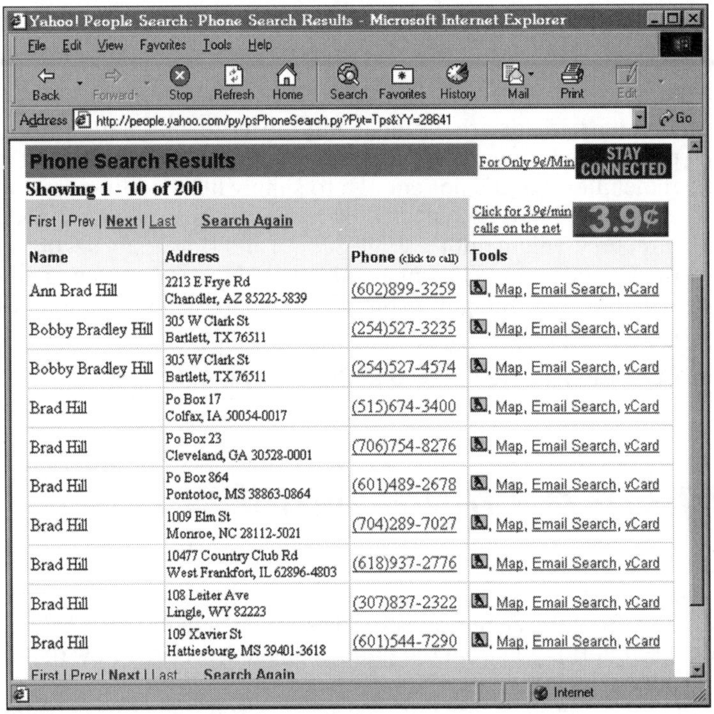

Figure 15-6:
The Phone
Search
Results
page. None
of these
Brad Hills
is I.

Getting Personal

All well and good, but searching for love is the thing. Yahoo! runs one of the most popular personal classified services on the Web. The classified service is only moderately sophisticated, but it has two great advantages over slick competing online personals sites. First, it's free. Putting up an ad, browsing, contacting someone — it's all free of charge. Second, it's fast. You can cover a lot of ground in your search for Mr. or Ms. Right without spending all night at it. After all, what you *really* want to spend all night doing is getting to know someone, not searching for his or her e-mail address. Yahoo! lubricates the process (so to speak).

Yahoo! Personals is part of Yahoo! Classifieds, which I dutifully explore in Chapter 23. I've separated the Personals section because personal ads are all about meeting people, whereas the other categories in Yahoo! Classifieds are about selling things.

Browsing personal ads

Here's how to get started browsing Yahoo! Personals:

1. **Click the <u>Personals</u> link on the Yahoo! home page (see Figure 15-7), or go directly to the following URL:**

   ```
   personals.yahoo.com
   ```

2. **Under the Welcome to Yahoo! Personals banner, click the metro area closest to your residence (or to the region where you want to browse).**

   You can also use the drop-down menu beneath the metro links to browse by state (United States only). International browsing isn't available.

3. **On the next page (see Figure 15-8), under the Browse By Type of Relationship banner, choose a relationship type and click the gender-preference code that appeals to you.**

   M is for Men and W is for Women, so the links under each relationship are cryptic but decipherable. <u>M4W</u> means Men looking for Women. <u>W4M</u> means Women looking for Men. M4M and W4W are same-gender ads. I don't know if anyone has ever clicked the <u>All</u> link, except perhaps androgynous folks with very broad tastes. However, for the purpose of unbiased illustration, I'm clicking it in this example.

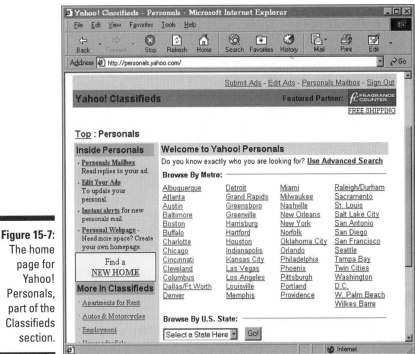

Figure 15-7:
The home page for Yahoo! Personals, part of the Classifieds section.

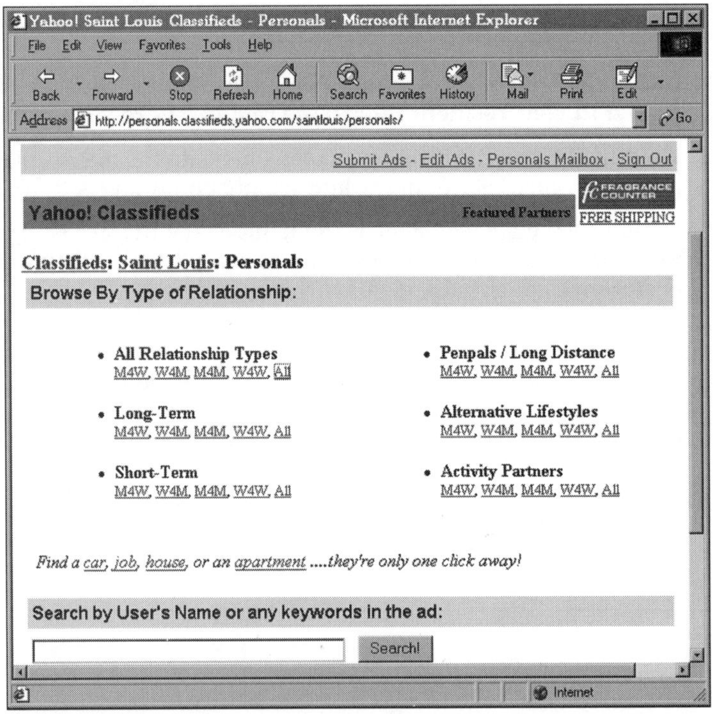

Figure 15-8:
This page is where you choose the relationship type and gender you're looking for.

4. **On the Search Results page, begin reading ads or consider searching with keywords.**

   Figure 15-9 shows the page containing personal ads (10 to a page), plus the search fields in the left-hand sidebar. The search options exist on every page of ads, and I describe how to use them in the next section.

As you can see from Figure 15-9, each personal ad consists of three parts:

✔ A header, which includes the relationship type being sought, the advertiser's age, ethnicity, religion, education, and employment status, and a profile of body type, height, and a few other tidbits. Some of these informational nuggets are provided at the discretion of the advertiser, so they aren't all present in every ad.

✔ A description makes up the body of the notice.

✔ Contact information is presented at the bottom. The Contact link is the advertiser's Yahoo! ID — click it to see the person's Yahoo! Profile. Use the <u>Reply to Ad</u> link for an e-mail form automatically addressed to the advertiser (see Figure 15-10).

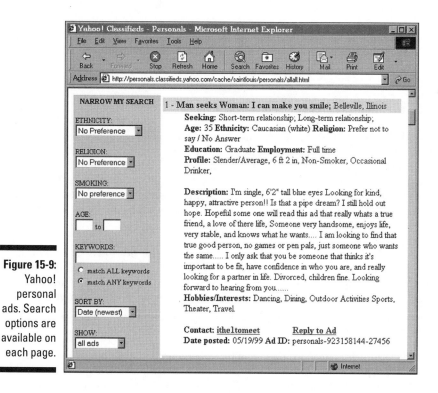

Figure 15-9: Yahoo! personal ads. Search options are available on each page.

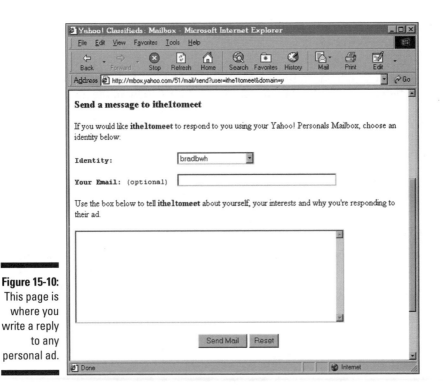

Getting picky

Use the NARROW MY SEARCH sidebar options to weed out elements you don't want to see in a classified ad. You can't determine in advance whether a new romantic interest will criticize your haircut. (Life is dangerous.) But you can force the search engine to find ads from people of a particular ethnicity, religious inclination, and age. You can eliminate smokers or non-smokers. You can sort the messages by date or age of the advertiser. And you can filter out older ads, which is usually a good idea.

The KEYWORDS field searches not only the Description body of the ad but the Yahoo! ID as well. Use the radio buttons to determine whether the search engine should find all your words or be satisfied with matches to just one word. Entering more than one word does not clue the engine that you're thinking of a phrase, however. If you want to match a phrase, put quotation marks around it.

If the standard search options aren't delivering your soulmate to the front door, you can try the Advanced Search page (see Figure 15-11). Although the Advanced Search page has an impressive layout (the figure shows only part of the page), it adds only a few features to the standard search options. For example, you can distinguish between drinkers and non-drinkers, and people of different body types.

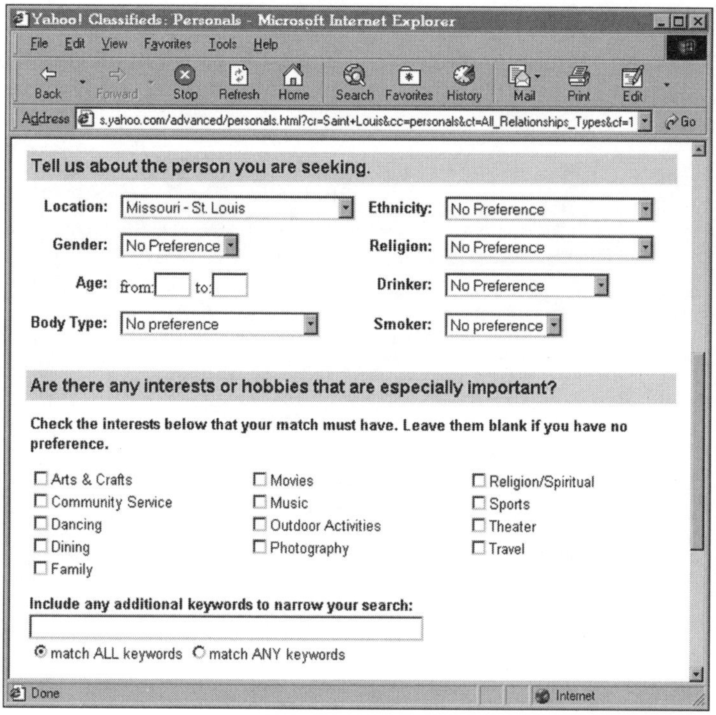

Figure 15-11:
Use
Advanced
Search to
match up
with a
person's
hobbies.

In addition to everything found in the left-hand sidebar of each search page, you can now match up with hobbies as listed in the ads. You can't write in your own hobbies, though — sad news for those who collect dried fiddle-heads. Use the check boxes next to the preset hobbies, and check as many of them as you want. The hobbies are so broad, most list nearly all of them in their ads.

Yahoo! Personals sets up a special Personals Mailbox for you, distinct from your Yahoo! Mail account. Personals mail is *not* mixed in with your regular Yahoo! mail, unless you give someone your Yahoo! Mail address.

Placing a personal ad

Browsing, writing responses to ads, hoping for replies — all is well and good, but you can cut to the chase with a more assertive approach. Consider placing your own Yahoo! personal. Here's how:

1. On the Yahoo! Personals home page, click the <u>Submit Ads</u> link.

The link takes you to the general submission page for Yahoo! Classifieds.

2. **Click the <u>Personals</u> link.**

3. **On the submission page (see Figure 15-12), fill in all required informa-tion fields, plus whatever optional information you want to share.**

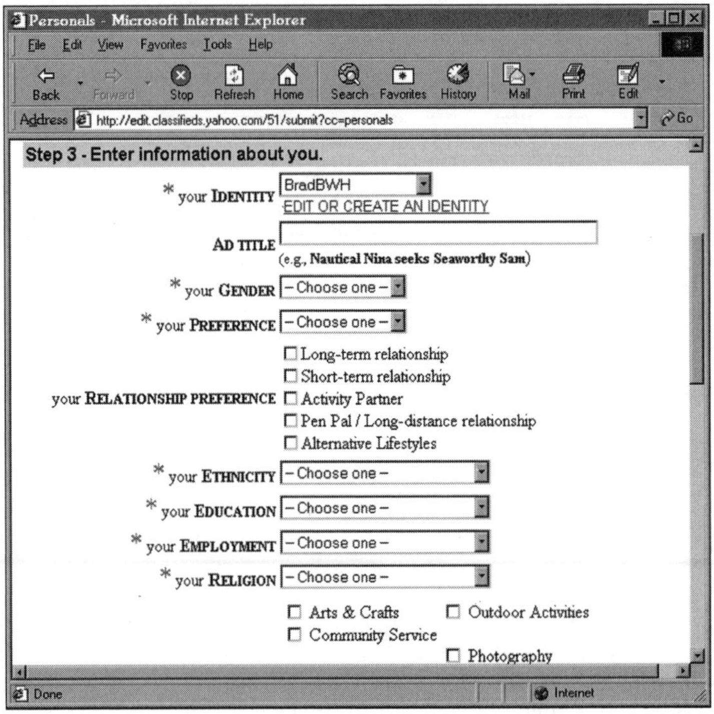

Figure 15-12:
Fill in all the required fields to place an ad.

4. **In the large text field (scroll down to see it), write your message.**

5. **Click the Submit entry button near the bottom of the page.**

   Your ad is automatically positioned in the geographical directory that best matches your zip code.

Responses to your personal ads go directly and automatically to your Personals Mailbox. They are not mixed with your Yahoo! Mail. Some people set up a separate Yahoo! ID for Personals communications, to assure that all Personals correspondence remains separate from other letters. Your Personals Mailbox is accessed in a few different ways, including from My Yahoo! (if you choose the link to appear there) and from Yahoo! Messenger. You may also click the <u>Personals Mailbox</u> link on the Yahoo! Personals home page (refer to Figure 15-7). Of course, at any time, you can shift a correspon-dence from your Personals Mailbox to another address by giving someone another of your e-mail addresses.

Part V

At Your Service, Yahoo! Style

The 5th Wave   By Rich Tennant

"Children— it is not necessary to whisper while we're visiting the Vatican Library Web site."

In this part...

This part explores the bridge between Yahoo! and the physical world. Yahoo! builds that bridge with services such as helping you plan trips and make travel reservations, play interactive games online, publish your resume, and shop for a new car. This part unlocks your understanding of Yahoo! services.

Chapter 16

Non-Computer Destinations

● ●

In This Chapter

▶ Imagining future travel destinations with Yahoo!'s help

▶ Planning a trip and booking tickets

● ●

*Y*ahoo! Travel is a double-faceted travel site, incorporating destination info with reservation and ticketing services. As such, it's appealing to armchair travelers and also useful for determined ticket-buyers. The destination content is wonderfully literate and interesting — great text, minimal pictures. The ticket-reservation service operates much like others on the Web, finding the least expensive options automatically and enabling online purchases of plane tickets, hotel reservations, and rental-car reservations.

Get to the right portion of Yahoo! by clicking the <u>Travel Agent</u> link on the home page or by entering this URL in your browser:

```
travel.yahoo.com
```

The Yahoo! Travel home page (see Figure 16-1) links to both the destination content and the reservation service. This chapter explains the high points of each.

Armchair Traveling

I don't know about you, but I like reading about foreign places and imagining I'm visiting them. (I try not to imagine cramped train seats, unpalatable food, vexing language problems, and bewildering currency exchanges, though.) Yahoo! Travel features great travel writing, especially when it comes to the history and culture of a place, and also preparatory information for soon-to-be travelers. Following is the best way to dive into this part of Yahoo! Travel:

1. **On the Yahoo! Travel home page, click any <u>By Destination:</u> link.**

   Don't be fooled by the search form above the links — it leads only to Yahoo! directory pages, not to travel destination pages. You could search on the keyword *computer*, but that's not what you came to Yahoo! Travel to accomplish.

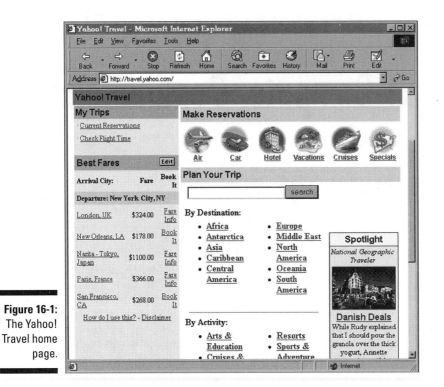

Figure 16-1:
The Yahoo!
Travel home
page.

2. On the next page, click any <u>Featured Countries</u> link.

Not many countries are left off these lists; the destination section is grat-ifyingly complete. You may also use the map in the left sidebar. Click on the map to display a larger version, which is interactive. On the larger map, click any country to proceed.

3. On the country destination page (see Figure 16-2), begin your explo-ration of that country's cities, weather, attractions, and culture.

The country destination page is an information hub that you might want to bookmark if you're involved with ongoing research into a destination. Most country pages include the following sections:

✔ **Destination Pages.** Some countries feature pages dedicated to cities or regions. Each of those pages presents information for travelers about dining, transportation, nightlife, local attractions, and other points of interest. Usually, a featured article from National Geographic Traveler or Kroll Travel Watch help convey the flavor of a destination.

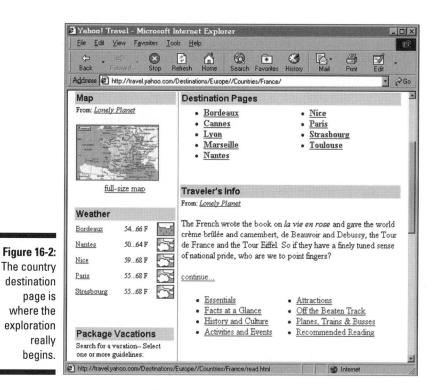

Figure 16-2:
The country destination page is where the exploration really begins.

✔ **Traveler's Info.** The Traveler's Info links, provided by the Lonely Planet travel site, are an incredible, valuable resource. This is where armchair traveling gets really satisfying. I've lost myself in this section, learning about the cultures of far-off places. All editorial content behind these links is composed with style and humor. The Facts at a Glance page is a dry political and economic cheat sheet, but the other sections bring countries to life with rich descriptions of history and current atmosphere. The History and Culture page is a definite keeper — I've hopped from country to country in Yahoo! Travel just reading that page.

✔ **Map.** The tiny map in the left-hand sidebar expands with a click, but it's not interactive. It's nice to see a country's layout, though.

✔ **Weather.** Nothing brings a place to life like knowing what the weather is doing *right now*. Click any city link under the Weather banner to get a five-day forecast, so you can plan your imaginary residence in a foreign land.

✔ **Package Vacations.** Scroll down the page to see this feature, in the left-hand sidebar. It's positioned on each country destination page, but it has nothing to do with the country. It's a generic Yahoo! Travel feature that allows you to search for tour packages according to destination, price, duration, and theme.

> ✔ **Currency Converter.** This interactive puppy is convenient. See at a glance how the destination country's national currency stacks up against German, British, American, and Japanese monetary units, or use a drop-down menu to convert other currencies.

At any point in your exploration of destinations, if you feel inspired to actually travel somewhere (you have to get out of that armchair sometime), click the <u>Travel Reservations</u> link on the Yahoo! Travel banner to shift over to the ticket-buying portion of Yahoo! Travel.

The Real Thing

Time to get out of your imagination and into a real airplane? Yahoo! Travel has you covered when dreaming turns to reality with an online reservation service that covers plane travel, hotel stays, and car rentals. Other sections specialize in vacations, cruises, and bargain travel packages.

Buying plane tickets online is safe, convenient, and empowering. I dumped my human travel agent years ago. I liked him, and he did a good job, but you can't beat the ease and flexibility of researching your own options and making the purchase from home.

As with other e-commerce, you buy plane tickets with a credit card. Yahoo! transfers your personal information from your Yahoo! ID account, then asks you for your credit card number at the "point of purchase" — on the screen where you actually buy the tickets. However, you can have a Yahoo! Travel account without having a Yahoo! ID. It's just that if you have the ID, opening the travel account is a little easier.

As of this writing, the Yahoo! Travel reservation service is available for American and Canadian residents only. This restriction will probably change — that's my personal prediction, not the Yahoo! company line. Personal predictions are offered free of charge.

Reserving a plane trip is somewhat complicated, but not difficult. You just need to persevere through a number of screens. You may bail out of the process at any time by clicking a Cancel button if one is on the page, by surfing your browser elsewhere, by logging off the Internet, or by throwing your computer out the window. (The last option is an act of desperation, and should be reserved for moments of pure despair.) Seriously, you're in no danger of becoming inextricably involved in the reservation process or inadvertently buying a ticket until the final purchase page, which I mark clearly in Step 11. Here's what to do:

1. **On the Yahoo! Travel home page, click the <u>Air</u> link.**

   The Roundtrip Flight Search page appears (see Figure 16-3).

2. Fill in all the information fields.

The important thing to remember on this complex page is that you can't make any bad mistakes. If you leave something out, Yahoo! tells you about it and prompts a correction before proceeding. Throughout the planning of an itinerary, you have the ever-present option of returning to this page and changing your settings — so don't agonize over whether to leave in the morning or afternoon. If you're planning something more elaborate than a simple roundtrip excursion, click the <u>Multi-City</u> link. Skip over the Show me Airlines button for now — it's a diversion that I discuss right after this instruction list.

3. Scroll down to find the How should we search? (OPTIONAL) banner, near the bottom of the Roundtrip Flight Search page, and select "Show me all flights so that I can build my own itinerary."

This is important. If you don't click this selection, Yahoo! Travel sends you down a path that is unnecessarily confusing for most trip planning. I cover the features of that path right after this instruction list.

The <u>Terms and Conditions</u> link directly above the Show me available Flights button regurgitates standard legal language about the use and abuse of the flight reservation service. (Smoking the service is considered abuse.) Clicking the button is, legally, your acknowledgment of the Terms and Conditions, so you might want to glance at them.

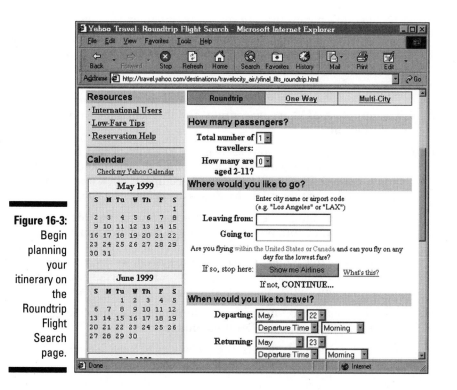

Figure 16-3:
Begin
planning
your
itinerary on
the
Roundtrip
Flight
Search
page.

4. **Click the Show me available Flights button.**

   The Select a Flight page appears (see Figure 16-4). Don't panic — clicking the Buy button doesn't charge your credit card. You can still back out. The Hold option usually lets you reserve an itinerary for 24 hours. If you're ready to buy tickets during this session, proceed with the Hold button. In some cases, Yahoo! Travel doesn't present complete roundtrip itineraries at this stage — when this happens, you are asked to choose an outgoing flight by clicking the Select button. The next page asks that you do the same for the returning flight.

5. **Click the Buy or Hold button to continue planning your trip.**

   The Review the ticket price information page appears.

6. **Click the Rules button for either leg of your trip to review the ticket restrictions and requirements.**

7. **Click the I Agree button — unless you're having second thoughts, in which case it would be a good time to click the Cancel button.**

   The Ticket Delivery Options page appears. E-Tickets are convenient, but don't offer the tactile reassurance of a physical ticket. The E-Ticket eliminates the possibility of the stomach-dropping experience of arriving at the gate and realizing you forgot your tickets. The lower portion of this page describes general rules and conditions of traveling. It explains that flights are sometimes deliberately overbooked, that you should show up early, and other details that are second nature to experienced travelers.

8. **Select whether you'd like an E-Ticket, normal mail delivery of a paper ticket, or FedEx (fast) delivery of the ticket by clicking the button of choice.**

   The Complete the passenger information page appears.

9. **Adjust any fields that are inaccurate, and then click the Information Is Correct button.**

10. **On the next two Choose your seats pages (the first of which is shown in Figure 16-5), select seats from the airplane diagram, and click the Continue button. Or if this is getting too complex, click one of the radio buttons, and then click the Bypass Seat Maps button.**

    The Enter billing and delivery information page appears. This is the do-or-die page. If you Continue past here, you're going on a trip. Or, at least, your credit card will be billed, whether you go or not. So be careful. You may have come this far just to see how the system works, but this is where the safe exploration ends. Don't let your mouse cursor anywhere near the Continue button unless you intend to buy these plane tickets.

11. **Type your credit card information, billing address, and delivery address, and then click the Continue button.**

    If you don't want to buy tickets, the safest way to back out is to click the Cancel button.

Figure 16-4:
Select your
itinerary
from this
page.

Reserving an airplane flight is the most complicated procedure in Yahoo!
Travel. Reserving a car or a hotel requires filling out the same sort of information (city, date, time, credit card payment), using the same sort of drop-down
menus and text-entry fields. You may use the <u>Car</u> and <u>Hotel</u> links from the
Yahoo! Travel home page to get started with those reservations, even if you
already have plane tickets, purchased through Yahoo! Travel or elsewhere.

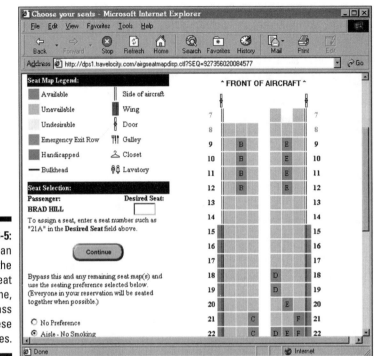

Figure 16-5:
You can
select the
exact seat
on a plane,
or bypass
these
pages.

Chapter 17

What's This, the Real World?

. . . .

In This Chapter

▶ Looking for a job

▶ Shopping for a house

▶ Looking for a new car

. . . .

I remember the real world, though it's been a long time since I ventured into it. Bright light emanating from the giant flameball in the sky, fresh air, changing seasons almost as pretty as my screensaver. Large metallic contraptions that move people around, gigantic shelters made of wood and plaster, and places to go where people give you money to perform tasks. I don't remember the real names for these things, but I do know Yahoo! helps you obtain them.

This chapter illuminates Yahoo!'s contribution to the bridging of the online and offline worlds when it comes to job hunting, house shopping, and car buying.

Getting a Job

I don't know if the entire job-hunting odyssey will ever be replaced by online services. It's hard to imagine an effective job interview being conducted without a face-to-face meeting. But when it comes to resume sharing and sorting through local or national listings, nothing beats the data-crunching power of computers or the networking facility of the Internet. Online job searches are a big deal, for employers and employees both.

Yahoo! Employment (see Figure 17-1) exhibits links to editorial and database content that helps you learn about and pursue new careers. The first step is to surf to the following URL or click the <u>Employment</u> link from the Yahoo! home page:

```
employment.yahoo.com
```

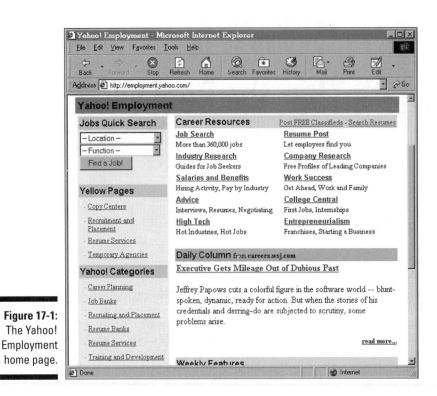

Figure 17-1:
The Yahoo!
Employment
home page.

Most people who enter Yahoo! Employment are looking for a job. You can get a fast start by using Jobs Quick Search in the left-hand sidebar. Use the drop-down menus to select a location (at the state level) and a job type, and then click the Find a Job! button.

Use the Job Search link to conduct a more advanced search, following these steps:

1. **On the Employment page, use the drop-down menus and text-entry fields to describe the location and job type you're looking for.**

   This form gets company-specific if you want, though you don't need to fill in any of the text-entry fields. The Keywords field might be the most crucial to an effective search. Use that field to enter a job specialty, such as *information technology*, so you can define your expertise more specifically than the Function drop-down menu allows. Another option is to use keywords to specify a location within a state — a city, for example. Basically, use the Keywords field to search for any helpful matches that may occur in the text of a job listing.

2. **Click the Search button.**

The Search Results page appears (see Figure 17-2).

3. **Browse your results and click links in the FULL LISTING column to see details about any job.**

Yahoo! Classifieds - Employment - Microsoft Internet Explorer

File   Edit   View   Favorites   Tools   Help

| ⇦ Back | ⇨ Forward | ⊗ Stop | ↻ Refresh | ⌂ Home | 🔍 Search | ⭐ Favorites | History | Mail | Print | Edit |

Address cr=national&ce_f=&cpo=&cpj=&ck=information+technology&g=&cs=time+2&cc=employment&cf=1&za=and   Go

| Tabled Results | Detailed Results |

Showing **1 - 10** of more than **2500** listings.   Too many to choose from? Not enough? **Use Advanced Search.**

Sort by clicking column header. Use *Advanced Search* to further reduce or increase the number of listings.

▼DATE	COMPANY	FUNCTION	TITLE	LOCATION	FULL LISTING
05/20/99	Space Telescope Science Institute	Other / Not Specified	Software Engineer - Hubble Space Telescope	Baltimore, Maryland	Details from CareerMosaic
05/20/99	Mckesson/HBOC	Sales	Sales Exec-Physician Practice Software	Houston, Texas	Details from CareerMosaic
05/20/99	The Lynn Borne Employment Network	*Information* Systems	*Information Technology* Consultants	Boston, Massachusetts	More detail
05/20/99	Sykes	*Information* Systems	Software Quality Assurance	Saint Louis, Missouri	More detail
05/20/99	The Computer Merchant, Ltd.	*Information* Systems	Y2K Remediation-Phase 2 (FLT)	Boston, Massachusetts	More detail

http://employment.classifieds.yahoo.com/yc?cc=employment&cs=time+2&cf=3&cr=nati   Internet

Figure 17-2:
The Search Results page shows your keywords in bold type.

You can adjust your search on any results page, using the Modify Your Search table at the bottom of the page. Click the DATE, COMPANY, or FUNCTION link to sort your results chronologically or alphabetically according to that column. (Sorting by date gives you a jump on new listings.)

Clicking the Detailed Results link above your search results displays a whole new look (see Figure 17-3). On this page you can modify your keywords and sorting options in the left-hand sidebar. The main body of the page displays full listings, with your keyword matches in bold type.

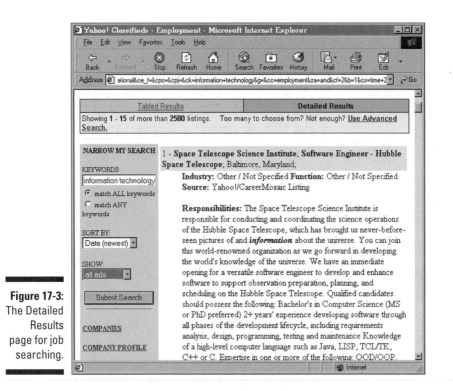

Figure 17-3:
The Detailed
Results
page for job
searching.

The flip side of cruising job listings is distributing your resume. In other words, instead of finding a company, let the companies find you. Yahoo! Employment provides a resume bulletin board, which may or may not prove effective. Using it is simple, though, and you don't need a prepared electronic resume, so it's worth a try. Here's what to do:

1. **On the Yahoo! Employment page, click the <u>Resume Post</u> link.**

   The Employment Wanted Classifieds page appears.

2. **Fill in all the information fields.**

   On this page, asterisks indicate required fields, which must be filled in or your resume won't make it to the listings. You probably want to spend the most time on the large text-entry fields, in which you can write, free form, about your career objective and why a company should hire you.

3. **Click the Submit entry button.**

The remainder of the Yahoo! Employment home page is filled with links to helpful articles and a few interactive tools. One fun (and possibly depressing) gadget lurks behind the <u>Salaries and Benefits</u> link — it's a Salary Calculator, which lets you compare your current salary (or salary requirement) in two different cities. In other words, you learn the equivalent of your salary in, for example, New York or Nashville. It's an amusing catalyst for fantasies, but also a useful tool if you're planning to relocate.

Gimme Shelter

Yahoo! Real Estate contributes to a growing trend of house buying and house selling over the Internet. With person-to-person contact becoming both more global and more precise, people are increasingly taking into their own hands what they used to entrust to professionals. At the grass roots level, Net-empowered individuals are buying and selling real estate as well as cars.

The Yahoo! Real Estate section contains articles and helpful educational readings. But the meat of the section consists of the listings themselves, part of the Yahoo! Classifieds system. I've separated real estate classifieds from other classifieds described in Chapter 22 because . . . well, because houses cost a heck of a lot more than other things people are selling. And because the shopping for real estate is an online activity many people are particularly interested in.

The link for Yahoo! Real Estate is usually positioned near the bottom of the Yahoo! home page. You can also get started by surfing directly to this URL:

```
realestate.yahoo.com
```

The Yahoo! Real Estate home page (see Figure 17-4) presents home-buying news, help articles, and links to a search engine and directory of ads. You may browse or search, for both houses and apartments, either purchases or rentals. If you're looking for a house to buy, here's the drill:

1. **On the Yahoo! Real Estate home page, click the <u>Houses for Sale</u> link.**

2. **On the Find a Home section of the next page, use the drop-down menus and text-entry fields to define what you're looking for.**

   In this search form, if you don't fill in the City or Town field, you're likely to be steamrollered by an unmanageable number of results. Narrow them down with a city. Of the three selections in the Category menu, Resale Houses by Owner is probably the most requested — Internet home shopping is all about connecting individuals and sidestepping realtors. Still, the Resale Homes by Agent/Broker category might be worth exploring for your locality of choice. On this page, if you decide you'd rather browse a directory than conduct a pinpoint search, scroll down to the Browse by Metropolitan Area section and click the regional link closest to your target location.

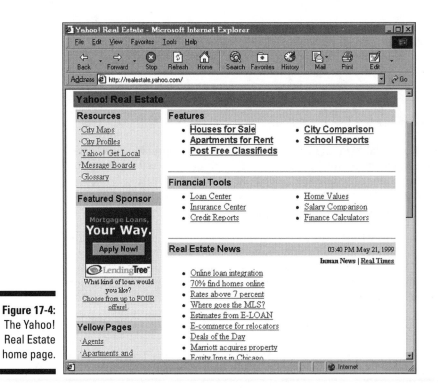

Figure 17-4:
The Yahoo!
Real Estate
home page.

3. Click the Search! button.

The Search Results page appears (see Figure 17-5).

4. Click any link in the FULL LISTING column to see more information about a listing.

The <u>DATE</u>, <u>PRICE</u>, <u>BEDS</u>, AND <u>BATHS</u> links help you sort your search results by category — click any one to sort the list chronologically or numerically according to that category. If you want to change your search requirements, scroll down to the Modify Your Search table and enter new information. Remember that only ten matches are displayed on each page; click the <u>Next 10 Ads</u> link to see more. The <u>Detailed Results</u> link presents full listings instead of this summarized list. You can toggle back and forth between Tabled Results and Detailed Results, and modify your search on either page.

If your searching efforts are delivering too many houses, you can cut through the excess with a more sophisticated search form. Click the <u>Use Advanced Search</u> link on the results page (Tabled or Advanced) to use a form (see Figure 17-6) that lets you specify the number of bedrooms and bathrooms and the way you want to sort your results.

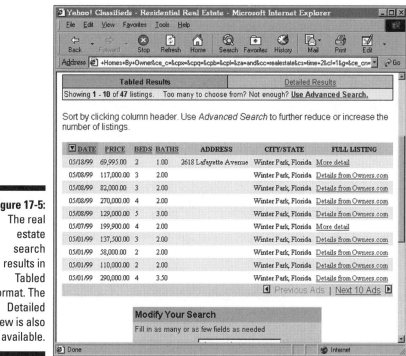

Figure 17-5:
The real estate search results in Tabled format. The Detailed view is also available.

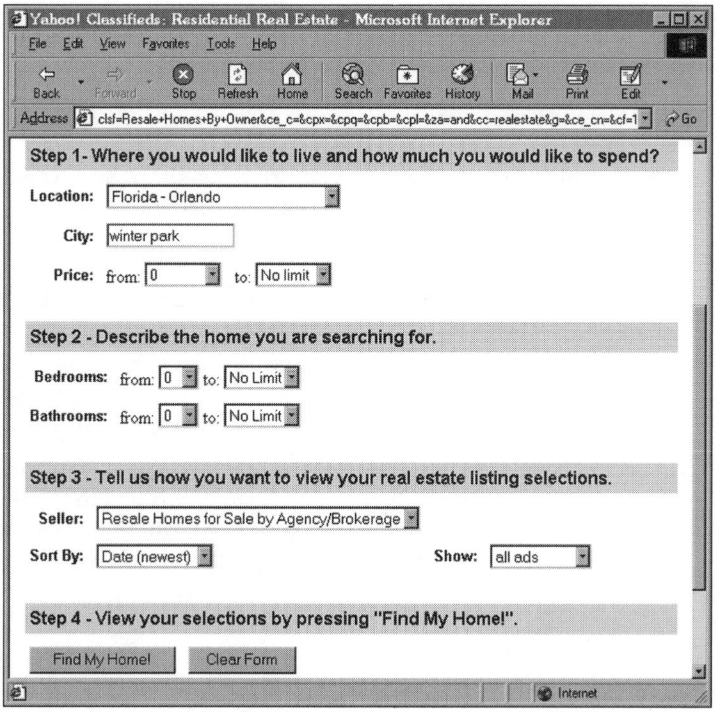

Figure 17-6:
The Advanced Search form helps you find the right house.

Apartments are nice, too. You can search for available rentals in your locality of choice, in much the same way as searching for houses. On the Yahoo! Real Estate home page, click the Apartments for Rent link, and then fill out the search form on the next page or browse the geographical directory of listings.

Beyond the Tin Lizzy

If real estate is a hot Internet topic, car buying is blazing. Cars got a jump-start on homes in the frenzy to gain efficiency through the Internet. Cars are less expensive, of course, and the buyer-seller transaction is simpler than closing on a house. Furthermore, the brutal ritual of buying a car (in the United States, at least) was begging for improvement when the Web came along. In the last few years (since about 1997), the momentum of auto sales over the Net has grown to the point that almost everyone with any online experience knows you can get a better, probably friendlier, car deal online than offline.

Yahoo! Autos is partly about used cars, and offers the same hook into Yahoo! Classifieds as the real estate and employment sections described earlier in this chapter. But Yahoo! Autos is more heavily weighted toward researching new cars and obtaining financing. To this end, Yahoo! has licensed editorial content and research tools from around the Web, and the result is an impressive, well-rounded resource for car shoppers of all kinds.

To get to Yahoo! Autos (see Figure 17-7), click the Autos link on Yahoo!'s home page or send your browser directly to this URL:

```
autos.yahoo.com
```

Yahoo! Autos provides a few ways to comparison-shop for new cars, but they all lead to the same data. Following is the quickest and most accurate way to get results:

1. **On the Yahoo! Autos home page, click the Research and Compare New Cars link or browse.**

   You can scroll down to the Car Guides section to browse car models. Browsing takes longer if you know the exact model you'd like information about, but it's the way to go if you're unfamiliar with model names.

   However, if you're *really* in the dark about cars and all you know is what features you want, you're better off following this link to the Research and Compare New Vehicles form (see Figure 17-8), where you can enter those preferences and let Yahoo! tell you which car models qualify.

Used cars and figures and loans, oh my!

A few other features of Yahoo! Autos are worth checking out. Almost everything in the car-buying experience is represented by an online service, from comparing models to financing a new car. If you're serious about buying a car over the Net, you should explore every link on the page. Here are some highlights:

✔ Click Auto Loan Quotes for a loan calculator. That's just the beginning — after you determine what's affordable, you can actually apply for a loan and receive the check in the mail.

✔ More calculators are lurking behind the Loan Calculators link. This page is especially useful if you're considering leasing a car, and want to compare the relative merits of leasing and buying.

✔ Car insurance is always a vexing topic. In many American states, insurance is confusing and expensive. The Auto Insurance page (click the Insurance link) dishes up some clarifying articles and an insurance quote machine that tells you what you should be paying. (The quote engine doesn't work for all states.)

✔ Search or browse for used cars by linking to the Yahoo! Classifieds section (Search New and Used Vehicles link). List your own used car for sale with the Sell Your Car link.

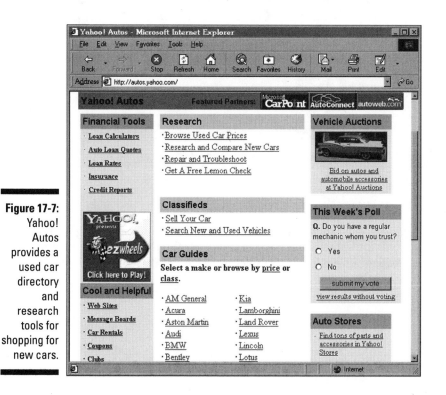

Figure 17-7:
Yahoo! Autos provides a used car directory and research tools for shopping for new cars.

You may return to this invaluable form a few times. You can angle into the Yahoo! Auto database from a few different angles. One day you might decide that price is crucial, and define your shopping universe on that basis alone. The next day you might be influenced by a friend's recommendation, and search only for cars of a certain make. On a day when you're thinking about ecology, you might focus on the mileage requirements above all else.

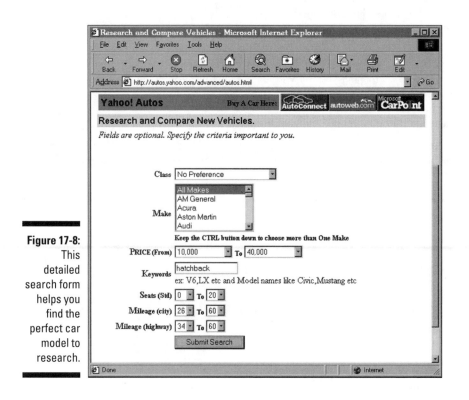

Figure 17-8:
This detailed search form helps you find the perfect car model to research.

2. **Define what car you're looking for.**

   Ideally, use several information fields in combination. In Figure 17-8, the fields are set to deliver any brand of hatchback within a modest price range of 10,000 to 15,000 dollars and a mileage rating of at least 26 MPG in the city.

3. **Click the Submit Search button.**

   The search results page appears (see Figure 17-9).

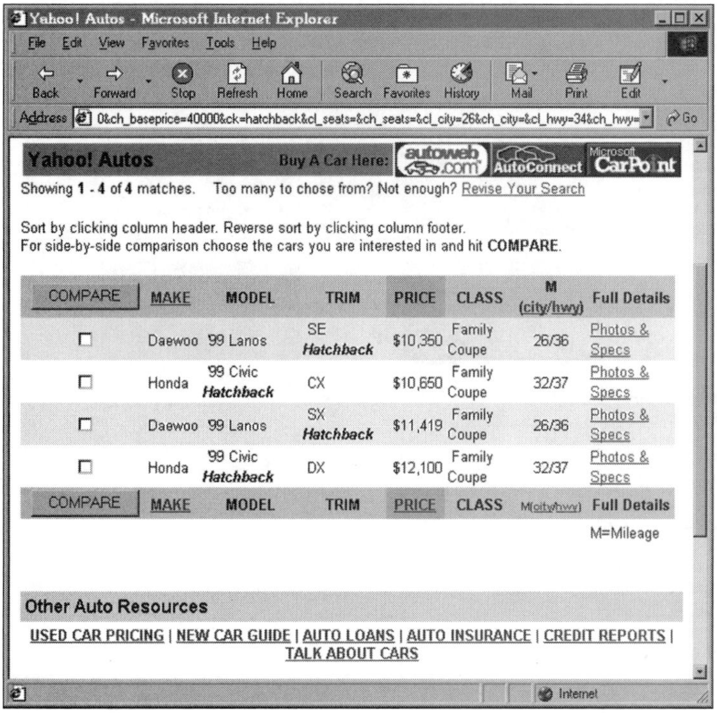

Figure 17-9:
The search
results page
when using
the
Research
and
Compare
feature.

4. **Click the <u>Photos & Specs</u> link to see a technical rundown of any model.**

   Yahoo! Autos displays a photo of the car model, and an overflowing basketful of data about its features and specifications. The base price is given (before optional), and in most cases, the dealer invoice cost — very useful for seeing how much the price is marked up. This is a useful page to print for comparison. Speaking of comparison, Yahoo! performs that comparison for you from the Search Results page. Just check the boxes next to models of interest, and then click the Compare button. You can see the result in Figure 17-10 — a side-by-side rundown of two or more models. The page gets a little crowded when comparing three or more models, so widen your browser window to the max.

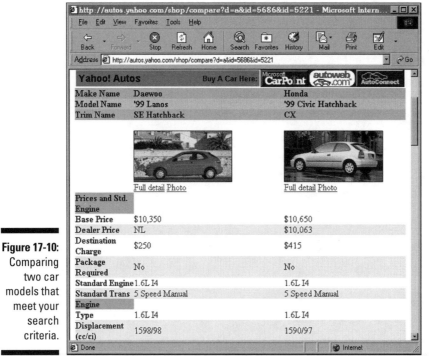

Figure 17-10:
Comparing
two car
models that
meet your
search
criteria.

Chapter 18

Backgammon, Anyone?

. . . .

. . . .

*Y*ahoo! isn't *all* fun and games, but one portion is devoted to pure interactive recreation, and that's Yahoo! Games. If you don't care for the violence of computer games, you have nothing to worry about. The most violent thing that transpires at Yahoo! Games is when a King gets checkmated. Yahoo! Games features board and card games that you can play with other Yahoo! members in real time. This chapter walks you through one game, illustrating the basic gaming software common to all the games. You don't need to install anything on your computer to play.

Rules of the Game

Yahoo! Games is the most heavily Java-dependent portion of the entire Yahoo! service. Other aspects of Yahoo! use Java, but not exclusively. For example, Java Messenger is just a supplement to the full-featured, downloadable Yahoo! Messenger. And the Java chat rooms are backed up by HTML chat rooms for computers that don't run Java easily.

Java is a software language that can be understood and used by different computer platforms. It's convenient primarily because it delivers applications to your computer by means of very quick downloads — usually just a minute or two, if that. Java is most often used to create a program or screen environment independent of your browser. Although Java runs on different computers — a facility known as *cross platform* — it can't overcome certain obstacles. Primarily, it needs a 32-bit operating system and a local hard drive to hold the Java program.

Because of Java's requirements, and because playing in Yahoo! Games is completely dependent on Java-readiness, certain home computer systems have trouble or are completely unable to participate in Yahoo! Games. They are

- ✔ **Windows 3.1.** Versions of the Windows operating system before Windows 95 are 16-bit systems, and cannot run Java.

- ✔ **WebTV.** WebTV systems (Classic and Plus) do not have local hard drives that can accept downloads of Java programs.

- ✔ **America Online.** The built-in AOL browser stumbles over many Web sites, and Yahoo! Games is no exception. AOL users should download a standard browser (Navigator or Internet Explorer) and use it rather than the default AOL browser.

After you have any Java problems squared away, Yahoo! Games provides really good playing environments for ten card games and five board games. Spades is the surprise popularity winner among the card games, but you can also play poker, gin, bridge, hearts, and a few others. Chess is the clear winner on the board side, but the backgammon and checkers rooms are usually bustling with activity as well.

The Yahoo! Games home page (see Figure 18-1) lists all available games and is the place to start meeting other people and playing a few games. Click the Games link on the Yahoo! home page, or go directly to

games.yahoo.com

Playing a Game

Most Yahoo! games operate in basically the same way, with variations due to the different natures of the games themselves. Every game involves a Java download and a succession of windows. Using mouse clicks, you proceed from the game page in your browser to a room window that's part of a Java download, and from the room window to a game window, which is also part of the Java program. These three windows (browser window, room window, and game window) are independent and operate autonomously.

The following steps take you through the process of beginning a game of checkers (or watching a game without playing). Other games differ in cosmetic details, but the same basic windows apply to them all:

1. **On the Yahoo! Games home page, click on the Checkers link.**

   The Checkers game page appears, as shown in Figure 18-2. Each game page lists several rooms you can enter immediately, usually in a lounge called Social. On some game pages (such as the page shown in Figure 18-2), rooms are grouped by playing level: Beginner, Intermediate, and Advanced.

Figure 18-1:
The Yahoo!
Games
home page.

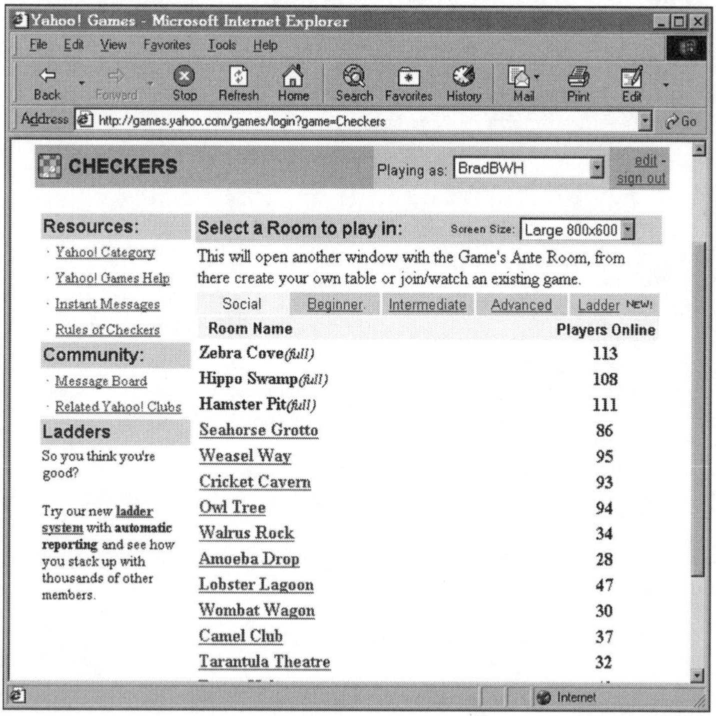

Figure 18-2:
The
Checkers
game page,
where you
select a
room to
play in.

2. **Select a screen size.**

   The Screen Size box lists two options: 800x600 pixels (the default size) and 640x480 pixels (the smaller size).

3. **Click on a room or on a level of play.**

   A Java download starts, which might take a minute or two to complete through telephone modems or a few seconds through a cable modem. The next thing you see is a room window, independent of your browser window. Figure 18-3 shows the Checkers room window.

4. **Click any Watch button to observe a game in progress, or click any Join button to play.**

   A new window opens — the game window — independent of both the room window and your browser window. In two-person games, such as Checkers, clicking a Join button matches you with the listed opponent, and you begin the game by each clicking a Start button. In group games, such as Poker, the Join button gets you a seat at the table — you can also click the Watch button to observe the table and then Join from there. Figure 18-4 illustrates a checkers game window as a player sees it. I am red (the dark pieces) in this game. Note that I am losing miserably.

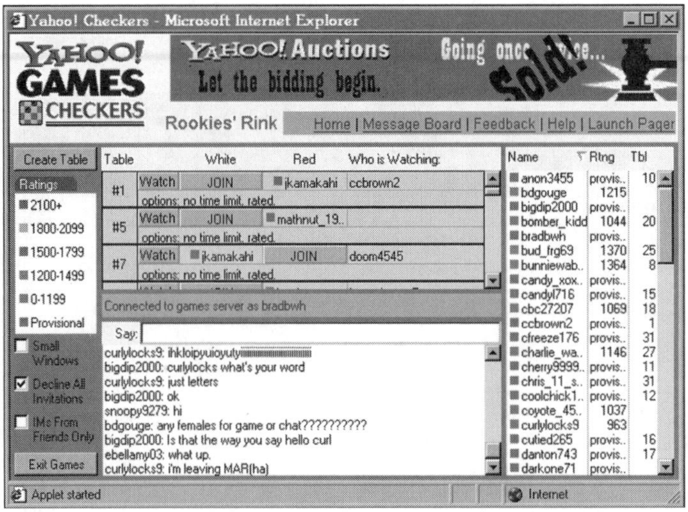

Figure 18-3: The Checkers room window, where you select a partner to play with or a game to watch.

Chatting with players is featured throughout all the Java room windows and game windows. You don't have all the fancy options included in Yahoo! Chat (see Chapter 11), but it's polite to say hi. If you're playing a timed game, chatting is often kept to a minimum.

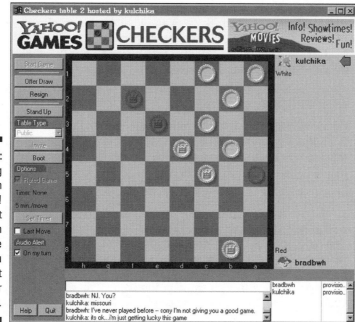

Figure 18-4:
Playing
checkers in
Yahoo!
Games. At
the bottom
of the
window, you
can chat
with your
opponent.

Rules for the games can be found on most of the game pages in your browser window. I say *most,* because, shockingly, at least one game page (poker) is missing a rules section. Generally, Yahoo! Games assumes a basic familiarity with the rules and with navigating the game window. Board games are played by clicking and dragging pieces from one position to another. The poker game window supplies preset buttons for calling, raising, and folding.

The room window contains the more complex set of features of the two Java windows. As you can see in Figure 18-3, the room window packs a busy screen into a small space. (You can resize the window.) Here are some important points about this window:

✔ The color-coded ratings in the left-hand sidebar are maintained automatically in Yahoo! Games. Whenever you enter a game room for the first time, you are given a provisional rating that moves up and down as you win and lose games. Notice how each name in the Name column has a rating color next to it.

✔ The Create Table button lets you establish a new playing station, which other people can join and to which you can invite anyone to play.

✔ Look at the Name, Rtng, and Tbl columns. A small arrow is next to one of these columns at all times. Click the header of any column to organize the names according to that column's criterion, and move the arrow next to the column header. This feature is especially helpful in listing potential players in order of their rankings.

✔ Check the Small Windows box to confine all game windows to the smaller 640x480 pixel size.

✔ Check the Decline All Invitations box to stanch the flow of Join invitations that's bound to arrive if you don't check it. (Keep reading to find out how to create a table and invite players.)

✔ Check the IMs From Friends Only box to receive Instant Messages from only your Yahoo! Messenger friends (see Chapter 11).

✔ All the items on the link menu near the top of the room window (except for <u>Launch Messenger</u>) open browser windows to various Yahoo! locations. <u>Home</u> goes to the Yahoo! Games home page; <u>Message Board</u> surfs your browser to the relevant board in Yahoo! Messages (see Chapter 12); <u>Feedback</u> displays an e-mail form with which you can write to Yahoo!; and <u>Help</u> takes you to an explanation page of many of the features of Yahoo! Games. The <u>Launch Messenger</u> link opens Java Messenger, not the full-featured Messenger (see Chapter 13).

✔ Double-click a player's name to pop open an options window (see Figure 18-5). That little window tells you the player's game history and rating. You can also send an Instant Message to that person. Check the Ignore box if you don't want to receive an Instant Message from that person. The Ping button send a data pulse to that person's server and back to your server — sort of Internet radar. The Ping test is for determining how much delay exists between two network points. Why have the Ping test in Yahoo! Games? Because when playing timed games, it's important that there be a quick network connection between the two players. If the Ping test results in a delay of more than a few seconds, frustrating lags might slow a game with that person. The Profile button opens a browser window displaying that person's Yahoo! Profile.

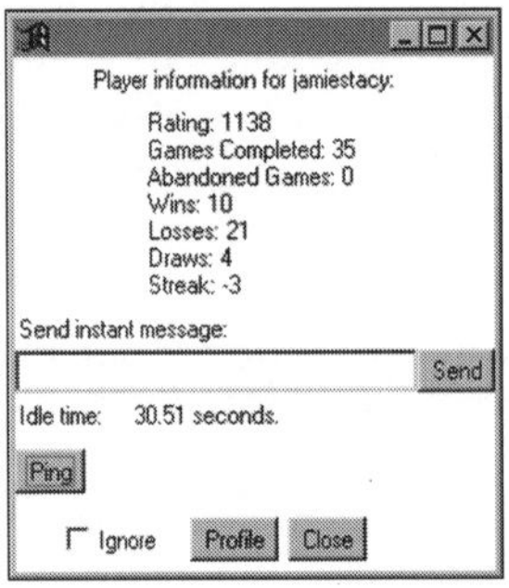

Figure 18-5:
Double-click any name in the room window to see a player's ranking and history.

Player information for jamiestacy:

Rating: 1138
Games Completed: 35
Abandoned Games: 0
Wins: 10
Losses: 21
Draws: 4
Streak: -3

Send instant message:

[   ] Send

Idle time: 30.51 seconds.

Ping

☐ Ignore   Profile   Close

You can get involved in a game in two ways: Join someone's table or create your own table. Both are accomplished in the room window. Click the Join button of any room that needs a player, or click the Create Table button in the left sidebar to establish a new game.

Creating your own table is the only way to set the game timer (if one exists for that game) and invite particular players to join you. The following list continues in the Checkers windows, but is essentially the same as for the other games:

1. **In the room window, click the Create Table button.**

    A game window opens (see Figure 18-6). In some games, a pop-up box asking for timing and other settings precedes the game window.

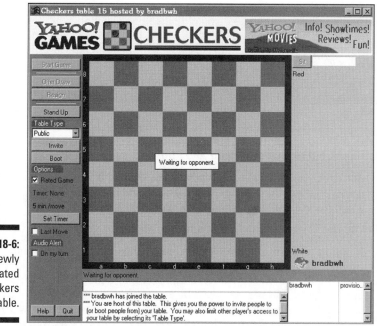

Figure 18-6:
A newly
created
checkers
table.

2. **Using the drop-down menu, select the Table Type.**

    Public tables may be joined by anyone who wants to play and watched by anyone who wants to observe a game in progress. Protected tables may be watched by anyone, but players can join only by invitation. Private tables are invisible to other members, and can be joined or observed only by invitation.

3. Click the Set Timer button to establish a time limit for games.

The default timer setting for checkers is unlimited time for the complete game, with a limit of five minutes per move. (It takes deep strategic thinking to ponder a checkers move for five minutes. Falling asleep helps, too.) Clicking the Set Timer button pops open a Set Timer window (see Figure 18-7). The Initial time setting is an overall time limit for a game. The Increment is the number of seconds added to each player's clock after every move. (Called a *fisher clock* in chess, this timing feature prevents a quick-moving player from ever running out of time.) Use the check box to set a five-minute per-move deadline. After entering your settings, click the OK button.

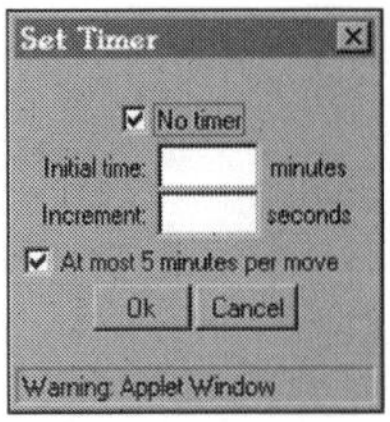

Figure 18-7:
The Set
Timer
window
places time
limits on
games.

Set Timer

☑ No timer

Initial time: [   ] minutes

Increment: [   ] seconds

☑ At most 5 minutes per move

[Ok]   [Cancel]

Warning: Applet Window

4. Check either or both audio alert boxes.

Actually, you can leave both boxes unchecked if you'd rather not be pestered by audio alerts. I find them convenient. You can get alerted when it's your turn or when your opponent has made a move.

5. Use the Invite button to ask another player to your table.

A pop-up window appears with a list of players currently in the game room. As in the room window, you can sort the names by rank — just click the Rtng column header. If a player has a table number next to his or her name, that player might be engaged in a game. Click a player's name once, and then click the Invite button. A pop-up window appears on that player's screen with an invitation to join you, as well as Accept and Decline buttons.

6. Click a Sit button to take your place at the table.

In checkers (and other board games) you get your choice of color. In multiplayer card games, you get your choice of position around the table. Click the Stand Up button to relinquish your place at the table.

The Boot button does not simulate your slamming a shoe on the table. It *does* give you the power to remove a player from your table. Click on any player's name and click the Boot button to give that person the heave-ho. The expelled person receives a "You have been removed from the table" notice, and the game window disappears from that person's screen. Be careful! It is actually possible to boot yourself from your own table — an ego-bruising experience.

Throughout Yahoo! Games, you might see Ladder rooms. This new feature brings an element of competitiveness to the game rooms. Ladders are session rankings for people who want to see how they match against other players in the room. As you play games, Yahoo! moves you up and down the room ladder as you win and lose. It's a fun feature, especially if you plan to play several quick games during a single session. However, don't confuse Ladders with Rankings. Rankings are adjusted in all rooms and carry over from one session to another. Ladders exist only in marked rooms and apply to only a single session.

Feeling antisocial? Do you prefer solitary games? The Yahoo! Crossword (click the <u>Crossword</u> link on the Yahoo! Games home page) is a single-person game. Additionally, Hearts can be played against computerized opponents. From any Hearts room window, create a table with the Create Table button and invite three robots to play with you. Robots are identified as *~robot1*, *~robot2*, and *~robot3*.

Chapter 19

The Yahoo! Companion

*Y*ahoo! offers several compelling features and products that aim to make it central to your entire Internet experience. The Yahoo! Messenger (Chapter 13), My Yahoo! (Chapter 2), and Yahoo! E-mail (Chapter 3) are effective, enjoyable, and useful anchors to the Yahoo! service. One other gizmo, the Yahoo! Companion, is designed to keep every important and customized portion of Yahoo! as close as a click in your Web browser.

Yahoo! Companion is a menu bar that attaches to the Internet Explorer browser (version 4.0 and later). This attachment tells you when you have Yahoo! e-mail and links to just about every portion of Yahoo!. Furthermore, you can use it to supplement (or replace) the Favorites bookmarking system in Internet Explorer. (Yahoo! Companion doesn't work with the Netscape Navigator browser.)

I am happily addicted to Yahoo! Companion, but am the first to admit that it's a tool for the dedicated Yahoo! user. If you have Internet Explorer, the Companion is worth a try. It's free, easy to install, and this chapter walks you through its features.

Activating the Companion

Yahoo! Companion is downloaded over the Net. Installing it is much easier than regular program downloads and doesn't require selecting a location on your hard drive or going through an involved installation procedure. You just activate it from a special Web page, and wait for it to appear in your browser. If you use Internet Explorer (version 4.0 or later), follow these steps to give it a try:

1. **On the Yahoo! home page, click the <u>more...</u> link above the directory topics.**

   The More Yahoo! page appears.

2. Click the <u>Companion</u> link.

The Yahoo! Companion page appears (see Figure 19-1). Notice the small window containing the Terms of Service agreement. More legal talk — in a *very* small window that makes it extremely difficult to read. Essentially, this typical agreement specifies that you can't make multiple copies of the software or sell it; that Yahoo! offers no technical support for Companion (thank goodness for this book, eh?); and that Companion is free for now (my prediction is that it will remain free). Clicking the activation link is a legal acceptance of the Terms of Service, so if you're concerned about legal fine print, scroll through the document to read it all.

You can skip the first two steps by going directly to

```
edit.yahoo.com/config/download_companion
```

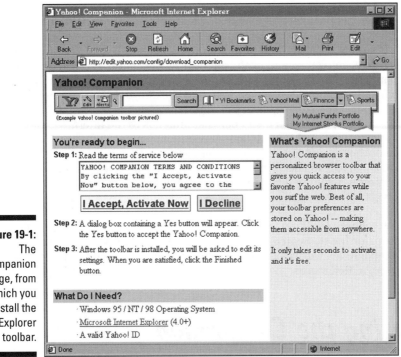

Figure 19-1:
The Companion page, from which you install the Explorer toolbar.

3. Click the <u>I Accept, Activate Now</u> link.

4. If a window appears asking whether you want to download and install the Yahoo! Companion, do the following:

  a. Click the Yes button.

  A new browser window appears displaying the Edit Yahoo! Companion page.

b. Close your old browser window.

The new window will, after completing the next step, incorporate the Companion. From that point on, every new browser window you open contains the Companion.

5. **On the Edit Yahoo! Companion page, click one of the preset toolbar radio buttons.**

Companion offers five ready-to-go configurations plus a <u>Make My Own...</u> link. I describe how to make your own settings a bit later in this section.

6. **Because you haven't made any customized settings at this point, register your permission by clicking the OK button, and then click the Finished button.**

Yahoo! Companion appears below the links bar and above the radio bar of Internet Explorer version 5.0. If you disable those two bars, it appears directly under the address bar (see Figure 19-2).

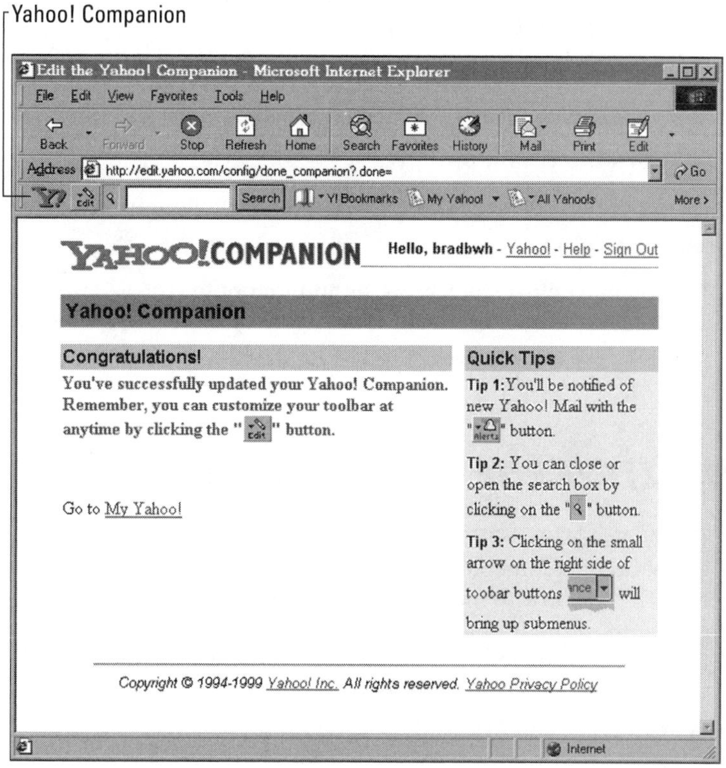

Yahoo! Companion

Figure 19-2:
The Yahoo!
Companion
in action.

Pretty insistent for a companion

As you can see from the tedious Install/Uninstall process, Yahoo! Companion is for dedicated Yahoo! users. The Companion is insistent — after you download it, you're stuck with the extra bar on your browser until you uninstall it. The Yahoo! Messenger, on the other hand, hooks conveniently into various parts of the service but resides as an independent program in your computer, so you can run it or not as you please.

I like Yahoo! Companion and usually use it. It doesn't appear in most of this book's figures because I didn't want to convey the impression that anyone must use Companion to enjoy Yahoo!.

The Companion bar can't be removed in the standard Internet Explorer fashion, by right-clicking a bar and selecting one of the checked bars. In fact, the Companion isn't really an option as long as it's installed. The only way to remove it from your browser is to Uninstall it, as follows:

1. **Click the Edit button of the Companion.**

2. **Select Uninstall.**

   A pop-up confirmation window appears.

3. **Click the Yes button.**

   A pop-up window notifies you that Companion has been uninstalled.

4. **Click the OK button.**

   You must close your browser and reboot for the Companion to disappear. You may activate it again at any time by following the first set of steps in this chapter.

Customizing the Companion

Like My Yahoo! (see Chapter 2) and Yahoo! Messenger (see Chapter 13), Yahoo! Companion comes to life when you customize it to your own preferences. Here's how to make the Companion most useful:

1. **After you install the Companion, click the Edit button near the left edge of the Companion toolbar.**

2. **Click the Edit My Toolbar selection.**

   The Edit Yahoo! Companion page appears.

3. **Click the <u>Make My Own...</u> link.**

The Customize Yahoo! Companion page appears (see Figure 19-3).

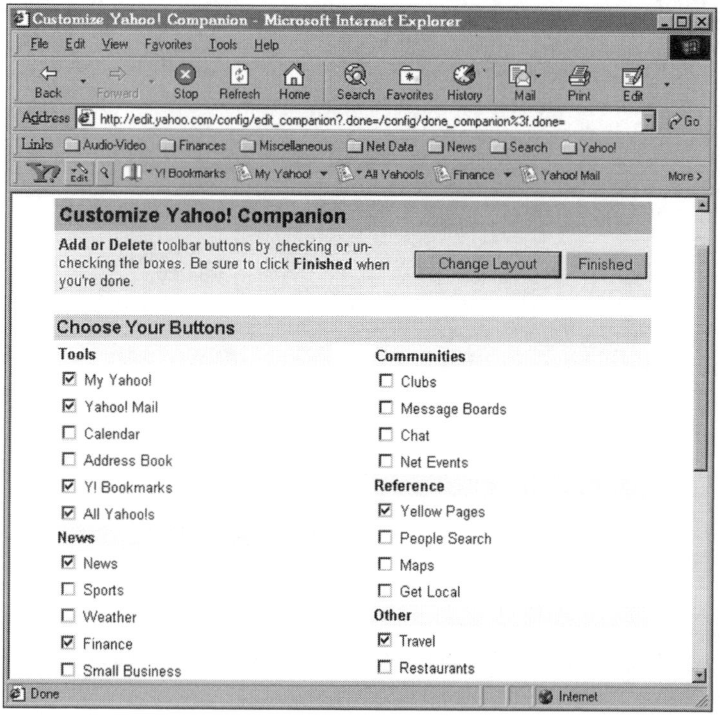

Figure 19-3:
Use this page to select which buttons appear on your Companion.

4. **Check the boxes next to the buttons that you want on the Companion bar.**

5. **Click the Change Layout button.**

The Customize Yahoo! Companion Layout page appears (see Figure 19-4).

6. **Change the order in which Companion buttons appear on the toolbar by selecting from the list and using the arrow buttons.**

Click any button appearing on the list, and use the up and down arrow buttons to shift its position in the list. Use the X button to eliminate a button from the toolbar.

7. **Click the Finished button.**

The Companion is like a glorified Favorites list for Internet Explorer, but dedicated to Yahoo! locations. (The Y! Bookmarks button houses links to more than a dozen outside sites, but I'll get to that a bit later.) Keep the following major points in mind when using Companion:

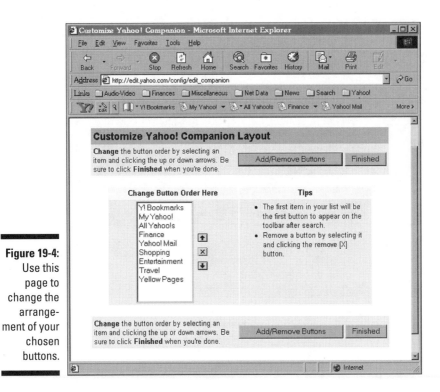

Figure 19-4:
Use this
page to
change the
arrange-
ment of your
chosen
buttons.

✔ Click the Y! button on the left edge of the Companion toolbar to display the Yahoo! home page.

✔ Click the magnifying-glass button to reveal a keyword search form. It operates just like the one in the main Yahoo! directory (see Chapter 5).

✔ An Alert button appears when you get a new e-mail or Yahoo! Personal mail. Click the button and select the alert you want to view. Click Refresh under the Edit button to reset your alerts.

✔ Click the More button on the right edge of the Companion to reveal your other selected buttons that don't fit on the toolbar. If you want different buttons on the toolbar, use the preceding instructions to change the toolbar layout.

✔ Some buttons have small arrows. Click the arrow to reveal specific Web page links for that button.

Y! Bookmarks (under the Tools section when you're configuring your Companion options) is a special button in three respects. First, it links to sites outside Yahoo!. Second, you can organize its links into folders. Third, the button is configurable and (in my opinion) improves the Favorites system of Internet Explorer.

Follow these steps to take advantage of the Y! Bookmarks button of the Companion:

1. **With the Yahoo! Companion installed, click the Edit button.**

2. **Click the Edit My Toolbar selection.**

   The Edit Yahoo! Companion page appears.

3. **Click the <u>Make My Own...</u> link.**

   The Customize Yahoo! Companion page appears.

4. **Under the Tools section, check the Y! Bookmarks box.**

5. **Click the Finished button.**

6. **On the Companion toolbar, click the Y! Bookmarks button.**

   A menu drops down with several default links.

7. **Click the Edit Bookmarks/Folders selection.**

   The Edit your Bookmarks page appears.

8. **Check all boxes next to the default links that you want to remove from Y! Bookmarks, and then click the Delete button.**

   You can check out the sites before deleting them from your Bookmarks list by clicking the site links.

9. **If you want to alter the Bookmarks listing of any link, click the Edit icon next to the link.**

   The Edit Bookmark page appears (see Figure 19-5).

10. **Make the alterations you want, and click the Save button.**

    You can change the URL, the name of the link as it appears in your Bookmarks list, and any comment that you want to appear on the Edit your Bookmarks page. (Comments do not appear on the Y! Bookmarks list when you pull it down in the browser.)

11, **Create a new folder by clicking the <u>New Folder</u> link.**

    The Add Folder page appears.

12. **Type a folder name and any comments you want to attach to it. Click the Save button or the Save & Add Another if you want to create multiple folders.**

13. **Click the <u>Add Bookmark</u> link to add a single site link to the Y! Bookmarks list.**

14. **When you've finished making alterations to your Bookmarks, click the Finished button.**

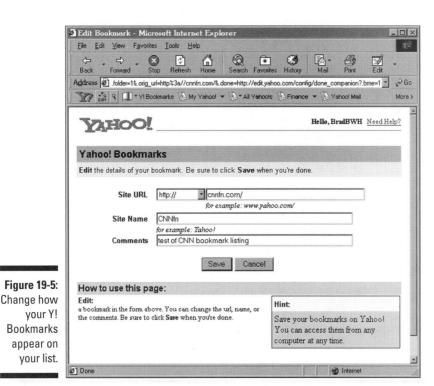

Figure 19-5:
Change how
your Y!
Bookmarks
appear on
your list.

Your Y! Bookmarks settings are saved on Yahoo!'s computers, not on your PC. This excellent feature makes it easy to access your bookmarks from any computer with an Internet connection. For anyone who travels, even to an office for work, having a Net-stored, completely portable bookmark system is a gigantic advantage over saving Favorites in Internet Explorer. (Of course, you must use Internet Explorer on the remote computer for this feature to work.) The downside is that creating a new item is more cumbersome in the Y! Bookmark list than in Explorer — much more cumbersome. I use Y! Bookmarks for my *essential* bookmark sites, the ones I never want to be without.

The Yahoo! Companion responds to the sign-ins and sign-outs to and from Yahoo! through the browser. When you sign out of your Yahoo! ID while running Companion, a Sign in button appears on the Companion toolbar. That button takes your browser to the sign-in page, but doesn't assume you want to sign in with the ID that previously used the browser. Sign in with any Yahoo! ID and password. Your Companion settings are keyed to a single account password. If somebody else using the computer signs in with a different Yahoo! ID and password, the Companion stays attached to the browser in default format, ready to be edited. Your settings disappear until you sign in with your ID and password.

Part VI
Buying and Selling

The 5th Wave   By Rich Tennant

"I have to say I'm really impressed with
the interactivity on this car wash Web site."

In this part...

The chapters in this part explain how to do what every-one likes best — shop. Yahoo! provides several venues for buying and selling stuff. Yahoo! Stores are explained from the shopper's perspective, and the chapter on Yahoo! Auctions describes how to be a bidder or a seller.

Chapter 20

Shopping at the Yahoo! Mall

. . . .

In This Chapter

▶ Understanding the Yahoo! Shopping concept

▶ Browsing and searching the Yahoo! Shopping directory

▶ Using the shopping cart and buying things

▶ Comparing prices when buying books, music CDs, and videos

. . . .

*I*t sometimes seems that the entire point of the Internet is to give consumers another way to shop. Is the visionary aspect of the Net dead?
Where once futurists proclaimed a new era of planetary shrinkage, citizenry
in the virtual global village, and equal self-expression for all, now people
speak of the unstoppable rise of e-commerce. Is the Utopian ideal nothing
more than a dying ember in the human imagination? Heck, who cares, just
give me a credit card and a secure online connection.

Actually, no vision of cyberspace society has been sacrificed to the gods of
commerce. There's room for everything in a realm without boundaries. It is
true, though, that the *convenience* of the Internet is emphasized strongly
these days, and online shopping is a big part of saving time as we shift into
the new millennium.

E-commerce has benefited my day-to-day life in any number of ways. Simple
gift buying is greatly eased in some situations. Holiday shopping isn't nearly
as grueling as it used to be. When planning a serious purchase, researching
brands and prices has never been such a breeze, nor have so many stores
been within easy reach. On the Net, all stores are a single click away, so mer-
chants must compete by offering good prices and reliable service.

The modern Internet is a gravy train for consumers, for now at least. Online
stores subsidize their businesses not only through sales, but also through
advertising on their sites. As a result, some e-commerce sites sell merchandise at or below wholesale to attract traffic, driving up their ad rates. How
long this precarious business model will last is anybody's guess, but for the
time being we're in the midst of a golden age of Internet shopping.

Yahoo! contributes to consumer-friendly Internet mania in a unique way, and it is one of the major hosts for virtual stores. Although many Internet portals offer directory services to shopping around the Net, Yahoo! maintains its own mall, made up of stores that use its hosting and shopping-cart services. So, although Yahoo! provides a directory of online stores, they're all Yahoo! stores. This under-one-roof system has a few advantages:

✔ You can search for and locate specific products easily.

✔ Price comparisons are easy to see, though you are limited to Yahoo! stores as opposed to Net-wide price shopping. But Yahoo! helps you compare prices outside the Yahoo! collection of stores, too.

✔ Buying stuff from multiple Yahoo! stores is simple, thanks to the universal on-screen shopping cart that links them together. You can buy a music CD, a box of chocolate, and a computer mouse in a single session. (Authors love receiving chocolate as a gift.)

✔ Yahoo! places hooks from the shopping area to Yahoo! Auctions (see Chapter 21) and Yahoo! Classified (see Chapter 22), so your shopping has other dimensions.

If the Yahoo! system has a downside to, it's that visitors might get the impression they are shopping the entire Internet, when in fact the experience is limited to Yahoo! stores. Fortunately, Yahoo! has a lot of stores. I have found the trade-off to be more than fair, and definitely useful.

This chapter explains how to navigate through Yahoo! Shopping, from browsing to buying.

Hanging Out at the Mall

The fun begins on the Yahoo! Shopping home page (see Figure 20-1). Click the Shopping link on the Yahoo! home page, or go directly to this URL:

```
shopping.yahoo.com
```

Figure 20-1 shows the categories in the Yahoo! Shopping directory. Yahoo! stores sell a broad range of stuff. If you know exactly what you're looking for, the search form is useful. The drop-down menu next to the Search button lists all the shopping categories of the directory. Just select a category, enter your keyword(s), and click the Search button. The search engine works best with specific queries as opposed to general ones. So *air conditioner* and *fruit basket* are better keywords than *books* or *toys*. Searching for authors and recording artists is productive when buying books and music CDs.

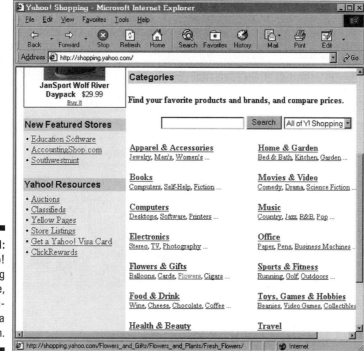

Figure 20-1:
The Yahoo!
Shopping
home page,
with a direc-
tory and a
search form.

Browsing in the Yahoo! Shopping directory is like sailing along the rocky
shoals of temptation. Not a directory page goes by that doesn't toss pictures
and top-selling ideas in your face. Each top-level directory category leads to a
page of subcategories, helping you narrow your selections. Figure 20-2 shows
the Chocolate directory page in the Food and Drink category, from which you
can either proceed more deeply into the directory or go directly for any featured products. (Any one of which would be an appropriate gift to a
hard-working author.)

Whether you search with keywords or drill down into the directory, your goal
is a product page. Figure 20-3 shows the Patterned Neckties page of the Men's
Apparel section of the directory. Each necktie selection leads to a store —
and the particular page of that store — selling ties. You can click the main
product link, any of the necktie pictures, or the <u>matches</u> link to the right.
They all lead to a store page from which you can select merchandise, add it
to your shopping cart, and eventually buy it. (Before buying, you can always
remove items from your shopping cart or alter the quantity of any item.)

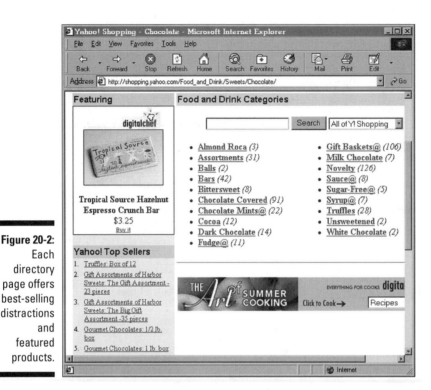

Figure 20-2:
Each directory page offers best-selling distractions and featured products.

Figure 20-3:
A product page gives you a choice of stores.

All Yahoo! stores look different but have identical shopping carts. In fact, it's really just one shopping cart (yours) that you carry around from one store to another, even though you can't see it. If you place something in your cart, and then shop some more and eventually place a second item in your cart, both items appear in the cart. Your shopping cart continues to hold your items until you sign out of Yahoo, close your browser program, or turn your computer off.

Break out of the confines of Yahoo! Shopping with the <u>Search Stores on the</u> <u>Web</u> link at the bottom of each product page. This link places the product page name (*patterned neckties* in our example) in the search engine and sets it loose searching for relevant products all over the Web. Now, the search engine is smart, but no genius. It knows enough to look for products, but not necessarily the exact type of product you want. For example, in the *patterned neckties* example, one of the results is a book on neckties sold at the Barnes & Noble online store.

Speaking of searching, you can initiate a new search from any product page. Just scroll down to the search form at the bottom, choose a category with the drop-down menu, enter keywords, and click the Search button.

Shop Till You Drop

Time to get down to business. It's one of those days — you have to spend some money. Forget the mall with its teen throngs and Day-Glo ambience. Bathe your face in the serene light of your monitor, place your credit card within easy reach of your quivering fingers, and log on to Yahoo! for some serious shopping.

The preceding section explains browsing and searching in Yahoo! Shopping. However you get there, at some point you find something you simply must own, and the consuming begins. Let's assume the object of your desire is a half-pound box of gourmet chocolates, so that *consuming* can take on a double meaning.

If you have a Yahoo! ID, it makes sense to sign on to Yahoo! with that ID before beginning your shopping. When you confirm your purchase, Yahoo! takes your address and plugs it into the on-screen order forms, saving you time. If you anonymously buy several items from different stores, each store needs to prompt you for shipping and billing information — it's a drag.

Figure 20-4 shows the purchase page for the chocolates. I show this not to tempt you unduly or to plant ideas of the perfect author's gift in your mind, but to illustrate the Order buttons. (Honestly.) No matter what store you're in within Yahoo! Shopping, you always begin the buying process with that Order button. (Shopping for books, music CDs, and videos works a little differently, as described in the next section.) Following are the step-by-step instructions from any product purchase page.

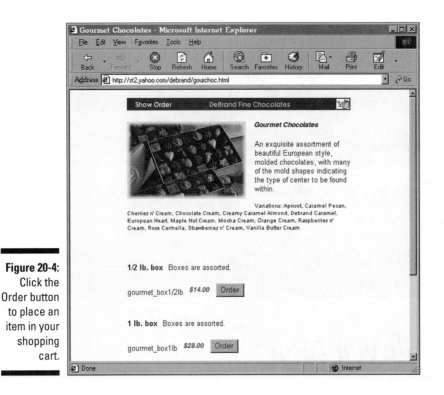

Figure 20-4:
Click the
Order button
to place an
item in your
shopping
cart.

1. **On any product purchase page, click the Order button.**

   The Yahoo! Shopping Cart page appears, and your item is placed in your shopping cart (see Figure 20-5).

2. **Check the Item, Unit Price, and Quantity to make sure you selected the correct product.**

   The shopping cart doesn't make mistakes, but it's always possible that, in a chocoholic fever, your trembling hand clicked the wrong item. If you've made a mistake, click the Remove button. You can revisit the product purchase page by clicking the item name or go to the store's home page by clicking the name of the store.

   In the Quantity field, enter the number of items you'd like, or leave it alone to receive one item. (You might want to get one for yourself in addition to the one you're so generously sending to me.) If you do change the number in the Quantity field, click the Update Quantities button to update the price.

   Note that at this stage, shipping charges have not been added to your total. Each store adds its own shipping charges during the order confirmation process.

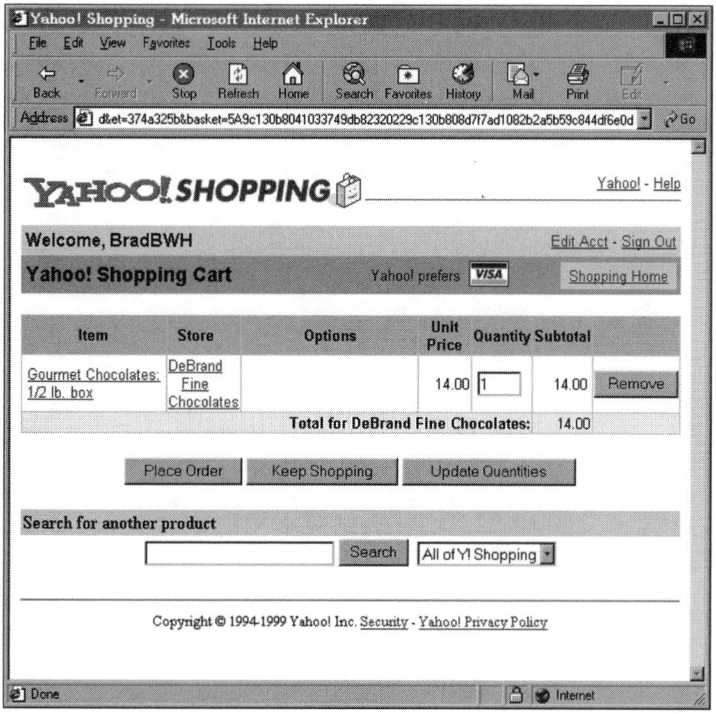

Figure 20-5:
The Yahoo!
Shopping
cart, holding
one item.

If you're using Yahoo! Shopping without signing in with your Yahoo! ID, an extra button appears on the Yahoo! Shopping Cart page called Place Order Without Registering. Yahoo! Shopping lets you proceed up to a certain point anonymously, but then demands that you either sign in or start a new account.

3. Click the Place Order button or the Keep Shopping button.

Use the Place Order button if you've finished shopping. (So soon?) If you'd like to keep the spirit of greed alive, click the Keep Shopping button. You can also cut to the chase by initiating a product search using the keyword entry form at the bottom of the shopping cart. Figure 20-6 illustrates a fine, upstanding shopping cart holding the results of a modest spree from three stores. You may remove any item, change any Quantity field, or revisit the product purchase page. At some point, weary at last, you must click the Place Order button to purchase the items in your cart.

4. On the Yahoo! Shopping Check Out page (see Figure 20-7), verify your shipping address for the first item in your cart, and click the Continue button.

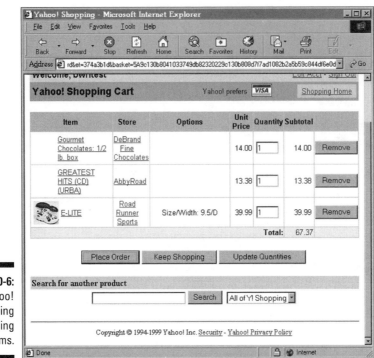

Although you have one shopping cart, you're buying products from different stores, and each store handles its own shipping. You use your credit card only once, and Yahoo! passes the orders to the stores. Your card is billed separately by each store.

5. **On the next Yahoo! Shopping Check Out page, enter a billing address or click the Same radio button to use your shipping address from the previous page.**

6. **Check the E-mail box to receive an order confirmation at your e-mail address.**

   Make sure the listed e-mail address is correct; if not, replace it with a correct or preferred address.

7. **Enter a credit card number, and use the drop-down menus to select a card type and an expiration date.**

8. **Click the SEND THIS ORDER button, unless you want to cancel your order.**

   You know what this means. This is the actual order page, and clicking that button sends the order to the Yahoo! Store. This page is your final chance to back out. If you want to cancel the order, click the Do Not Order button. Then, in good conscience, you must resign from the Frenzied Shoppers Guild.

9. **Repeat steps 5 through 8 for the remaining items in your shopping cart.**

As you receive order numbers for each item you buy, jot them down somewhere. You receive those numbers in an e-mail as long as you select the E-mail box in Step 6, but it doesn't hurt to have a handwritten note in case you accidentally delete the e-mail confirmation. You need that order number if you want to check the status of your order. To check an order, use the Order Status link on most Yahoo! Shopping pages.

As you're shopping, you can always view your shopping cart by clicking the View Cart/Check Out link on most Yahoo! Shopping pages. I've found it makes sense to pile stuff in the cart while browsing, and sort it out later. You don't want to see something interesting, decide to buy it later, and then not be able to find it again. The Order button is not a purchase button, and it's impossible to get charged for clicking it. Because you can easily remove items from the shopping cart, placing things in the cart is a convenient way to organize your shopping.

Buying Books, Music, and Videos

Three categories in Yahoo! Shopping operate a bit differently from the others. They are Books, Music, and Movies & Video. In each of these categories, Yahoo! makes a greater effort to provide price comparisons. A number of Yahoo! Stores sell products in these three categories, so Yahoo! helps you get the best deal by showing what each store is asking for any music CD, book, or video you look at. Furthermore, Yahoo! stretches the price comparison out to the Internet at large upon demand.

Because these three categories are essentially identical to each other, if different from the other categories, the best way to illustrate them all is to step through a purchase in one of them. Follow along, then, in a purchase of a computer book chosen at random:

1. **On any search or directory page, click a book product.**

   The Yahoo! Book Shopping page appears (see Figure 20-8).

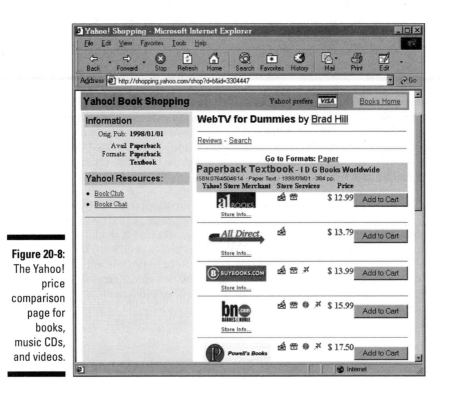

Figure 20-8:
The Yahoo! price comparison page for books, music CDs, and videos.

2. Compare the competing prices for your book.

Note the small icons next to each store. Those little graphics indicate store services such as free shipping, gift wrapping, the availability of express delivery, and customer service over the phone. Scroll down the page to see a key to the icons.

3. Click the Compare Prices for this product on the Web link to see what prices you can get outside Yahoo! Shopping.

A new page appears with prices from non-Yahoo! stores. The search might take a few seconds or a minute.

4. Decide on a store, and click the Add to Cart button.

This step assumes you choose a Yahoo! Store. If you go to an outside store, follow whatever procedure the store requires, but remember that you are then separated from your Yahoo! Shopping Cart. (You can return to it, though, and continue shopping, as long as you don't sign out of your Yahoo! ID.) Selections are not added to it from the outside store, and purchases become an independent credit card transaction. If you stay within Yahoo! Shopping to buy a book, a CD, or a video, continue with the purchase process as described in the preceding section.

Chapter 21

Going Once . . . Going Twice . . .

*M*illions of people have discovered the odd, unique, exhilarating kick of winning an online auction.

When you think about it, it's strange that buying something through an auction is called *winning*. A sign of the sweepstakes-oriented, consumer-intensive culture? Certainly, buying through an auction can be a victory when you get a bargain. Some products sold in this fashion, though, don't have fixed prices, and in those cases it's not clear whether you've secured a bargain or participated in an expensive garage sale.

Two types of Internet auction sites are available. *House auctions* provide the merchandise and accept bids on it. These sites stock their own inventory, which can range from new products to second-run items, overstocked merchandise, and used or refurbished equipment. *User-to-user auction houses* simply provide the cyberspace and the software for bidding and selling — the visitors supply the goods. Yahoo! Auctions is this second type of auction house. You can use it to buy from other individuals or sell your own stuff in an auction format.

In this chapter, I provide the details on registering for Yahoo! Auctions, bidding, and selling stuff in your own auction.

Registering for Yahoo! Auctions

The first step is to find the Yahoo! Auctions home page. Easy enough. Just click the <u>Yahoo! Auctions</u> link on the Yahoo! home page or go directly to

```
auctions.yahoo.com
```

You need a Yahoo! ID to buy or sell in Yahoo! Auctions. Even if you already are a registered Yahoo! user, you must complete a separate registration form as an auction participant. Follow along:

1. **At the top of the Yahoo! Auctions home page (or any Yahoo! Auctions page), click the <u>Customize</u> link.**

   The sign-in page appears.

2. **Fill in your Yahoo! ID and password, and then click the Sign in button.**

3. **On the next page, fill in your e-mail address, notification preferences, the notice to winning bidders if you plan to sell anything, and information about you for a seller's profile.**

   Some of these categories are irrelevant if you don't ever sell anything in Yahoo! Auctions. Folks interested in browsing, bidding, and buying should fill in the Email Address and Notification Preferences sections. Bidders and sellers can both receive e-mail and Yahoo! Messenger alerts when certain things happen in their auctions. Check the boxes next to information you want to receive, in the column that represents how you want to receive it (e-mail, Yahoo! Messenger, or alphanumeric pager).

4. **Click the Update button.**

Finding Auctions and Bidding

Yahoo! Auctions is organized in directory fashion (no surprise), like most other portions of the service. The Yahoo! Auctions home page (see Figure 21-1) shows you an overview of the auction types available. This page gets you involved by either browsing or searching for an auction. If you're wandering around for the first time, or are new to Internet auctions in general, you might want to take the directory route. Just click a main topic area or one of the subcategories to begin drilling into the directory.

Some directory topics extend several layers down before you see any auction listings. Subcategory pages get you close to specific types of objects being sold. In Figure 21-2, the auction page for Indian-head American nickels, shows a seventh-level page of the auctions directory. Had you known you were looking for precisely such a numismatics auction, you could have used the search form with the keywords *indian head nickel*.

Figure 21-1:
The Yahoo!
Auctions
home page.

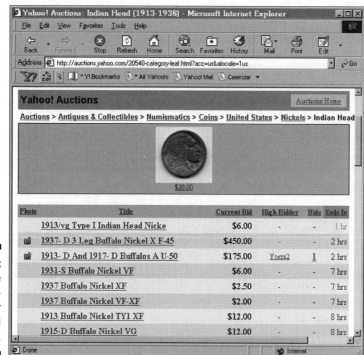

Figure 21-2:
Some of the
listed auc-
tions for
Indian-head
nickels.

Search forms are located on every directory page in Yahoo! Auctions. Use them to enter specific items you're looking to buy, such as *keyboard synthesizers*, *baby clothes*, or *whitney houston cd*. (As you can see in these examples, you don't need to use capital letters to get good matches.) Be aware, though, that your keywords are matched against the descriptive text of the auction pages, not just the auction titles, and also that sometimes just one keyword is matched. I often search with the keywords *cd collections*, hoping to scarf up lots of music from somebody liquidating his or her collection. Inevitably, the search results match with computer systems for sale with CD drives.

The auction directory pages (refer to Figure 21-2) show you the auction name, the current bid, the remaining time in the auction, and the high bid if there's been any bidding at all. (Because Yahoo! Auctions holds so many auctions, many transpire without a single bid. Lack of bids can indicate a too-high minimum price, or a great bargain that has become lost in the crowd. To see an auction page in progress, click any auction title.

The auction page (see Figure 21-3) presents a bundle of information plus an opportunity to place a bid. Here are the major points to look for:

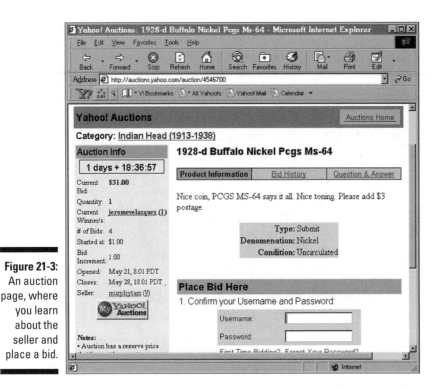

Figure 21-3:
An auction page, where you learn about the seller and place a bid.

✔ Look at the left sidebar for information about the auction, including a running clock ticking off days, hours, minutes, and seconds until the virtual closing gavel. The Current Bid is the high, or winning, bid of the moment, and therefore your minimum bid should you enter the auction.

✔ Click the seller's name to read an auction profile (not a generic Yahoo! Profile) describing the seller's background with auctions or business. (Many sellers are auction dealers or other small business people who have migrated their retail operations to Yahoo! Auctions.) All of the seller's current auctions (some people have dozens going on at once) are listed on the seller's page and linked.

✔ Click the <u>Bid History</u> link to see a log of the bidding so far.

✔ Click the <u>Question & Answer</u> link to query the seller about the auction item, and read any previous dialogue that's been posted.

✔ Scroll down to the Place Bid Here section to participate in the auction. Enter your Yahoo! ID in the Username field and your password below. Then type your bid in the Max Bid Amount field. In the Comment field, you may add a comment, which will appear next to your bid in the Bid History list. Click the Place a Bid button when you've filled in everything.

Yahoo! Auctions uses a system called Automatic Bidding. Yahoo! understands that if you enter a bid higher than one dollar above the current winning bid, you want the system to manage your bidding for you. Yahoo! continually monitors the auction and bids up your figure to remain just above any new bids. Automatic Bidding continues in this fashion until your limit (the amount you typed in the Max Bid Amount field) is reached. Then, if someone tops your maximum amount, you're out of the auction. Until then, your are kept on top of the heap. Naturally, with the system helping everyone in the same fashion, popular auctions reach the highest maximum bid very quickly. You can always enter an auction again if you're pushed out by higher bids.

When you place a bid for the first time in Yahoo! Auctions, the system throws a long Terms of Service agreement on your screen. I've breezed past many of these agreements in other chapters of this book, but if you're going to read one of these legal documents fairly carefully, this should be the one. In it, Yahoo! describes exactly what its role is in the Auction process, and what its responsibilities are and aren't. Yahoo! provides the auction space and underlying software, but has no involvement in actual transactions and money exchanges. Yahoo! doesn't warrant or endorse the sellers in any fashion. Basically, you're on your own, and have no recourse to Yahoo! if you meet a shifty seller or don't get the item you paid for.

What happens if you win? When you win a Yahoo! Auction, Yahoo! brings you together with the seller and steps out of the picture. The seller contacts you by e-mail and arranges the details of your transaction. Each auction page (on the bottom left) indicates what forms of payment the seller accepts. Small-business sellers often take credit cards, but individuals running auctions as a hobby usually take checks or money orders, and may implement precautions such as not shipping until the check clears. Each seller determines individual shipping and handling costs.

To see a list of all auctions in which you're participating, as a bidder or a seller or both, click the <u>My Auctions</u> link on the Yahoo! Auctions home page.

Selling Something in an Auction

Just as bidding is open to anyone in Yahoo! Auctions, so too is creating an auction. (The only requirement is that you have a valid credit card. However, I want to emphasize that creating an auction is free. The credit card is just a verification procedure.) Follow these steps to create an auction:

1. **On the Yahoo! Auctions home page, click the <u>Submit Auctions</u> link.**

   The category selection page appears.

2. **Click a product category that best fits your item.**

   Some selections take you to subcategory pages. Continue selecting the niche most appropriate to your item.

3. **Click the <u>Submit to this Category</u> link.**

4. **On the Instant Yahoo! Account Verification page, click the Secure Account Verification button.**

   You might wonder what this is all about. Yahoo! is about to ask you for credit card information. You can't put anything up for bidding in Yahoo! Auctions without a valid credit card. Your credit account is *not* charged in this process. Selling something through Yahoo! Auctions is free.

5. **On the Yahoo! Account Verification page, fill in the fields with your contact information, credit card number, and card expiration date, and then click the Finished button.**

   The Yahoo! Account Verification — Complete page appears.

6. **Click the <u>Continue to Yahoo Auctions</u> page.**

   The Submit an Item page appears (see Figure 21-4).

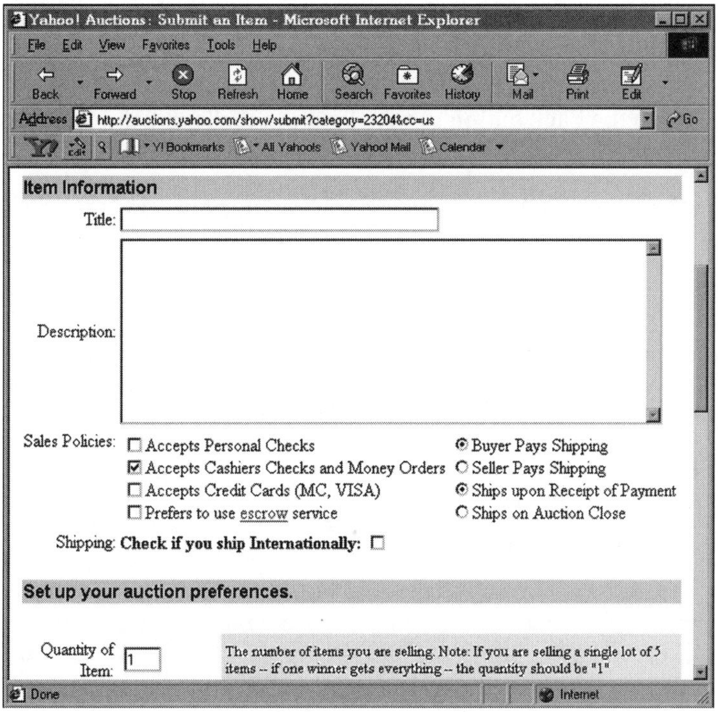

Figure 21-4:
Part of the
Submit an
Item page,
where you
create and
define your
auction.

7. Fill in the information fields.

This page is where you name your auction and describe what it is you're selling. The Sales Policies boxes let you check what kind of payment you accept and determine who pays shipping. (It's assumed you will not ship internationally, but a check box allows you to invite international orders.) In the Set up your auction preferences section, fill in your quantity of items, your starting price, and the length of the auction. (Bids below the starting price are automatically rejected by the system.) The Additional Options are useful for configuring how your auction operates. You can control the minimum selling price (higher than the starting price), and a Sell Price at which the auction closes if bidding reaches that level. ***Note:*** You must enter at least a title, a description, and a starting price. If any of those fields are left blank, Yahoo! pesters you until you fill them in.

8. Click the Continue button.

The Preview Item Submission page appears. This page is how your auction will appear.

9. **Check everything for accuracy, and then click the Submit Auction button.**

If you spot any mistakes or change your mind about any information, use the Back button of your browser to display the Submit an Item page (refer to Figure 21-4) and adjust your information.

On the Thank You! page, under the View your Auction banner, click the URL to see your auction page. You can also use that URL to promote your auction around the Internet. E-mail it to friends, post it in relevant message boards, or promote it on your Web site.

You may add a photo to your auction page; doing so makes a big difference in attracting bids. If you have a digitized (scanned) photo of your item, follow these steps:

1. **On the Submit an Item page (see Step 7 in the preceding list), click the Add Photos link.**

The Upload Photo(s) page appears (see Figure 21-5).

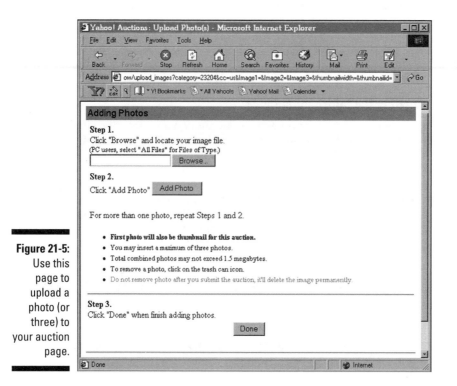

Figure 21-5:
Use this page to upload a photo (or three) to your auction page.

2. **Click the Browse button.**

   At this point, your operating system prompts you to locate the graphics (photo) file on your hard drive, preparatory to uploading it to Yahoo!. I've written the next steps from the viewpoint of a Windows 95 user.

3. **In the Choose File window, locate your scanned photo, click it, and click the Open button.**

4. **Click the Add Photo button.**

5. **If you have more than one photo to upload, repeat Steps 2 through 4.**

6. **Click the Done button.**

If you have a Web site and you want to avoid the Yahoo! upload process, which can be a little slow, simply post the photo to your site using whatever upload procedure you're accustomed to. Then, on the Submit an Item page, place the URL in the information that describes your item.

You are limited to three photos per auction, and the cumulative file size cannot exceed 1.5 megabytes. However, most photo files aren't that big.

Chapter 22

Yahoo! Classifieds: The Neighborly Way to Shop

- -

In This Chapter

▶ Navigating the Yahoo! Classifieds directory

▶ Posting your own classified ad

- -

*Y*ahoo! Classifieds is primarily about selling stuff. Yahoo! users can put up notices about any kind of product, item, or service, from a book to a house. The Classifieds are more homegrown than Yahoo! Auctions, which is populated by dealers as well as individuals. Nevertheless, some stores advertise their wares in the Classifieds. In fact, the Autos & Motorcycles section of the Classifieds directory has a portion dedicated to new and used car dealer ads.

This chapter guides you through the Classifieds directory and explains how to post an ad of your own. I extracted two portions of the Classifieds, and put them in other chapters. You can find out about the Personals in Chapter 15, and looking for real estate is covered in Chapter 17. It's fun how these explanations are scattered throughout the book, isn't it? Well, anyway, that's where those two topics are.

Shopping the Ads

The starting point for browsing and placing ads is the Yahoo! Classifieds home page (see Figure 22-1). Click the <u>Classifieds</u> link on the Yahoo! home page, or go directly to this URL:

```
classifieds.yahoo.com
```

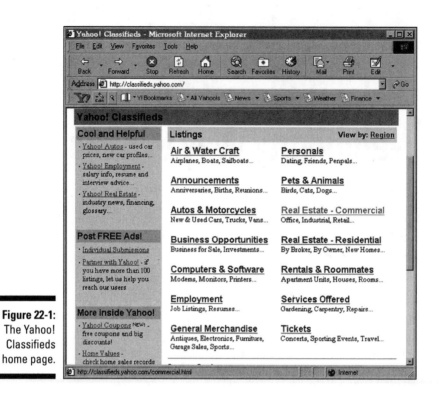

Figure 22-1:
The Yahoo!
Classifieds
home page.

Among the main topic headings in the Yahoo! Classifieds directory, the General Merchandise section is probably the most packed with items and the directory portion most people turn to for general browsing. I'll use General Merchandise as an illustrative example of the other sections.

When you click any main directory heading, you get a second-level page with a search engine and a geographic guide (see Figure 22-2). At this point you have three choices:

- ✔ Use the drop-down menus and keyword entry form to search for items for sale in certain geographic regions.

- ✔ Ignore the drop-down menus and use the keyword entry form to search for items across all geographic regions.

- ✔ Use the geographic directory to browse for all sorts of items for sale in a specific locality.

Your goal is to eventually reach the actual classified ads. Figure 22-3 shows what they look like. Note that the left sidebar of the ad pages contains a keyword form and Submit Search button for revising your search.

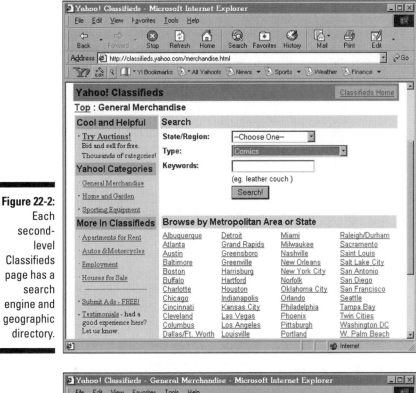

Figure 22-2:
Each second-level Classifieds page has a search engine and geographic directory.

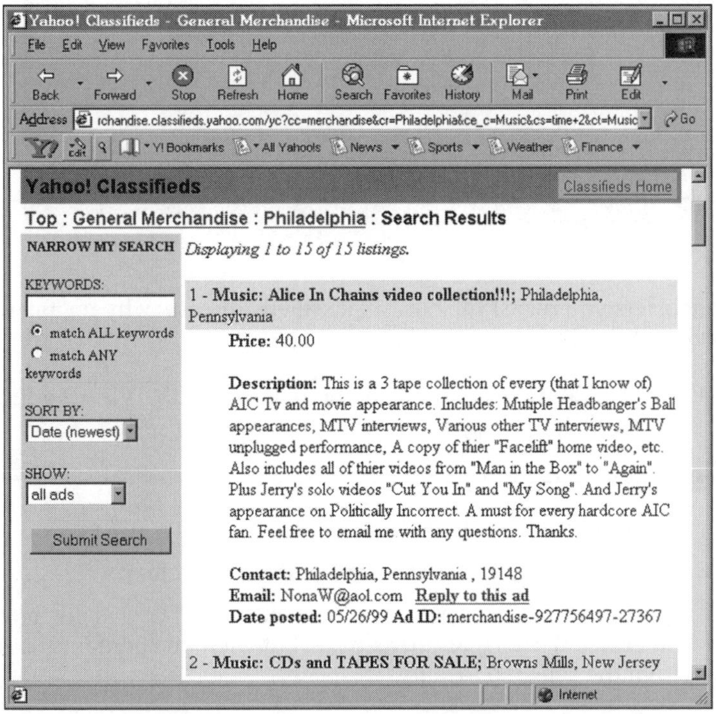

Figure 22-3:
A classified ad.

Clicking the Reply to this ad link displays the Reply to Ad page (see Figure 22-4), on which you write a response to the author of the classified ad. The form puts your Yahoo! e-mail address in the From header, assuming you're signed into your Yahoo! ID and have an e-mail account (see Chapter 3). Feel free, however, to change that default address to another of your e-mail addresses if you prefer. You can click the recipient's e-mail address link to open a Compose Mail window in whatever your default e-mail program is, if you prefer using that method.

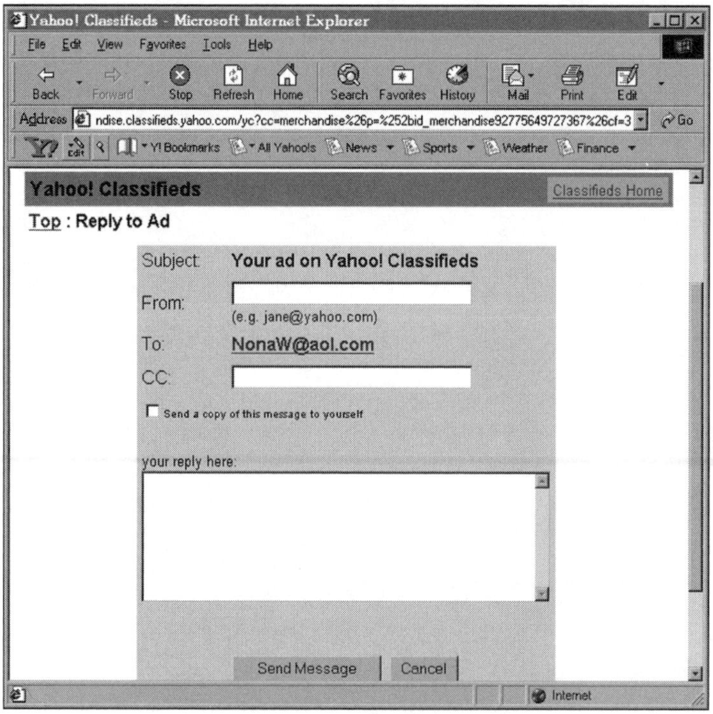

Figure 22-4:
Use this page to reply to a classified ad.

Yahoo! Classifieds   Classifieds Home

Top : Reply to Ad

Subject: **Your ad on Yahoo! Classifieds**

From:
(e.g. jane@yahoo.com)

To: NonaW@aol.com

CC:

☐ Send a copy of this message to yourself

your reply here:

Send Message | Cancel

Yahoo! lets you recast the entire Classifieds directory by region, with a simple click of the mouse:

1. On the Yahoo! Classifieds home page, click the View by Region link.

The Yahoo! Classifieds — By Region page appears.

2. Click a Metro link.

The (Metro) Classifieds page appears.

3. Continue browsing as if from the main directory.

All main directory categories from the Yahoo! Classifieds home page are on each (Metro) Classifieds page, but each one contains listings only from the selected locality.

Submitting an Ad

The flip side to buying somebody's old comic-book collection is posting your own ad. Want to unload that stack of psychedelic vinyl from the hazy days of your youth? You can either auction it off in Yahoo! Auctions or sell it through the Classifieds. Use Yahoo! Auctions (described in Chapter 21) when you're willing to accept a range of selling prices, and when you're in the mood for the extra work of setting up the auction page. Use Yahoo! Classifieds when you have a non-negotiable price and crave the relative simplicity of posting an ad.

Here's how to proceed:

1. **On the Yahoo! Classifieds home page, click the <u>Individual Submissions</u> link.**

   The Submission page appears.

2. **Click any category.**

   Some category links lead to subcategory pages. Just continue selecting the best niche for your item.

3. **On the next page, fill in your zip code, a description of the item, and your contact information.**

   Only a few fields are required — the ones with asterisks next to them. Different categories have varying requirements. Figure 22-5 shows the information fields for the Announcement category, in which nothing is being sold. If you're selling something, you need to fill in at least one means of contact, such as your e-mail address. (You might not want to list your mailing address or phone numbers.)

4. **Click the Submit entry button.**

   Yahoo! shows you your ad. Your listing is automatically placed in the correct geographical location of the directory, according to your zip code.

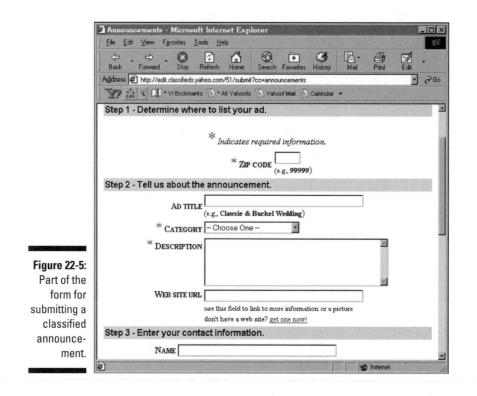

Figure 22-5:
Part of the form for submitting a classified announcement.

Part VII
The Part of Tens

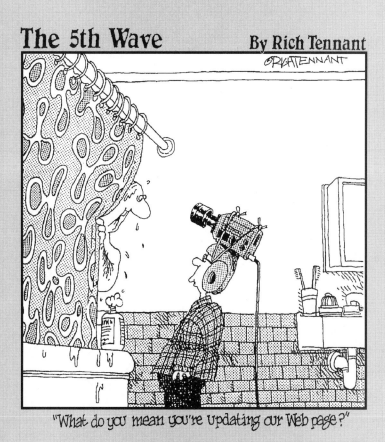

The 5th Wave   By Rich Tennant

"What do you mean you're updating our Web page?"

In this part...

This part tops off the book with a couple of lists. One offers ten Yahoo! directory pages that serve well as bookmarks for future searches. The other points you toward ten popular Yahoo! Clubs you might want to join.

Chapter 23

Ten Directory Pages Worth Bookmarking

In This Chapter

▶ Finding Internet radio stations

▶ Saving a list of online encyclopedias

▶ Bookmarking a directory of online auctions

▶ Keeping an index of online brokerages

▶ Saving humor links

Multilevel Marketing

```
dir.yahoo.com/Business_and_Economy/Business_Opportunities/
              Multi_Level_Marketing/
```

*I*f *multilevel marketing* (sometimes known as *network marketing*) leaves a bad taste in your mouth, stop licking this page. Also, you might want to update your conception of this particular type of business opportunity. Once associated with illicit pyramid schemes, multilevel marketing has gained increasing legitimacy through the 1990s, especially as the trend toward self-employment and entrepreneurism has accelerated. We're not talking chain letters here, and it's not just Amway, either. (Although Amway has its own Yahoo! directory page.)

These days, a self-motivated individual can sell darn near anything during his or her spare time, from vitamins to cosmetics, from telephone service to utility service. Computer technology generally, and Internet networking in particular, have motivated tremendous growth in multilevel marketing as an employment option. Veterans sometimes sell multiple product lines, all the while recruiting others to join the distribution network. Some of these business plans operate entirely online; others require face-to-face selling and postal service.

The Yahoo! Multi-Level Marketing directory page (see Figure 23-1) provides an eye-popping overview of opportunities for network marketing. The page includes large subcategories devoted to health products (one of the biggest multilevel marketing sectors) and telecommunications (another one of the biggest). The alphabetical list of site links might give you some surprises.

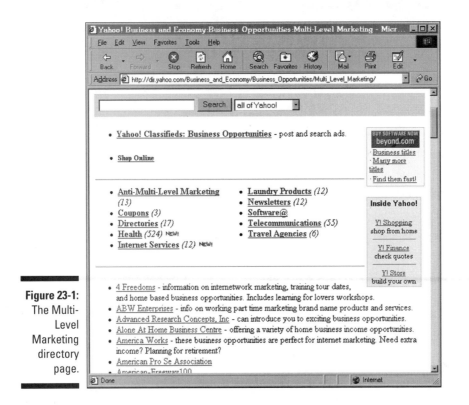

Figure 23-1:
The Multi-Level Marketing directory page.

Internet Radio Stations

> dir.yahoo.com/News_and_Media/Internet_Broadcasts/Radio/
> Stations/Web_Directories/

Internet radio is coming of age. If you aren't familiar with its pleasures, now might be the time to explore this entertaining sector of Internet life. Internet radio uses *streaming audio* of one kind or another — a few competing formats are available. All required software is free for the asking (and the downloading), and some of it might be included in whatever browser you're using.

Three audio players dominate the streaming audio scene, and if you want to enjoy a seamless experience of Internet radio, it's a good idea to equip your system with all three. Two are plug-ins that integrate with your browser, and one is a stand-alone program that you activate independently of the browser. Here they are, with the Web addresses from which you may download them:

- ✔ **RealAudio Player.** The RealAudio player, from a company called Real Networks, is a downloadable plug-in. It handles not only RealAudio streaming audio, but also RealVideo streaming video. Get information and the player itself from the following site:

  ```
  www.real.com
  ```

- ✔ **Windows Media Player.** The Media Player is positioned as part of the Microsoft Windows 95 and 98 operating systems, so you might already own a copy. It's a good idea to upgrade to current versions of this and all other audio stream players. (The quality of Internet radio keeps improving.) You can download new versions here:

  ```
  www.microsoft.com/windows/windowsmedia/
  ```

- ✔ **Winamp MP3 player.** Winamp isn't the only MP3 player you can download, but it's one of the most popular ones, and it comes bundled with good features. Hundreds (maybe thousands) of *skins* (glorified color schemes for the program) are available for quick downloading, which adds to the fun. You can get Winamp at many MP3 sites, including the following:

  ```
  www.winamp.com/
  ```

Yahoo! has a directory page of Internet radio stations, but that's not what I'm recommending here. The list is substantial, but far from comprehensive. However, I *do* suggest that you bookmark the Web Directories page in the Radio:Stations subcategory. This page features hub sites that direct you to Internet radio outlets from all over the world. In other words, it's best to rely on sources outside Yahoo! for lists of Internet broadcasts. This is the best Yahoo! directory page for finding those outside sources.

Encyclopedias

```
dir.yahoo.com/Reference/Encyclopedia/
```

The Internet is supposed to be the world's greatest information resource, right? I've referred to it as such many times myself. If you're online more for the information than for the entertainment, the Yahoo! directory page of online encyclopedias (see Figure 23-2) will light up your eyes.

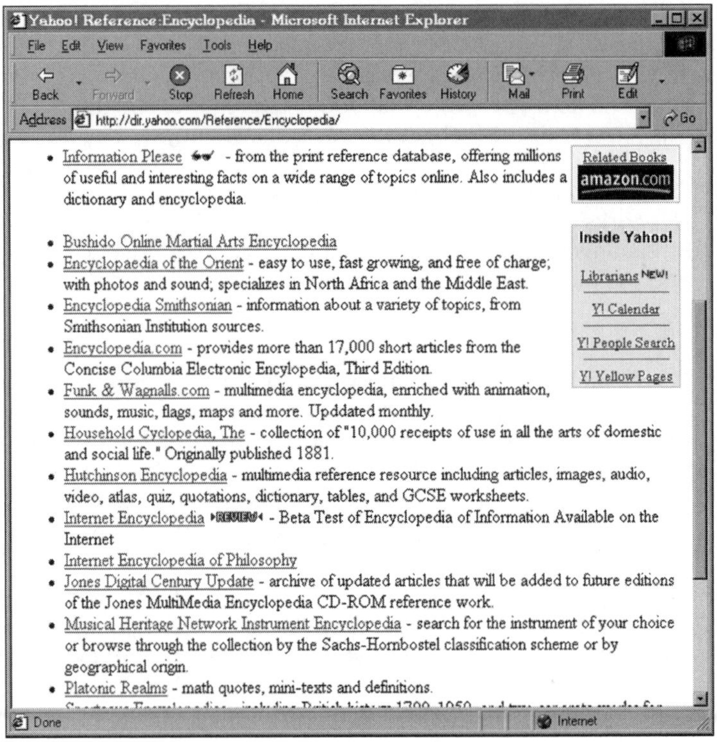

Figure 23-2:
The Yahoo!
directory
page of
online ency-
clopedias:
an info-
junky's
dream.

This page is not concerned with online supplements to CD-ROM encyclopedias. Rather, it's devoted to all-virtual products such as the Encyclopedia
Smithsonian and the experimental Internet Encyclopedia.

While you're in an academic mood, try the Yahoo! listing for dictionaries. The
following link takes you to the directory page of English-language dictionaries, but you can click one level up for a more general directory to all kinds of
dictionary subcategories. (See Chapter 4 for details on navigating around the
directory.)

```
dir.yahoo.com/Reference/Dictionaries/English/
```

Online Auctions

```
dir.yahoo.com/Business_and_Economy/Companies/Auctions/
                    Online_Auctions/
```

You might have heard that online auctions have become popular. Perhaps you've dipped your toe into the pleasure of bidding on merchandise over the Internet. Maybe, in fact, you're a dedicated addict of the virtual "Going, going, gone!" Whatever your status regarding online auctions, from mildly curious to power bargain hunter, the Online Auctions directory page at Yahoo! is bound to open your eyes.

Many have heard of eBay, plenty of people use OnSale, and the hourly Flash Auctions appeal to fans of First Auction. Yahoo! perpetrates its own auction action as described in Chapter 21. But this directory page stunningly reveals that the virtual auction scene is in raging epidemic mode. The breadth and variety of cyberspace bidding is glorious. Dedicated auction houses gavel up office equipment, antiques, fine art, rare wines, vintage automobiles, clothes, old coins, power tools, and — sure to appeal to every casual user — cargo containers. Don't forget Magic Auction, which conducts a weekly bid session for magic supplies.

The best part of this directory page is that almost every listing has a description — a distinct lack on many Yahoo! subcategories. Figure 23-3 shows a small portion of the Online Auctions directory.

Who knew there were so many ways to spend money on the Internet?

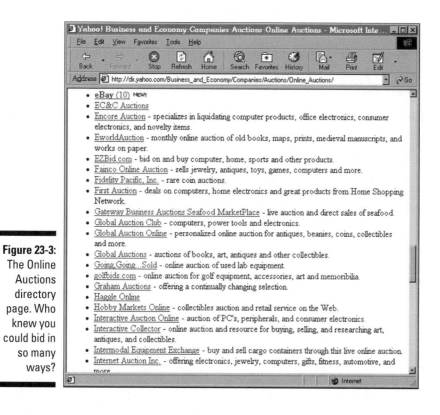

Figure 23-3:
The Online
Auctions
directory
page. Who
knew you
could bid in
so many
ways?

Internet Trading

```
dir.yahoo.com/Business_and_Economy/Companies/
        Financial_Services/Investment_Services/
        Brokerages/Internet_Trading/
```

During the past few years, online investing has evolved into one of the primary attractions of the Internet. The reasons for this growth in interest are many; it's not just technology. For many people, brokerage accounts replace traditional savings accounts, so we have more investors than ever before. The raging United States bull market of the 1990s has helped too. The growth of online services and the Internet have contributed to a new standard of investor empowerment. One result is the online brokerage — an automated system of buying and selling stocks and other securities, which fits right in with the Net's delivery of investment data.

Even having followed the evolution of online investment, I am astounded by the sheer number of online brokerage companies that have popped up. Choosing among them presents one of the most urgent predicaments for newcomers. The Internet Trading directory page doesn't offer advice, but at least it furnishes an overview of the options. Most of the listings include descriptions that give you a general sense of the brokerage's specialty. Click on the Reference and Guides subcategory link to find sites that will help you make sense of it all.

Movie Guide

```
dir.yahoo.com/Entertainment/Movies_and_Film/Titles
```

Does the Internet have movie envy? Maybe. There's no question that movies are a huge topic online. Two main types of movie sites are available. Official sites are produced by movie studios and remain active for the duration of the movie's theater life. The other type are the fan sites, which are likely to remain obsessively alive forever.

Official movie sites tend to be high-gloss productions, full of atmosphere, lots of production pictures, and usually video clips. They are essentially promotion sites — high on glitz, low on community. Fan sites are often more fun and sometimes just as informative. No P.R. agency in the world can deliver the goods like a manic fan.

The Movie and Film: Titles directory page is fairly high up in the Yahoo! directory (third level), and I'm pointing you there as a launching pad for all kinds of movie site explorations. This page has no site links, only subcategory breakdowns (see Figure 23-4). I'd avoid the <u>Complete Listing</u> link unless you want to overwhelm your computer and cause it to run into the next room whimpering. You can zero in on the type of film you're interested in with the subcategory links, and find your way to specific movies on subsequent pages. Notice also the alphabetical directory above the subcategories — a handy feature found on only a few Yahoo! pages. Use it when you don't need to browse, but want to laser your way directly to a particular movie.

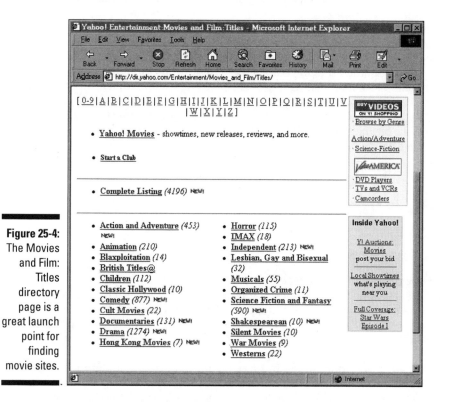

Figure 25-4:
The Movies and Film: Titles directory page is a great launch point for finding movie sites.

After you get to the lists of movie titles, you might be surprised to see that many movies have their own directory pages. They deserve entire directory listings because fans have made so many sites for them. I tell you, the Net is a great place for movie lovers. Have fun!

Personal Home Pages

```
dir.yahoo.com/Society_and_Culture/People/
        Personal_Home_Pages/Groups/
```

The Web is a highly commercial realm, but it wasn't always like that. At the beginning, college students primarily embraced the Web, and they created simple home pages to share interests and links. Corporate America soon discovered the marketing potential of the Web, thus beginning the commercial joy ride that has led us to the transcendental pleasures of e-commerce. But during this evolution, the Web has kept its allure as a medium for personal expression and sharing. In fact, with the advent of page-building communities such as GeoCities, personal home pages are more popular than ever.

In an environment dominated by high-profile corporate sites, it can be refreshing to surf among amateur, personal pages. It can even be a way to meet people, because most personal pages contain e-mail links. That's why I'm recommending the preceding link to the Groups directory page in the Personal Home Pages category — the pages tend to be topical and the links have descriptions. The quality of the sites listed on this directory page is definitely homegrown and informal. Some of the "groups" are couples. You can also find bicycle groups, dormitories, and clusters of friends. Don't miss the Falafel Knights page.

Internet Humor

```
dir.yahoo.com/Entertainment/Humor__Jokes__and_Fun/By_Topic/Co
             mputers_and_Internet/Internet/
```

One of the delights of being online is that the Net is a funny place. Unintentionally funny at times, but beyond that, humor is circulated among the online citizenry at a lightning pace. And hundreds of deliberately funny sites archive public domain humor or make attempts to get you laughing with original material.

I must warn you that the Net has a rampant "shaggy dog" humor mentality, in which utterly senseless sites are created just for the fun of it. For example, a site for dead links invites people to memorialize links that no longer work. Online humor also slices into the mindspace with a sharp edge, as with the Hatemail in a Box site, which provides tools for flaming authors of bad pages. You have to have a strong constitution to roam the dark alleys of the Net, but you can get some good laughs along the way if you know where to look.

This Yahoo! directory page tells you where to look. Tons of site links take you directly to some of the most hilariously pointless locations you can imagine, such as the Anti-Banana Society. Subcategories divulge lower-level directory pages devoted to fake awards, ugly pages, various humor archives, and parodies.

Cool Sites

```
dir.yahoo.com/Computers_and_Internet/Internet/World_Wide_Web/
          Best_of_the_Web/Sites_of_the___/Day/
```

Long, long ago, someone named Glenn Davis decided the Web had attained utter coolness and was inspired to officially commend it. The Cool Site of the Day award was born, and the benefactor's site became ragingly popular. Herds of people eager to attain surfer coolness trampled into the Cool Site page every morning to begin their day with a blast of hip design and cutting edge content. They devoured the daily links like attitude vitamins. They built bookmark lists that positively glowed with cooldom.

And the idea was copied. Now dozens of award-giving sites fall into the generic category of "Cool Site" pages. The Cool Sites of the Day directory page offers a rundown of the now-bewildering assortment of sites that presume to arbiter coolness. Niches have developed, such as the Cool Dog Site of the Day, the Cybersmith Site of the Day, the Harsh Site of the Day, and the Incredibly Useful Site of the Day.

As a parallel trend, many award sites have sprung up that don't deliver daily links, but instead bestow honors upon sites as they are encountered. These non-timetable award sites are grouped on another Yahoo! directory page, at the following URL:

```
dir.yahoo.com/Computers_and_Internet/Internet/World_Wide_Web/
          Best_of_the_Web/Awards/
```

Firsts

```
dir.yahoo.com/Entertainment/Cool_Links/Computers_and_Internet
          /Classic_Oldies/Firsts/
```

I've saved the Firsts for last because this page must be one of the quirkiest subcategory directory pages in all of Yahoo!. Located in the Entertainment: Cool Links category, Firsts is a concise listing of several landmark Web sites that have been copied endlessly since their inception. The original Cool Site of the Day is here, for example. In the spirit of capriciousness, so is the Hamster Dance site, which probably has never been copied.

For Internet veterans, this directory page is like a memorial to milestone Web sites of the past five or six years, all of which (on this list, anyway) are still going strong. For newcomers, it's a Web history lesson.

Chapter 24

Ten Yahoo! Clubs Worth Joining

Rendezvous

clubs.yahoo.com/clubs/rendezvous

*B*ecause Yahoo! Clubs are designed to be social gathering places (though they function quite well as business settings); it's no surprise that social clubs have lots of members. Rendezvous, which is listed under the Sex & Romance category in the Clubs directory, is among the most popular meeting place for singles. If you're concerned about adult content, I believe Rendezvous to be safe and fairly wholesome. Although I haven't examined every photo submitted by its over 5,000 members, I have never encountered anything racy. That goes for the message boards as well as the photos.

Rendezvous is a hangout for young singles primarily — the under 30 crowd. There's nothing stopping someone of any age from joining. (I, for example, had no trouble entering this sanctum of youth, but if you think I'm going to divulge my age, either in the club or in this book, you are grievously mistaken.) The atmosphere is friendly, inquisitive, and bustling with activity. The interactive calendar is oddly empty — most people are interested in photos and messages. The chat rooms are often quiet.

Rendezvous was founded in September 1998, and enjoys a membership growth rate of about forty new people each day. It's a good club for young singles to cruise, with a high chance of developing e-mail relationships.

Emotional Support

`clubs.yahoo.com/clubs/emotionalsupport`

One of the beauties of the online experience is in its capacity to connect people with common interests, problems, or hardships. Online support groups in a variety of formats have received quite a bit of publicity both for their remarkable way of bringing people together in a safe (cyber)space, and for their occasional aberrations. In 1998, for example, one Internet support group hit the headlines when one of its members confessed to a murder and most of the group members declined to notify authorities. The incident drew criticism that online groups operate in a world of their own, taking the "safe space" operational maxim to absurd lengths.

Such incidents generate publicity, but so do plane crashes. In my long experience with virtual communities, stretching back years before the Web was invented, I developed profound respect and admiration for the positive impact that online connections can have on people's lives.

The Emotional Support club at Yahoo! does not define itself according to any particular ailment, condition, or addiction. Instead, it positions itself as a warm, caring community that invites its members to relax into a comforting, supportive atmosphere. It's a virtual shoulder to lean on, as the opening message puts it. Emotional Support was founded by four people, thirtyish to fortyish, and they established a sympathetic haven for almost 200 members.

Apocalyptica

`clubs.yahoo.com/Entertainment___Arts/Humor/`

Note: The above URL has three underscores between Entertainment and Arts. Don't ask me why.

Don't be put off by the dire name of this club. It's not about the end of the world, unless you plan to die laughing. Apocalyptica is a humor club, where members are invited to relax, socialize, and post jokes on the message board. (Posting jokes isn't a requirement.) There is no bawdiness filter in place here, so don't join if you have tender ears. But if the club's motto sounds appealing ("All For Fun, Fun For All"), give it a try.

Apocalyptica is primarily a messaging community — the chat rooms aren't used very much, the calendar is empty, and photos of members, though welcomed, are less common than in other social clubs. Apocalyptica garnered 300 members in its first two months, and is growing quickly in popularity.

Genealogy Research Club

clubs.yahoo.com/clubs/genealogyresearchclub

Online information access has given birth to many new hobbies and enlivened others. One activity that has definitely benefited from the information age is genealogy. Searching for one's family lineage is facilitated by a number of online tools. The Genealogy Research Club can point you to the resources — and provide lots of encouragement.

The message board is where the action happens in this club. The 1,300 members use messages to request information about Internet resources, to announce what family or geographic area they are researching, and to help each other out. The ambience is friendly, but the active members are serious hobbyists. Anyone just starting out can learn a lot here, make some friends, and possibly discover some relatives.

Snail Mailers United

clubs.yahoo.com/clubs/snailmailersunited

In a fine twist of irony, a Yahoo! Club has been formed to resist e-mail. Online veterans refer to postal mail as *snail mail* because of its non-instantaneous pace compared to e-mail. Snail Mailers United gathers people interested in traditional pen-pal correspondences. The club's tagline — "Use a stamp — Go postal for a change!" — says it all.

It's not surprising that the various electronic features of a Yahoo! Club don't have much appeal for this membership of almost 1,000 folks. The message board is used actively to trade physical-world addresses. The club has proved a surprising success, growing at a clip of almost 500 members per month.

Y Chess

clubs.yahoo.com/clubs/ychess

Y Chess is one of several in-house Yahoo! Clubs, meaning that Yahoo! created it and staffs it. In theory, Y Chess (and the other Y Game clubs) supports the chess portion of Yahoo! Games. (See Chapter 18 for more information about Yahoo! Games.) But in fact, the discussions in Y Chess range broadly on the subject of the game and the various sites at which you can play chess online.

The tone of the message board is serious but friendly — devout chess players talking shop. Newcomers and beginners are welcome, and elementary questions are answered with the same down-to-earth geniality as advanced topics. Don't miss the Links page, with pointers to chess sites.

To see other Y Game clubs, check out this Yahoo! Clubs directory page:

```
http://clubs.yahoo.com/Games/
```

Time Out for Parents

```
clubs.yahoo.com/clubs/timeoutforparents
```

Several Yahoo! Clubs are devoted to parenting and expected parenthood. Time Out for Parents was recently formed, at the time of this writing, but I'm impressed by its friendly, clublike feeling and especially by the highly organized message board. The staff of this club creates weekly topics for discussion, daily topics, and twice-daily chat sessions. The small membership contributes to the intimate feeling of the club, but that might change as more people become aware of the good quality here. (I guess I'm not helping to keep it small.)

Time Out for Parents has eight founders, and the unusually high number makes for a real team effort. These founders are very active on the message board, both in setting conversation topics and answering the many questions that spring up.

Lost Purple Wizard of the Nada

```
clubs.yahoo.com/clubs/lostpurplewizardofthenada
```

Take a guess. Nope — guess again. Never mind, I'll tell you. The Lost Purple Wizard of the Nada is a spirituality club representing a "guild of ancient metaphysical wizards." The club has attracted a fairly large membership, perhaps due to the curiosity factor, or maybe because of the flashy logo on the front page, or perhaps the mystically friendly mood of the message board helps.

Tarot card reading is popular in this club, and readings are sometimes conducted and reported in message format. Wicca and magick topics hold forth prominently in the discussions, but any question about metaphysical occurrences is dealt with seriously and kindly.

The Thinking Human

clubs.yahoo.com/clubs/thethinkinghuman

The Thinking Human is a current events discussion forum. The club's introduction openly invites challenge and debate, but in fact the message board remains fairly polite. And thoughtful. Conversations range all over the map of current events at any given time, with some members holding the floor with long analyses of modern problems and suggested solutions.

This is not a particularly social club, and nobody is angling for pen pals or out-of-club communication. It is singularly faceless, with exactly zero photos posted in the club's first eight months. Ideas are the currency of this community.

Web Page Making

clubs.yahoo.com/clubs/webpagemaking

This club has an attitude. Fronted by a great graphic and a brief declaration of the dos and don'ts of Web page design, Web page making is a clearinghouse of shared information about how to make good Web sites. Feel free to ask a question on the message board about JavaScript, creating drop-down menus, or changing images with a MouseOver. Or post your link and ask for opinions.

Index

Notes

Notes

Notes

Notes

Notes

Notes

Notes

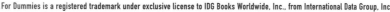

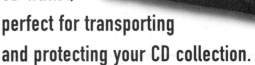

WWW.DUMMIES.COM

Discover Dummies Online!

The Dummies Web Site is your fun and friendly online resource for the latest information about ...*For Dummies*® books and your favorite topics. The Web site is the place to communicate with us, exchange ideas with other ...*For Dummies* readers, chat with authors, and have fun!

Ten Fun and Useful Things You Can Do at www.dummies.com

1. Win free ...*For Dummies* books and more!
2. Register your book and be entered in a prize drawing.
3. Meet your favorite authors through the IDG Books Author Chat Series.
4. Exchange helpful information with other ...*For Dummies* readers.
5. Discover other great ...*For Dummies* books you must have!
6. Purchase Dummieswear™ exclusively from our Web site.
7. Buy ...*For Dummies* books online.
8. Talk to us. Make comments, ask questions, get answers!
9. Download free software.
10. Find additional useful resources from authors.

Link directly to these ten fun and useful things at
http://www.dummies.com/10useful

For other technology titles from IDG Books Worldwide, go to
www.idgbooks.com

Not on the Web yet? It's easy to get started with *Dummies 101*®: *The Internet For Windows*®*98* or *The Internet For Dummies*®, 6th Edition, at local retailers everywhere.

IDG BOOKS WORLDWIDE

Find other ...*For Dummies* books on these topics:

Business • Career • Databases • Food & Beverage • Games • Gardening • Graphics • Hardware
Health & Fitness • Internet and the World Wide Web • Networking • Office Suites
Operating Systems • Personal Finance • Pets • Programming • Recreation • Sports
Spreadsheets • Teacher Resources • Test Prep • Word Processing

IDG BOOKS WORLDWIDE
BOOK REGISTRATION

Register This Book and Win!

We want to hear from you!

Visit **http://my2cents.dummies.com** to register this book and tell us how you liked it!

- Get entered in our monthly prize giveaway.

- Give us feedback about this book — tell us what you like best, what you like least, or maybe what you'd like to ask the author and us to change!

- Let us know any other *...For Dummies*® topics that interest you.

Your feedback helps us determine what books to publish, tells us what coverage to add as we revise our books, and lets us know whether we're meeting your needs as a *...For Dummies* reader. You're our most valuable resource, and what you have to say is important to us!

Not on the Web yet? It's easy to get started with *Dummies 101*®: *The Internet For Windows*® *98* or *The Internet For Dummies*®, 6th Edition, at local retailers everywhere.

Or let us know what you think by sending us a letter at the following address:

...For Dummies Book Registration
Dummies Press
7260 Shadeland Station, Suite 100
Indianapolis, IN 46256-3945
Fax 317-596-5498

**BESTSELLING
BOOK SERIES
FROM IDG**